D1529144

STALKING

THE

HOLY

STALKING ——·—— THE ——·——
HOLY
THE
PURSUIT OF
SAINT
MAKING

——·——

MICHAEL
W. HIGGINS

Published in 2006 by
House of Anansi Press Inc.
110 Spadina Avenue, Suite 801
Toronto, ON, M5V 2K4
Tel. 416-363-4343 Fax 416-363-1017
www.anansi.ca

Distributed in Canada by
HarperCollins Canada Ltd.
1995 Markham Road
Scarborough, ON, M1B 5M8
Toll free tel. 1-800-387-0117

Distributed in the United States by
Publishers Group West
1700 Fourth Street
Berkeley, CA 94710
Toll free tel. 1-800-788-3123

House of Anansi Press is committed to protecting our natural environment.
As part of our efforts, this book is printed on Rolland Enviro paper: it contains
100% post-consumer recycled fibres, is acid-free, and is processed chlorine-free.

Pages 277 and 278 constitute a continuation of this copyright page.

10 09 08 07 06   1 2 3 4 5

Library and Archives Canada Cataloguing in Publication Data

Higgins, Michael W.
Stalking the holy : the pursuit of saint-making / Michael W. Higgins.

Includes index.
ISBN 0-88784-181-3

1. Canonization. 2. Christian saints. I. Title.

BX2325.H53 2005   235'.24   C2005-905163-9

Cover design: Bill Douglas at The Bang
Text design and typesetting: Beth Crane, Heidy Lawrance Associates

Canada Council   Conseil des Arts
for the Arts   du Canada

*We acknowledge for their financial support of our publishing program the
Canada Council for the Arts, the Ontario Arts Council, and the Government of
Canada through the Book Publishing Industry Development Program (BPIDP).*

Printed and bound in Canada

To Krystyna,
my wife, lover, and partner, who,
if she wasn't a saint when we were married in 1973,
is surely one now

The only sadness is not to be a saint.
— Léon Bloy

. . . the dreadful gift of pity for the many
is granted only to saints.
— Primo Levi

Contents

Acknowledgements

NO PROJECT EVER emerges fully formed from the head of its creator. It is the result of numerous collaborations, some major and some minor, but all necessary.

I am indebted to Jacques Goulet, Professor Emeritus, Religious Studies, Mount Saint Vincent University, in Halifax, Nova Scotia, who provided me with the title for this project. Several years ago, when I was the Seton Lecturer at the university, I encountered Jacques as I meandered down the corridors and when he saw me he blurted out with his customary Gallic charm that "there was that Higgins fellow ever stalking the holy." I liked that phrase and resolved to store it in my memory to be retrieved some time in the future. Well, the future is now.

I am indebted to Kevin Burns, editor, producer, and friend, who has worked closely with me on the companion undertaking — the CBC Radio One *Ideas* series "Stalking the Holy."

I am indebted to Carolyn Dirks, Librarian at St. Jerome's University, who provided regular and reliable assistance on numerous occasions.

I am indebted to Kieran Bonner, immediate past Vice-President and Academic Dean at St. Jerome's University, who assumed some of my duties while I was away engaged in research for the book.

I am indebted to Becky Thompson, Administrative Assistant to the President, for her equanimity and perseverance.

I am indebted to Rebecca Higgins, Rosemary O'Hearn, and Manuela Popovic for their expert transcriptions of the interview tapes.

I am indebted to Kevin Linder, Managing Editor at House of Anansi Press, for his sage advice.

And, most importantly, I am indebted to Krystyna Higgins, my most rigorous critic, for her fair and judicious commentary.

INTRODUCTION

FROM THE BEGINNING, I have been haunted by saints. No exorcism will work, so I have simply given in to their irresistible power. I have no other choice.

Still, I can try to understand something of their mesmerizing allure. And to that end, I have written this exploration of the holy ones with the intention of discovering what it is in them that holds so many of us in their thrall.

This, then, is a personal search, a stalking of the holy, that hopes to uncover the many dimensions that define sainthood. And one of these dimensions is the pursuit of happiness, "the initial thirst for a more authentic life, the impulse that led so many saints . . . to rebel against the 'deadness' of their surrounding culture and its false rewards."[1] It is a gallimaufry, or ragout, that draws upon juicy bits of anthropology, politics, theology, spirituality, psychology, history, truth, and fantasy to make up a stew that is, all at once, enjoyable to digest, filling, good for you, and memorable. In addition to being a personal quest — a *peregrinatio*, or experience of going forth into strange lands — it will also be a state-of-the-art examination of the process, the players and the politics of saint-making itself. How does one go about becoming a saint; or better yet, how do one's followers or admirers go about doing it on your behalf — the official part, I mean?

Many years ago, while walking along the Via Vittorio Emanuele in Rome, I came across a basilica that displayed the remains of one of the many *beati*, or blessed ones, waiting for that final stage of approval called canonization. His body, or what remained of it, was on show, not because of an Italian affection for the morbid, but because this was but one way to hurry along the process of sainting — a way, if you like, of encouraging that final miracle so necessary for the Vatican's definitive seal of official sainthood.

Although I remember, as if it were only yesterday, the shrunken remains of the saintly wannabe lying in public view in a centuries-old church on a Roman thoroughfare, what also remain fixed in the memory are my serial exposures to the venerable body parts of St. Oliver Plunkett (his head) in Drogheda, Ireland; of St. Teresa of Avila (her finger) in Spain; and of St. Anthony of Padua (his tongue) in Italy. These relics are meaningless outside the context of saintliness. In fact, they are more likely to occasion derision than veneration if they are not understood within that very context.

Before the body parts, there is the narrative, the heroic exploits, the singular witness that make up the compelling individual stories of sainthood. After all, what makes the saints so interesting for believer and non-believer alike is their rich diversity of background and history. No two saints are alike (unless, of course, they happen to be the same saint: more about that later).

From prepubescence to maturity, I have been drawn to particular saints. Their appeal has depended upon personal circumstances, and the ascension of one saint in my orbit of the holy has invariably been linked to the eclipse of another.

My first real saint — and there is now little evidence of his "realness" — was the boy martyr Pancratius. Put to death by the anti-Christian emperor Diocletian, Pancratius perished because of his devotion to the Eucharistic host he carried on his person, up to and including his death in the Colosseum. How I happened upon this pious story is even now a mystery to me. The drama of Pancratius's death formed the contents of my first award-winning public-speaking endeavour. To discover some years later that Pancratius can be found nowhere in the respectable annals of saintly lives was a source of despair for me. And guilt. Was I to return my trophy? Did I win on false pretences? Only scholarship could free me from the tyranny of falsehood.

After checking several authorities, I unearthed the following: there was a fourth-century Phrygian orphan martyred in Rome by the name of Pancras, and there was a first-century disciple of St. Peter, also called Pancras, who became the first bishop of Taormina in Sicily and died at the hands of brigands. The second Pancras was also known as Pancratius and is to this day also recognized as a saint by the Greek and Russian Orthodox churches. But he was not a boy of fourteen and did not perish during the reign of Diocletian.

Have the two Pancrases been collapsed into one? Is Pancras a composite? A pious invention? Once you start asking these questions, they lead you into interesting places — far more interesting than the sanitized biographies of the holy that so often pass as historical matter of indisputable veracity.

After Pancratius came Sebastian. I also won an award with his story — I was on a roll. I was also on safer ground. Or at least I *thought* so. Still an early adolescent when I discovered this soldier-martyr, I found the facts of Sebastian's life fascinating and inspiring. Little did I know at the time of Sebastian's checkered history and iconography.

A soldier who rose to the rank of captain of the Praetorian Guard, the Roman emperor's own personal bodyguard, Sebastian converted to Christianity and chose not to tell his boss, who was Diocletian. Frequently imperilling his own life by counselling and sustaining scores of future martyrs, Sebastian was eventually outed and ordered executed by an understandably irate emperor. Diocletian decreed that Sebastian was to die by arrows. In spite of being pierced several times by the imperial archers and then dumped into the Tiber, Sebastian survived. A less heroic chap would have taken this as a sign and left Rome for good. Not Sebastian: after taking time to recuperate, he returned to the court, scolded Diocletian for his cruelty, and invited the perplexed and furious emperor to do his worst. Diocletian didn't disappoint. This time the insubordinate captain would be mercilessly clubbed and then buried. Diocletian was nothing if not thorough.

Not unreasonably, Sebastian became the patron saint of archers (a saint, after all, should be forgiving), was often invoked during plagues, and became extremely popular during the Renaissance with visual artists, who depicted him in various poses of partial nudity, arrows strategically located throughout his muscular, lithe, and contorted body, his face often betraying a post-orgasmic look of unearthly satisfaction. In the nineteenth and twentieth centuries, Sebastian became the unofficial saint of homosexual writers and artists — Uranists, as they were known in the fin de siècle — even surfacing in underground gay movies. I suspect that this development was not what Rome had in mind for St. Sebastian.

But no saint has had quite the appeal for me as Thomas à Becket. I was a convert to the saint shortly before I saw the Hal Wallis film *Becket*, starring Peter O'Toole as King Henry II of England and Richard Burton as the courageous and defiant Archbishop of Canterbury. Based on the drama by French writer Jean Anouilh, the Edward Anhalt adaptation captures the drama, ambiguity, and mystique associated with sainthood. Sainthood, that is, which is the crown of shedding one's blood for the faith. Therein lies the drama. The film clinched my attraction to the Becket story.

There have been countless biographies, plays, poems, visual depictions, documentaries, histories, and films dealing with the Becket affair: his friendship with the king; his carnality; his politicking; his divided loyalties; his ambition; his causes. Becket was a complex man, and no natural saint — therein lies the attraction. It was his death at the hands of the boorish barons that ensured his sainthood and his literary fame.

At one time chancellor and principal confidant of his liege lord and friend Henry Plantagenet, Becket was appointed, with reluctance on his part (the degree of reluctance varying with the biographer), as primate of England. He was the premier of the

Lords spiritual in the realm. And that's when things began to turn sour.

He was no longer first and foremost the king's man but the church's, and Becket was nothing if not resolute. Many of the issues that divided the king from his bishops have not stood the test of time. Some of them were clearly not worth dying over. Yet die Becket did. And his death shook Christendom, brought a king to his knees, and guaranteed some considerable measure of church autonomy up until the time of another Henry — the Eighth.

Why is Becket so fascinating? Alfred Lord Tennyson wrote a play about him. The eccentric English writer, Baron Corvo, co-authored a life of him with the best-selling priest-novelist (before Andrew Greeley, that is) Robert Hugh Benson. Before Anouilh wrote about him, T. S. Eliot had written his verse drama *Murder in the Cathedral*. Why the interest?

I suspect the reason can best be seen in the drama of his life and office. The spectre of a leader murdered in his own cathedral during the celebration of vespers shocks today just as it did in the twelfth century. For a contemporary equivalent, think of the worldwide political and religious aftershocks of Archbishop Oscar Romero's assassination in San Salvador in 1980. Is there no sanctuary at all? No place, no figure, no position that is inviolable? In an age of terrorist murders noted for their capricious cruelty, in an age that views little as sacred in the service of either an autocratic or theocratic ideology, the memory of Becket seems painfully pertinent.

The particular details of the Becket–Henry squabble may no longer be relevant, and clearly they are not, but the spectacle of two men of power engaged in a struggle at great cost *is* relevant. The interests of the church and the state do collide — and on occasion *must* collide. When there is an easy compromise between the officials of the church and the state, when the church forfeits its critical and prophetic role, when the interests of the church and state conspire merely to serve each other, great trouble awaits them, as the Catholic hierarchies of Argentina, Nicaragua, and Chile discovered, to their shame.

The story of St. Thomas of Canterbury is a story rich in folly, heroism, and death. It is a story of great meaning. It is a story of our time: a contemporary drama.

It is not that difficult to imagine some disgruntled strong-man confiding to his henchmen, "Will no one rid me of this meddlesome priest?" Are there not places where such a request or order is only too plausible?

The memory of Becket lives on in the witness of Father Jerzy Popieluszko of Poland; the murdered Anglican Arch-bishop of Kampala, Uganda; the gunned-down Archbishop of Cali, Colombia; and countless others. The drama of Becket's life, with its epic dreams and foibles, its honour and its stub-bornness, is a story *for* our time, as well as a story *of* our time — a bloody time.

But why was Becket made a saint? Was it in part a political decision? Or, perhaps more tellingly, a political decision only?

In the first novel of his Deptford trilogy, *Fifth Business*, Robertson Davies has his crusty, idiosyncratic, immeasurably wise protagonist Dunstable Ramsay observe of saint-making:

> I have always found it revealing to see who gets to be a saint in any period; some ages like wonder-workers, and some prefer gifted organizers whose attention to business produces apparent miracles. In the last few years good old saints whom even Protestants love have been losing ground to lesser figures whose fortune it was to be black or yellow or red-skinned — a kind of saintly representation by popu-lation. My Bollandist friends are the first to admit that there is more politics to the making of a saint than the innocently devout might think likely.[2]

Political correctness is not something Ramsay, feisty old survivor that he is, is inclined to heed, but we should take note of his observation about the politics of saint-making when we consider the astonishing rise and fall and rise of one extraordinary woman: Joan of Arc.

Why the enduring interest in Joan? In the last two years alone, we have seen a miniseries and at least two films about this peasant girl. Art critic Joan Acocella, in a *New Yorker* article that provided an insightful and savvy overview of the burgeoning Joan industry, noted that over the past two centuries Joan has drawn the attention of such playwrights, novelists, and poets as Friedrich von Schiller, George Bernard Shaw, the Alexandre Dumas family, Thomas De Quincey, Anatole France, Mark Twain, Paul Claudel, Anouilh (a regular with saints), Charles Péguy, and Maxwell Anderson. Composers like Giuseppe Verdi, Peter Tchaikovsky, Charles Gounod, Arthur Honegger, and Richard Einhorn have been transfixed by the mystery and heroism of the Maid of Orleans. So, too, have film directors like Preminger, Bresson, Dreyer, and Besson.

It is evident that this fifteenth-century French girl of rustic origins, and illiterate to boot, electrified a war-besotted Christian world, obeyed heavenly voices, defied warriors and prelates, and in spite of being reduced to ash and cinder, continues to haunt not only my imagination but that of untold millions, half a millennium after her tragic death.

Trapped by political forces she only partly understood and by scheming churchmen whose motives she only dimly divined, Joan was captured, tried, and condemned to death by a far-from-impartial tribunal of religious and political judges. Remember that, for all her iconic status, courage, driving intelligence, and Promethean will, she was a child in so many ways. She was frightened of death, bewildered by the conflicting forces swirling about her, and devout.

She was persuaded to recant, to abjure her heresy/treason, but when she grasped the full significance of her recantation, she withdrew it and sealed her death by torching in a public square.

Shaw captures something of her pathetic and noble resolve to face death over perpetual imprisonment when he has her say in his drama *Saint Joan*: "I could do without my warhorse; I could drag about in a skirt; I could let the banners and the trumpets and the knights and soldiers pass me and leave me behind as they leave the other women, if only I could still hear the wind in the trees, the larks . . . the young lambs . . . the blessed church bells . . . my angel voices."[3]

Now, this is Shaw speaking, not Joan. And Shaw has a tendency to "improve" history (or mangle it) in order to best suit his dramatic purposes. But this passage, irrespective of its historical accuracy, encapsulates that visionary mode of knowing that sees into the heart of God and repudiates the guile and duplicity of power's reasoning.

Joan is the stuff of legend, albeit holy legend. Her burning in the marketplace of Rouen was an act that reverberates even now in politics, religion, and art. The list of those captured by the magic, seductive symbolism, or transparent holiness of the Maid who dragged a cowering dauphin to be crowned king at Rheims, who defeated armies and confronted canonists, is a list that includes, besides artists, neo-fascists like Jean-Marie Le Pen of France's National Front, monarchists and anti-republicans everywhere, and a wide array of feminist scholars and activists.

Acocella marvels at it all and sagely observes that our obsession with Joan will do her reputation no harm: "Her cult is big enough to absorb it."

Acocella also notes the growth of a scholarly discipline given over to the exclusive study of Joan, of her appeal to a broad spectrum of academics including "post-modern folk . . . women studies people, the queer-studies people, the deconstructionists."

She also has her own web site. In fact, she has several, as well as a St. Joan of Arc Anti-Defamation League, a "war game," and a rock group. It is indeed the Joan industry; a saint has never been so busy.

As Canadian visual arts critic Peter Goddard has noted: "In the Vatican, the saints are the action figures of Christendom; splendidly costumed and dashingly portrayed in roles they'll play out for all eternity." This is not only true of the saintly figures to be found on fresco or canvas, masterfully sculpted, towering in their representation in stone or pigment, but in their chronicled lives, holy mystique, and cultic significance. They are indeed the "action figures of Christendom."

And their fortunes rise and fall. If Joan had to wait centuries for her reward, others are still clamouring for a hearing — clamouring, that is, through their promoters, disciples, and earthly beneficiaries. Take Savonarola, for instance.

It is a chilling experience to stand inside the room in the Dominican convent of San Marco in Florence that housed the scourge of the Medici, the unbending friar Girolamo Savonarola. The room is a stark testament to his ascetic rigour. There is no warmth, no colour. His petrifying zeal knew no bounds, nor discretion, nor self-interest. He denounced all those who chose vanity over austerity, pleasure over mortification, corruption over purity. Savonarola denounced, in his unchecked zeal, both prince and pope, paying little heed to diplomacy, moderation, or practical discernment. In time, he paid a heavy price. He was excommunicated and executed, his ashes scattered on the River Arno, his achievements expunged like his life, all memory of him restricted to squabbling historians, inspired artists, disaffected friars, and puritans everywhere looking for a soulmate.

In 1998, five hundred years after he perished in flames in the Piazza della Signoria, Savonarola has been mooted as a future Florentine saint. The Archbishop of Florence opened his cause for beatification; his fellow Dominicans (only those of a particular disposition, mind) and a large body of admiring citizens (no doubt with an eye to the commercial and cultural benefits) have all come together to support the rehabilitation of the wronged author of the Bonfire of the Vanities. Such are the politics of saint-making.

But holiness speaks in sometimes muffled ways. The grand and controverted exhortations of a fiery Savonarola appeal to the few, in spite of their charismatic origin and theatrical delivery. It is, however, the quiet witness of a ragpicker that can speak with the greater clarity.

While occupied in the 1980s with co-authoring the biography of a leading Canadian prelate (*My Father's Business: A Biography of His Eminence G. Emmett Cardinal Carter*), I recall one occasion during our many conversations when he lamented the fact that several of his critics allowed him little room for consorting with the wealthy, the influential, the powerful. "Do they expect me to mingle with the ragpickers?" he asked with rhetorical scorn. Still reeling from that candid epiphany of prelatical hauteur, I went home and distracted myself by reading the Notebook section of *The Tablet* of England. Therein I discovered the following:

> Sister Emmanuelle Cinquin was once a professor at the Sorbonne. Now at the age of 78 she lives in a shanty town just outside Cairo among the ragpickers — the tramps who with their children collect the domestic rubbish of the city — and, she told Leila Farrah on a recent visit to London, feels she is "the happiest woman in the world." Born in Belgium, this Sister of Notre Dame de Sion still works "flat out." But she does not always sleep well at night, because the problems of the local ragpickers — who call her "Abieti," or big sister — are heavy to bear. . . . Her days begin early with the Mass. That is to drink from the true

source, she says, and "every morning my heart becomes really full with this bright water and during the day all it has to do is just to flow from my heart." Her life is based on a radical option for the poor. "I realised that if you want to help those in need, you have to share their life day and night. . . . What is important is to savour the moment, and the capacity to love which God gives. I might die tomorrow. I am actually very ill with broncho-pulmonary disease. But it doesn't worry me. I want life to be a fiesta."[4]

In the end, the model saint is capable of heroic self-emptying — *kenosis*, as the Greeks would have it — and it is the quiet drama of that act or mode of living that most inspires us. Still, the electrifying gesture that is martyrdom grabs our imagination with an immediacy that transcends the plodding beauty of a daily dying in love for others. In other words, the high drama of Oscar Romero's assassination is more gripping than the short, painful, and luminous witness of St. Maria Faustina Kowalska, John Paul II's first canonized saint of the third millennium.

Yet it is Romero, and not the cloistered nun-mystic, who has fixed the world's attention on the relentless fury of a love and faith sealed in blood.

Romero was a champion of human rights, nominated for the Nobel Peace Prize, a persistent voice for the voiceless, a tireless critic of government oppression, and a hierarch who took seriously the liberating summons to side in solidarity with the poor. As fellow Salvadoran Jon Sobrino has noted:

Archbishop Romero symbolizes so many things. He was murdered within the church, at the altar where he was about to offer bread and wine. Historians went back to look for a similar case, and they ended up with Thomas à Becket. It is true: the Archbishop of Canterbury was also assassinated in church — but there was a big difference between Becket and Romero. The way historians interpret the killing of Thomas à Becket revolves around his determined defence of church prerogatives and rights. In contrast, Oscar Romero never defended the rights and privileges of the church. In fact, he risked the very security of the institution itself, as we might know it. The radio station which broadcast his Sunday homilies was very often dynamited, interfered with, censured. But he never said: "Let's quit preaching this way because the interests of the Church are suffering." In fact, each time it cost him thousands of dollars to repair the station and, for that matter, his printing house. But resist he did. He had no choice. Not only that, but when he saw how his own priests were being killed he must have thought twice whether to go the same way or not. But he did go the same way. His faith and love for the poor made it impossible to do otherwise. It was as if he lived waiting for the bullets.[5]

I saw the place where he died while I was doing research with my colleague Douglas R. Letson on the Jesuits in San Salvador, just as I saw where the University of Central America (UCA) martyrs met their grisly deaths. I saw the photos of the shot Jesuits, their housekeeper and her daughter, the splattered brains, the crumpled bodies, and the blood, the blood everywhere. They were martyred because witness inspires witness. They died because Romero died, and he died because his assistant, Rutilio Grande, died. There is a holy, fearsome sequence to such noble deaths.

As I say, I have been haunted by the saints: the remote and dubious, like St. Pancratius, and the immediate and real, like Oscar Romero; the officially canonized, like St. Joan of Arc, and the unofficial holy ones, like the martyrs of UCA.

What goes into the making of the saints? Why do we need them?

In a culture that reverences the celebrity, that provides more than enough to feed the public hunger for gossip, that is prepared to see politics and entertainment as one, and that cannot escape the frenzy of the "now," the saints are both an attraction and a mystery. Books, videos, audio cassettes, CDs, and DVDs that focus on saints abound — as happened with angels a few years past — but, predictably, the quality varies wildly. Calendars, dictionaries, and the usual potpourri of lists, catalogues, and compact gems of saintly minutiae are ubiquitous. But do we understand the saints any better — their role in our personal and collective psyche, and the reasons behind the current resurgence?

Certainly, it helps that celebrities themselves are drawn to celebrities. Take, for instance, Jim Caviezel, the U.S. actor who portrayed Jesus in Mel Gibson's controversial *The Passion of the Christ*. Caviezel makes no apologies for his traditional Catholic devotionalism; in fact, he welcomes the opportunity to promote it. In his February 2004 article "Christ's Passion and Gibson's Lynching" for *New Oxford Review*, Michael Morris, a Dominican art historian, recounts his interview with the actor in which Caviezel's pious attachment to the saints was given full and sympathetic expression. He spoke to Morris of his conviction that Gibson and he were working as part of the Church Militant (that's us earthbound folk) struggling to bring the redemptive message of Christ to an unbelieving world, and that in order to do that as effectively and expeditiously as possible he wanted to engage the Church Triumphant (that's the heaven-sequestered folk). To that end, Caviezel amassed a number of relics from various saints, including Francis of Assisi, Padre Pio, Anthony of Padua, Maria Goretti (Caviezel has a special fondness for Italian saints), and — not unreasonably, given his profession — Genesius, a martyred Roman actor who became the patron saint of actors and who is sometimes confused with Genesius of Arles, also a martyr but with no discernible record of interest in the thespian arts. These relics he had sewn, along with his

Carmelite scapular, into the loincloth for the crucifixion scenes in *The Passion*. Determined to add a relic of the True Cross into the cinematic cross, Caviezel was delighted to achieve this end through the gracious assistance of an obliging Mother Angelica, founder and abiding spirit behind the Eternal Word Television Network. Perhaps both of these True Cross enthusiasts were unaware of Etienne Gilson's famous quip, made at a lecture series on species delivered at Toronto's Pontifical Institute for Mediaeval Studies in the early 1970s. Gilson, a Roman Catholic layman and intellectual of unimpeachable credentials, observed that "there are enough pieces of the True Cross in the world to build the Spanish Armada and enough phials of Precious Blood to sink it."

Canadian novelist, playwright, and actor Ann-Marie MacDonald has spoken of the high importance of storytelling in her youth, of how stories replaced geographical roots (she travelled extensively, as her father was in the military), of the priority of narrative over place in her life. The life of the imagination for MacDonald was inextricably tied to her religion, her interest in the saints nurtured by her love of their stories: "Although I was not allowed to watch *Perry Mason* on television, I got my sex, gore, excitement and violence from the lives of the saints like Agnes, Lucy, etc."[6] For many Catholics besides the author of *Fall on Your Knees*, the saints were a natural connection of faith and imagination in their youth, each feeding the other.

Adult faith in a postmodern world is at a clear disadvantage if it has jettisoned the saints because of some misdirected notion that there is no place for chronicles of mad heroism in a theological universe of right reason and lofty purpose. Ron Rolheiser, a theologian and spiritual writer, puts the case for saints starkly and urgently when he writes:

We're not lacking for solid ideas. What we're lacking is fire, romance, aesthetics, as these pertain to our faith and ecclesial lives. What needs to be inflamed today inside religion is its romantic imagination and this is not so much the job of the theologian as it is the job of the saint and the artist. We need great saints and great artists, ideally inside the same person.[7]

The saints — their stories, their witness, their lives — provide us with a solid dose of the romantic imagination. They are a worthy substitute for *Perry Mason*, an antidote to the sterile theologizing that mars much religious thought, and a spur to bold ventures of spirit and heart.

They are also a point of holy connection. In an interesting meditation on the Feast of All Saints, the polemicist, social activist, feminist theologian, and scourge of popes and patriarchs Joanna Manning reflects anew on the meaning of the communion of saints:

When Pope John Paul II came to Toronto in 1984, my son Nick was a student in Grade 7 at St. Michael's Choir School in Toronto and was chosen to sing the Gospel acclamation at the Papal Mass at Downsview. Because of the traffic restrictions in the city, he had to take the subway downtown to the Choir School early in the morning, and then board a special bus for transportation to the north end of the city. An hour after he had departed, the phone rang. It was a desperate Nick, calling from Dundas station. "Mom," he gulped, almost sobbing into the phone, "I've left my jacket on the subway and I am sure that they won't let me sing without my proper uniform." Already nervous because of the exigencies of the performance, he was now verging on the hysterical at the thought of facing the principal and explaining why he had come to school without the proper uniform on such an auspicious occasion.

An inspiration popped into my mind. "Now you remember me talking to you about your Auntie Ethel,"

I said. (In the heyday of her career, my late aunt sung with
the Covent Garden Opera Company.) "I know she's in
heaven now. Because she was a singer she'll understand the
way you feel. You just say a little prayer to her and ask her
to help you calm down," I continued, "and I'm sure something will work out." Little did I know at the time that
Auntie Ethel's reach was to extend beyond helping to calm
the stage fright of a small singer. A St. Michael's choirboy
travelling back into downtown from the other end of the
subway line sat in the very seat where Nick had left his
jacket, and so brought it into the school in good time to
reunite it with its owner.

A small miracle? Perhaps it was just a coincidence. . . .
The supportive kinship afforded by memories of past family
struggles can be an inspiration to persevere in the present.
The power of such subversive memory, which goes way
beyond what I was able to evoke for my son, has also
supplied me with the energy to continue along many a
difficult path. . . . This bond of companionship with those
who have gone before was activated for Nick in his hour of
need. And my feisty, sexy, singer aunt continues to inspire
and cheer us on as we, too, in the words of Paul, "race
towards the finish line and that glorious prize of heavenly
union" in the great community of God's beloved ones.[8]

Manning is not one inclined to sentimental Catholicism.
She is a severe and outspoken critic of the papacy of Pope John
Paul II, as you can quickly discover in her books *Is the Pope
Catholic?* and *Take Back the Truth: Confronting Papal Power and
the Religious Right*, and she has little stomach for pious piffle of
whatever concoction. As I say, a scourge of popes and patriarchs. But her personal anecdote about her son and deceased
aunt highlights that ineradicable sense of communion or time-

less companionship that is at the heart of the Catholic doctrine of the saints.

In his 1974 Massey Lecture *Nostalgia for the Absolute*, George Steiner notes that the decline of religion, the desiccation of theology, and the evacuation of inherited mythologies has resulted in a desperate "nostalgia for the absolute. . . . [a] starving for guaranteed prophecy."[9] I would argue that in our postmodern, globalized world, we hunger even more for communion, for connectedness, and in the ancient teaching on saints we can discover anew an antidote to the widespread feeling of existential loneliness, of cosmic isolation, that seems such an acute feature of our time. Sainthood as pap, as easy medicine for the frightened specks who inhabit the universe, is not quite what I have in mind. The saints are not fodder for the superstitious, nor commodities for those entrepreneurs with an eye for marketing to the devout. No, the saints are us, writ large.

For Roman Catholics, the saints are the holy ones. As U.S. theologian Richard P. McBrien observes regarding the Catholic tradition,

> there are at least four possible applications of the word "saints": (1) all those who have been sanctified, or made holy by the grace of Christ, whether they are living or dead, Catholic or non-Catholic, Christian or non-Christian, people of explicit religious faith or none; (2) those who, having been sanctified by Christ on earth, have entered into the joy of eternal life; (3) biblical figures in the time before Christ who lived by the Spirit of God and who became luminous examples of holiness; and (4) those whom the Church, either through popular acclaim or formal canonization, has declared to be members of the Church triumphant (i.e., those already in the company of God, the angels, and the saints in heaven) and who are

commemorated and invoked in the Church's public worship and private prayer.[10]

Stalking the Holy: The Pursuit of Saint-Making is concerned exclusively with the fourth application, and the next chapter will look at the history of the canonization process itself, a process that has undergone only a few changes in the last millennium. The script reads largely the same over the centuries, although there have been various changes to the set design, blocking, and dramatis personae. Let me briefly identify the key players in the sainting process at the same time that I remind you of what I mean by "making." Saints aren't actually made in the way that cardinals are created. The term "making" should be used with reservation, for saints are only *recognized* by human agency; it is the divine agency that does the actual making. Still, this official recognition is a kind of making replete with all those ingredients that go into any making: motivation, expertise, intentionality, insight, and risk.

Now, to the players: the individual or group that requests that a cause be opened for a particular candidate or candidates is called the *petitioner*; the one who has responsibility for all the legal, monetary, and procedural matters of the cause is called the *postulator*; the one who presides over the meeting of the theologians involved in the cause under review and is an official of the Congregation for the Causes of Saints (the Vatican body that has oversight over the entire process) is called the *promotor fidei* (promotor of the faith) or *praelatus theologus* (prelate theologian); the one who conducts a detailed review of the candidate's records and documents in the first stage, called the Diocesan stage, is the *promotor justitiae* (promotor of justice), who in an earlier incarnation was known as the *advocatus diaboli* (devil's advocate); the one who carries the heaviest burden in the second stage, called the Roman stage, and is responsible with a body of collaborators in preparing the major studies (*positios*) on the candidate's eligibility for final determination by the Congregation for the Causes of Saints is called the *relator*. These are the major players. There are minor actors as well: a cast of supernumeraries, a director (the Prefect of the Congregation for the Causes of Saints), subordinate directors, a producer (religious orders, a diocese, lay movements, etc.), and, of course, the executive producer (the pope). The following chapters will explore in greater detail the minutiae of sainting, the legal and historical changes in the process itself, alternating political and theological emphases, and why some of the rules have changed, but to help you map your way through the sometimes confusing terrain of this larger-than-life drama I thought it best to give you the list of characters before the end of Act One.

"Sainting" is not a uniquely Roman Catholic exercise or prerogative. Other churches in the apostolic and sacramental tradition — the Anglicans and the Orthodox — do likewise, although the elaborate liturgical, devotional, and juridical features of the Catholic iteration remain the pre-eminent model in Christian history.

Eastern Orthodoxy reminds its followers that saints make God attractive, conform their lives to Christ, and in keeping with the Greek word for saint, *hagios* (which means "not like anything else," "a person set apart"), exhibit in their lives a luminosity, transparency, or radiance that is unknown to them but clear to all who have eyes to see.

> Canonization in the Orthodox Church begins locally. Its first requisite is continuous and increasing love and veneration . . . by members of his community. The next step is reached when the hierarchy of a local church undertakes to examine all the records left by the holy man or woman, and if these prove satisfactory, then the last part of the act is performed and canonization is announced and other autocephalous churches are informed. This considered judgement of the Church is

essential, for sometimes people of exceptional spiritual gifts, but not necessarily of sound moral life and Orthodox faith, attract admiration and can mislead their followers.[11]

Although the notorious monk Rasputin, a man of undoubted spiritual gifts but utterly devoid of moral character, has never been raised to the altars, his principal employer, the Romanov family, has. Nicholas II, the last Tsar of All the Russias, and his family — Alexandra (the tsarina), Alexei (the tsarevich), and daughters Olga, Tatiana, Maria, and Anastasia — were all canonized during a special synod of the Russian Orthodox Church in August 2000. They were canonized with more than a thousand other Christians who had been persecuted for their faith during the seventy-year Communist tyranny. Efforts to canonize the Romanovs, who had been executed with four of their servants by the Bolsheviks at Yekaterinburg in April 1918, were met with considerable resistance by those Orthodox believers who felt that Nicholas's abdication in 1917 paved the way for the decades of Communist rule that were to follow. Others, including Metropolitan Yuvenali of the church's canonization commission, were initially resistant to the canonization of the tsar because there was no concrete evidence of miracle-working, although ecclesiastical officials eventually certified some of the miracles associated with the tsar, "including icon portraits of him that weep fragrant liquid. Such reports led the Russian Orthodox Church Abroad . . . to canonize Nicholas in 1981."[12] Debates among Orthodox hierarchs, both in Holy Russia and in the Diaspora, revolved not only around the various claims of miracle-making, but also the authenticity of the bones/relics of the Romanovs themselves. Doubts about Alexei prevailed to the end — they could find no conclusive evidence of his remains with the other massacred Romanovs — but the canonization proceeded nonetheless, under the assumption that the probability was high that he was executed with the others. In addition, the church authorities were at pains to insist that in canonizing the family they were not endorsing Nicholas's reign, nor arguing for the restoration of the monarchy. In the words of the synod proclamation, they were simply declaring the Romanovs to be a family "who sincerely tried to carry out the commandments of the gospels." The family was canonized as "passion-bearers," the lowest category of sainthood in the Orthodox Church, because of the "meekness, patience and humility" that defined their conduct in their last hours, conduct that was guided by "the light of an all-conquering Christian faith." Some Orthodox theologians argued that the Romanovs were martyred not for their faith but because of their imperial blood. At the time of the Romanov family canonization, some, both in Russia and abroad, were advocating for the cause of the more contemporary Russian "saint" Father Alexander Men, a parish priest, writer, and public figure who was brutally murdered with an axe on the morning of September 9, 1990, while walking through the woods on his way to catch a train to his church. He was mourned nationally and admired for his many gifts.

Alexander Men was not a profoundly original thinker: his genius was to communicate the best in Orthodox theology and spirituality in clear contemporary language, and to incarnate those values in his own life. Behind him stand the "way of the heart" of the Russian Fathers, the spiritual guides or *startsy* of the Optino monastery south west of Moscow, the late nineteenth-century and early twentieth-century renaissance of religious thought in the writings of Solovyev, Berdyaev, and Bulgakov, the witness of the cata-comb Church in which the young Alexander was nurtured, the Judaism of his mother's upbringing, and the martyr-dom of countless priests and lay Christians in Stalin's gulags. Through all this, Men characterizes his spiritual inheri-tance as "open to people, to their problems, their longings,

open to the world. . . . Men's testimony in 30 years of
ministry was to spiritual freedom, to mutual respect between
Church and State, and to dialogue between religions, but
above all to the power of love to transform human community, enhance human personality and fulfill the divine
creation.[13]

Whether Men is canonized or not is a matter for the politics
of saint-making. For many in the Russian Orthodox Church,
the time had come to vindicate the heroic witness, if not of the
tsar directly, then certainly of the butchered Romanovs — and
through them the countless thousands, perhaps millions, who
remained faithful to their Christian heritage in the face of the
Communist antichrist. Although dissent among Orthodox
Russians, as well as among those who profess no faith at all, on
the appropriateness of the Romanov canonizations will not be
easily laid to rest, there is no doubt that multitudes clamoured
for some form of recognition for the courage of those silenced
by Lenin, Stalin, and their brutal minions.

The Anglicans, too, have their way of acknowledging the saints.
Like the Roman Catholic and Orthodox churches, the Anglican/
Episcopalian communities worldwide have a *Common Worship
Calendar*. Although Anglicans are not bound to honour the saints,
invoke their intercession with the Divinity, or acknowledge the
papal prerogative in conferring official sainthood on a candidate, they do attach significant importance to the "great cloud
of witnesses," as the Letter to the Hebrews calls the saints.

The saints are the models of Christian life par excellence.

The saints maintained popular culture, providing drama
and human interest and stories of violence for generations
which knew nothing of television "soaps" or the Internet.
Inevitably the stories became embroidered and sometimes

muddled. . . . but their lives had the merit of *personalizing* theology . . . and providing models for others to follow.[14]

The Anglicans include in their list — their calendar — not only many of those historical figures sainted by the Roman Catholic Church, but many others who have not been added to the canon, *synaxaries* or *menologies* over the centuries. They include such prominent Anglicans as the seventeenth-century metaphysical poet George Herbert; the Oxford scholar-bishop Charles Gore; the slum worker and sister of William Morris, Isabella Gilmore; the Pre-Raphaelite poet Christina Georgina Rossetti; the founder of the nursing profession, Florence Nightingale; Dr. Samuel Johnson, the towering man of letters; the social and political activist Eglatine Jebb; and, always a subject of controversy, Charles Stuart, beheaded by Oliver Cromwell, Protector of the Commonwealth and regicide extraordinaire.

As you can appreciate, there are undoubtedly Anglicans of a more republican bent of mind who will wonder why King Charles I is included in their calendar of saints. Similarly, zealous disciples of the Iron Lady, Baroness Thatcher, may be disinclined to admire Anglicans of a socialist mould; Anglican readers possessed of a postmodern sensibility may be disposed to read the devotional poetry of Anglican saints through an unsympathetic lens; and founders of orders or communities of religious women may be viewed by some of their later coreligionists as unliberated neo-feminists. Fair game. After all, inclusion in the calendar is not commensurate with a high approval rating. Saints are products of their culture — historical beings, flawed pilgrims en route to final integration. They are heroic models, exemplars of holiness, icons of hope, and they are "sacraments, that is, both signs and instruments of grace. This is what the Church proclaims when it raises them, by whatever process, to the heights of sainthood."[15]

Publisher, writer, and justice advocate Robert Ellsberg has his finger on the pulse of many saints because he understands that we have frequently misread their importance. We have seen them as morose, flesh-hating, happiness-spurning loners keen on avoiding human contact and in love with suffering. Ellsberg sees them, by contrast, as more likely to be suffused with joy, guides to authentic happiness.

> The opposite of happiness is not sorrow, I learned from the saints, but deadness. Many of us know what that feels like: the dissatisfaction induced by a consumer culture that stimulates our sense and bombards us with largely meaningless choices, while leaving us starved for some deeper purpose. But this is not a new phenomenon. The desire to escape such deadness was one of the motives of the early desert fathers and mothers. They rejected a world whose agenda was defined by the pursuit of power, property, and pleasure. They went into the desert to tap into the source of life and to discover their own true selves. The story of such desert ascetics may appear harsh and off-putting to a contemporary audience. *The Life of St. Antony*, one of the earliest desert fathers, spares no detail of his ordeals in the wilderness — including hunger, sleeplessness, and the peril of wild beasts. Yet when he reappeared from the desert everyone was struck not only by his physical health but by the "soul's joy" that shone from his face: "He was never troubled, his soul being calm, and he never looked gloomy, his mind being joyous."[16]

Lest we conclude that the saints provide an easy route to bliss, that they are a sure guide to certitude in an age in love with doubt, that they are the perfect marketable item as progenitors of the ultimate "Chicken Soup for the Soul," psychiatrist Robert Coles reminds us that sainthood is no guarantee of perfection. The saints attest to the multiple ways that we seek God,

> the many ways of getting down on one's knees, in the hope (the hope against hope) that there is in this cosmos the listening, the watching, and, not least, the judging, the sorting, which so many of us, for so long have sought, prayed for, spent lives wondering about, waiting for — God in all the mystery of the word, in all the perplexity and frustration that the word can evoke.[17]

Because the saints have given themselves over to that "mystery, that perplexity and frustration" that we call God, and because they are the true stalkers of the holy, they speak to our collective need for transhistorical meaning, for perpetuity, to be "alone with the Alone." The saints are not an antidote to our agnosticism. They are a still point in the whirligig that is life, an aperture to wholeness.

Chapter One

THE PROCESS AND
THE CONTROVERSIES

NOVELIST, ESSAYIST, AND screenwriter Ron Hansen
puts it neatly when he says that "the hunger of our spirits is fed
by sharing in the glimpsed interiority of others."[1] We are drawn
to the lives of the saints because they give us access to their inner
struggles, defeats, and triumphs. Imitation may be the supreme
form of flattery, but it can be deadly with the saints. Think of
the martyrs.

Catholics have been exhorted to aspire to sainthood from
the beginning. In recent times they have nothing less than the
Second Vatican Council reminding them of the significance of
the saints:

> [T]o look on the life of those who have faithfully followed
> Christ is to be inspired with a new reason for seeking the
> city which is to come (cf. Heb. 13:14 and 11:10), while at
> the same time we are taught to know a most safe path by
> which, despite the vicissitudes of the world, and in keeping
> with the state of life and condition proper to each of us, we
> will be able to arrive at perfect union with Christ, that is,
> holiness.[2]

On the road to holiness are the saints, and they are there for
Catholics to imitate, venerate, and invoke. They have, in other
words, an active role to play in the life of the church. They are
more than travel agents to the Kingdom, and they are more
than simply guides. All Catholics are called to sainthood, and

many indeed are saints, but only a handful are officially recognized as such. This process of "sainting" involves several steps, but the ultimate one is known as canonization — adding to the canon, or the list of those officially declared as God's intimate companions. In some cases, canonization can follow fairly quickly after beatification — and by quickly I can mean a multiple of decades or a few centuries — but in many other instances the beatified, the *beati*, get to enjoy their interim status for an indeterminate period of time. Depending upon the time, the pope, and the saintly candidate's lobbying apparatus, the time before beatification can be considerably longer than that which elapses between the penultimate stage and the ultimate stage. Under Pope John Paul II, as we will see in greater detail later, candidates for officially recognized holiness had a streamlined and accelerated process. Canonization, one senior Vatican official outlines, includes such aspects as:

1) The majority of theologians considers canonization as an act of the infallible magisterium [teaching authority] of the Supreme Pontiff. In fact the text used in the declaration of solemn canonization declares: "We declare and define Blessed . . . is a Saint." 2) The subject of such a declaration is only a Catholic Christian. The Supreme Pontiff does not make such a declaration concerning persons not in full union with the Church of Rome. 3) The object of such a solemn declaration is that a person who has left this world, is actually in heaven, and now enjoys the beatific vision of God — Father, Son and Holy Spirit. 4) Therefore, the saint forms part of the heavenly communion of saints, can intercede for us before the Father, and is honoured with a solemn act of public, universal, and ecclesiastical cult, i.e., throughout the whole Church.[3]

This is the language of canon law, and the definition outlines the particular norms and conditions that must be met for a canonization to be valid. But the allure of the saint-candidate is to be found in the drama of his or her life and not in the licitness or validity of the cause. Fiction writers understand this better than canonists. As Ron Hansen notes:

> I am not sure I know what "heroic sanctity" is anymore, because all of my favourite saints are flawed in some deep way, so that when you examine their lives in a particular way you're going to unearth those flaws. I think that a lot of the biographies of the saints — the often-maligned hagiographies — that we had in the past painted the saints in such a way that we only had inconsequential peccadilloes to address. I think, however, that the saints have a general kind of angst gnawing away at them that they must battle all the time. My only problem with saints as they're "made" today is that the process is very selective. Whereas the populace at large has a very clear idea about what the saints are — Dorothy Day, Mother Teresa, the slaughtered Jesuits of El Salvador, Thomas Merton — we know that if you did a Devil's Advocate examination of these people's lives, you would always find something that would compromise their heroic sanctity. Certainly the people that we made saints in the early centuries were more often than not judged on how they lived at the end of their lives, not as they were as youths. I think, and certainly this is true of Day and Merton, that too much attention is paid to youthful indiscretions or to moments of bleakness or despair in middle age. This is problematic to me.

As it is for most moderns, to say nothing of most post-moderns. The canonization process that Hansen has difficulties

with has evolved over the centuries, and some of the most radical
changes in the history of canonization have been made in the last
twenty years. But from the very outset, as the Brooklyn-born
Monsignor Robert Sarno of the Vatican's Congregation for the
Causes of Saints makes clear, canonization has always been

> one of the most democratic processes in the church, in the
> sense that the church does not begin the cause for canon-
> ization until it asks the faithful of all levels — laity, priests,
> bishops — whether the person indeed has a reputation of
> holiness for having died the death of a martyr, or having
> lived a regular life dying a natural death and therefore qual-
> ifying as a confessor. In other words, the church does not
> really canonize before it discerns what God is doing among
> the faithful by raising in the minds and hearts of the people,
> through the power of the Holy Spirit, the conviction that a
> particular person is a genuine martyr or confessor. This
> conviction, if you like, of the potential saint's reputation for
> holiness is confirmed by God through what we call inter-
> cessory prayer, by which I mean that if the faithful believe
> that a person is holy and is in heaven they, the faithful, can
> pray for that person's intercession with God in times of
> need. And when God grants favours, graces, signs, and
> miracles through that person's intercession, God confirms
> that the Holy Spirit is truly working among the faithful to
> raise up the person as a model of imitation and as an inter-
> cessor in the very presence of God. First and foremost,
> then, the cause of canonization must be understood as the
> process of discernment, whereby the church discerns what
> the Holy Spirit is doing in the church itself. Mother Teresa
> used to say that she is "a pencil in the hand of God." Well,
> no one cares about the pencil. What they care about is the
> message that the pencil is writing, what God is trying to say
> to us through these holy individuals.

But how do you determine which "pencil" gets recognition? Certainly the process has mutated over time. The earliest saints were the "red" martyrs, those who paid the supreme price for their Christian faith during the Roman persecutions. But after the Peace of Constantine in 313 CE Christians began to venerate confessors, or the "white" martyrs — those who had suffered all kinds of hardships save death, and then others as well, including bishops, ascetics, persons from the Hebrew and Christian Scriptures, hermits, virgins, and teachers. Their tombs became places of cult or veneration where the faithful would gather on the occasion of the holy one's anniversary. The anniversary was not, however, that of the saint's birth but of his or her death and rebirth in heaven. There was no juridical tribunal, survey, judgement, or official inquiry. The declaration or conferral of sainthood was a spontaneous affair — canonization by acclamation, sainting via the *vox populi*.

The lack of official regulations and the emergence of factionalism, lobbying, and holy politicking resulted in the inevitable hodgepodge of shameless self-interest, nepotism, and simple piety. Things weren't looking good. Cults of dubious origin began to proliferate; *passiones*, or accounts of martyrdom, multiplied; official checks and balances were few; venal types with only a marginal interest in holiness outside of its marketability exploited the faithful's expanding taste for relics and pilgrimages; and to top it all off, various heretical martyrs were being promoted. It was time for action. The Church Council of Frankfurt in 794 decreed that one should only venerate those saints whose life was a certainty — a minimal requirement, one would have thought — and whose biography was credible. Nearly two decades later, the Council of Mainz forbade the *elevatio et translatio* (the disinterring of the body and its placement in a more worthy structure like a chapel or church) without the agreement of the prince and the permission of the ecclesiastical authorities. The bishops were now in control. They decided who was to be acknowledged and venerated as a saint. But as in all things Roman, the papacy wanted a bit — a big bit — of the action. In 973 we have the first documented case of a papal canonization: St. Udalricus, or Ulric of Augsburg. He is known as a zealous bishop — he had fifty years on the job, and, given the average lifespan of a male in the Dark Ages, that's a good innings — and he appears to have taken an active role in secular affairs and was reputed to have authored a letter against clerical celibacy (unsubstantiated and later proven to be a forgery). Pope John XV elevated him to the honours of the altar.

By the eleventh century, the Roman pontiff was eager to reserve the authority for controlling the sainting process to his august self. In 1170 Pope Alexander III wrote to the king of Sweden, reminding him of the pontifical privilege in the area of canonization — this was the first major plunge for exclusive claims — and by 1234 Pope Gregory IX cast nuance to the wind when he "expressly and exclusively" reserved to the Holy See the right of canonization. It was no longer a local episcopal privilege, but it was not until 1588, when Pope Sixtus V established the Sacred Congregation for Rites at the same time that he overhauled the Roman Curia (or command structure of the church) that there was an effort to firm up control of the hitherto localized process of sainting. From now on the suits, or rather the cassocks, take over. Sixtus ushered in the rule of the specialists, but it would not be until Pope Urban VIII (he of the Galileo condemnation) codified the practices in 1642 that we begin to see tight management from the centre. Urban issued decrees, in 1625 and again 1634, forbidding the public worship of persons not beatified by the Holy See. Although he beatified several during his pontificate, he canonized only two: Elizabeth of Portugal and Andrea Corsini.

A century later — in 1735, to be precise — Pope Benedict XIV published what would become a classic of its kind: *On the Beatification of Servants of God and the Canonization of the Blessed.*

This work remained normative for centuries and provided substantive material for the 1917 *Code of Canon Law*. Pope Pius XII (himself a candidate for canonization) "was moving to bring in changes and adaptations in line with the developments of modern science but he died before anything could be achieved."[4] There were rumblings at the Second Vatican Council (1962–1965) for decentralization of the process — beatification back to the bishops and canonization for the pope only — but nothing happened. At the Council, that is. In 1969, Pope Paul VI brought in modifications of his own: he eliminated ("suppressed," in canonical language) Sixtus's Sacred Congregation of Rites and set up two new ones, the Sacred Congregation for Divine Worship and the Sacred Congregation for the Causes of Saints. The latter was to concern itself with, in the words of the papal edict issued by Paul VI, "those things which in any way pertain to the beatification of servants of God; or to the canonization of (those declared) blessed, or to the conservation of relics." Other changes would occur as well, perhaps most earth-shattering the deletion of the adjective Sacred. To be fair, this was a congregation-wide adjustment and it suggests no disparagement of the duties of the office of sainting, only a rare spasm of dicasterial humility.

The tinkerings and modest tamperings that defined papal initiatives on the legislation governing sainting since Benedict XIV changed mightily on January 25, 1983, when Pope John Paul II both promulgated the new *Code of Canon Law* and issued the apostolic constitution *Divinus perfectionis Magister*, a work that generated major reforms in the centuries-long process of sainting.

Before we get to the document itself and the changes it occasioned, it will be profitable to consider John Paul's own penchant for saints, for no pontiff beatified and canonized more than he. In fact, the cumulative beatifications and canonizations of all John Paul's "predecessors of happy memory" don't equal his in

number, breadth, and daring. John Paul II is the saint-maker *par
excellence*.

The "why" for Kenneth Woodward, veteran *Newsweek* religion editor and author of the influential *Making Saints: How the
Catholic Church Determines Who Becomes a Saint, Who Doesn't,
and Why* (1990), is disclosed late in John Paul's career,

> when he asked in anticipation of the Jubilee Year 2000 that
> Catholics around the world draw up a list of twentieth-
> century martyrs who were Christian, but necessarily Catholic.
> That underscores his view that the martyrs are really the
> boast of the church. John Paul would be very much at home
> with the Early Church Fathers in this regard. I think that by
> doing this he shows a penetrating insight into the enduring
> significance of saints and particularly of the martyrs. If the
> saints, and the martyrs as a privileged form of heroic sanctity,
> are the special boast of the church, then maybe it's time that
> the church did some boasting — big time. Now, to go back
> in time, this explains his interest in using the mechanisms of
> canonization to point to people as examples for contemporary
> Christians. In addition, John Paul was a thespian in his early
> life and has a proper instinct for the dramatic. He also
> has an instinct for the universal symbolic. For instance, he
> has recognized that when you acknowledge a saint, espe-
> cially within a population of the church that doesn't have
> one, like Afro-Americans, he is binding this community to
> the church universal, and to the figure of the Holy Father
> himself as a living symbol of the Universal Church.

Robert Mickens, a pontifical university graduate, onetime
Vatican Radio translator and commentator, and Rome corre-
spondent for various publications, sees John Paul's theatrical
sense working in harmony with his traditionalist theology:

John Paul is a sacramental pope, by which I mean that he likes symbols, he likes the public square. He likes to make what we call teaching moments for the church. He likes to use examples and signs, physical things, momentous occasions, people, as a moment to transmit the truths of the Catholic faith. In this, as in many other matters, he is, I believe, a medieval pope. Some people wince when they hear the word medieval, but I think he is precisely that: medieval in the sense of mythic. He understands that the saints have mythic power themselves, that they are incarnational figures, that they bring faith, heaven and earth together in some magical configuration.

And epic was what John Paul especially liked. Consider the list of the holy he accumulated during his pontificate. John Allen, a feisty *vaticanista*, or Vatican-affairs expert, who files for the U.S. publication *National Catholic Reporter*, thinks the John Paul II record for sainting was remarkable on several levels.

John Paul is a man who experienced in his bones the suffering of the twentieth century. He experienced the consequences of National Socialism and the consequences of Soviet totalitarianism. Many of the people he has beatified or canonized are martyrs to some variation of twentieth-century despotism. I think that he feels a personal responsibility that goes well beyond his responsibility as pope, but he is pope, and most importantly he is the first Slavic pope and a man whose personal life experience reflects so much of the horrors, of the carnage, of the last century. I think that he feels an obligation to never let us forget, and I think that many of his beatifications and canonizations are calculated with that in mind.

As well, I think that he's a pope who is also very much in touch with currents in modern culture, the dominant ones in the West being such potent forces as secularization, dechristianization, etc. What we face is the detachment of the normal cultural ethos from its religious roots. In such a context as this, the church can no longer impose its moral teaching through the instrument of the state, so the pope has concluded that the world needs new models of holiness. By lifting up so many people from so many different lands and cultures, the pope is providing precisely such examples. Now, it is true that there is some debate as to whether or not he has been successful, since the overwhelming majority of the people beatified and canonized have been religious-order women and men and they are hardly representative of church as a whole. Still, he has made an attempt. But, and this is interesting, he has made a more successful attempt in the distribution of saints throughout various parts of the world. He has consciously chosen to make saints in Asia, Africa, and Latin America. If you look at the roll of the Roman Martyrology, which lists the some 6,000 recognized saints of the church, you will note that the overwhelming majority of them are European, but John Paul more than any of his predecessors has worked at spreading out the saintly demographics.

For Mickens, John Paul is medieval and for Allen he is attuned to contemporary cultural trends, but in either case, through whatever intellectual and emotional lens, the Pope understood that the life of holiness, in the words of his 1993 encyclical *Veritatis splendor*, "constitutes the simplest and most attractive way to perceive at once the beauty of truth, the liberating force of God's love, and the value of unconditional fidelity to all the demands of the Lord's law, even in the most difficult situations." (107) And the life of holiness is best exemplified by the individ-

ual lives of the holy ones. Hence, John Paul's unrivalled tally
of saints.

With *Divinus perfectionis Magister*, and the "Norms to Be
Observed in Inquiries Made by Bishops in the Causes of Saints"
issued two weeks following the promulgation of *Divinus*, it is
clear that a significant overhaul is underway. As John Paul wrote
in the preface: "Most recent experience . . . has shown us the
appropriateness of revising . . . the manner of instructing causes
and of so structuring the Congregation for the Causes of Saints
that we might meet the needs of experts and the desires of Our
Brother Bishops, who have often called for a simpler process
while maintaining the soundness of the investigation in a matter
of such great import." The Pope went on to observe that
involving the bishops more closely with the sainting process is
in keeping with the spirit of collegiality so enthusiastically
promoted and endorsed by the Second Vatican Council. Not a
few bishops can be excused if their wonder admixed with cynicism when they heard the Vatican express such interest in acting
collegially, given that they have little say on so many other
matters of "great import."

Sarno outlines the changes wrought by the new legislation,
changes that go some way towards downplaying the juridical or
adversarial approach of the past by substituting a more historical and pastoral approach for the advocacy role, an approach
that reintroduces the importance of local initiative and that
places greater focus on the use of a wide range of experts drawn
from all over the world:

> The first radical change which stands out is that the Holy
> Father has given the local diocesan bishop the authority to
> initiate a cause of canonization. He no longer needs the
> permission of Rome to introduce or start a cause. As a
> matter of fact, it would be important for people to know
> that Rome does not start a cause. I receive letters in my

office asking the Holy See to start the cause of this or that person and, invariably, we always write back reminding people that they must approach the local bishop, who has the direct responsibility for initiating causes, for discerning whether a proposed candidate has a true reputation for holiness as well as a demonstrated reputation for intercessory power on behalf of the faithful. This is the first radical change instituted by John Paul's legislation, although in a certain sense it was already anticipated by Pope Paul VI in 1969.

Another change is the express requirement that documents of any manner, shape or form that can serve as proofs either for or against the cause must be added to the process proper. Another change consists in the departure from the stark juridical nature of the canonization procedure as hitherto experienced. Various legal definitions and functions have been jettisoned in order to show that it — the canonization process — does not just involve the members of the Tribunal (the episcopal delegates, the promoter of justice, the notary etc.) but everyone who is involved in gathering the truth about the candidate and the cause. On this point we have a redimensioning, a reconstruction, of the old figure of the *advocatus diaboli*, or Devil's Advocate. At one time the D.A. had a special burden or assignment, both canonical and historical in nature, but with the elimination of this role, at least as performed by a single individual, we have an important and controversial change. Everyone now is the Devil's Advocate in the cause of canonization; everyone is obliged by moral law and by church law to contribute to the discovery of truth.

But not everyone is happy with this devolution. Woodward quite pointedly deplores the "dejuridicizing" of the process. As he notes, most people did not realize that as the canonization process unfolded over the centuries it became more and more juridical and adversarial, involving local players on one hand — increasingly canon lawyers — and Roman officials on the other hand — likewise canonists — who ended up, as lawyers do, batting back and forth on fine points of law. The process took forever. In an effort to expedite things and respond to the impatience experienced by many over the torturous unfolding of a case, the new legislation simplified matters by eliminating the double investigations — local and Roman — and redefining some of the responsibilities so that needless duplication can be avoided. Such is understandable. But the new legislation also got rid of the *advocatus diaboli*, and of his office, on the grounds that the process should move away from its adversarial function to a collegial one. This means that the model is no longer that of the courts but of the academy. Instead of a vigorously debated brief we now have a dissertation defence. Gone is the adversarial nature of the process, and my biggest complaint about this regrettable reform is that now everybody involved in the process has a stake in its positive outcome. There are no neutral players. The only person who can call a halt to the process is the *relator* — the dissertation supervisor, if you like — the figure under whom the life, virtues, investigation, the whole thing, has to be constructed. As you can see, he faces formidable obstacles, even of an emotional nature, for he is the one who is left to say: "Look, I'm awfully sorry, but your candidate simply has a fatal flaw. Tough." At the same time all the pressure is on him to make it work, the temptations to cut corners or avoid unwelcome critics omnipresent. I've seen it happen. The net effect of this reform has been to endanger the integrity of the process itself. And I am not alone in thinking this way.

For Woodward, as for others, the inadequacy of the new reforms was egregiously on show over the cause of the Spanish priest and founder of Opus Dei, Josemaría Escrivá de Balaguer. Escrivá's rapid ascent to sainthood disturbed his critics, exhilarated his disciples, and perplexed the majority of his coreligionists. Although Opus Dei is nothing like what Dan Brown says it is in *The Da Vinci Code*, it does succeed in stirring up conspiracy fears, wild notions of cultic intrigue, and fantasies of secret societies.

His cause for sainthood was a subject of heated debate, flagrant politicking, urgent intercessions, and full-assault manoeuvres by detractors from the very moment of the introduction of his cause. In fact, controversy accompanied Escrivá to his death.

Escrivá was born in 1902 and died in 1975, and during that time he saw his Spain undergo tumultuous changes, from monarchy to republic to dictatorship. Persuaded that he needed to respond to the toxic anticlericalism rampant not only in Spain but throughout large parts of Europe in the 1930s, he founded Opus Dei (Work of God), a corporate structure, or ecclesial movement, that has been variously throughout its history a pious association of laity, a pious union, a secular institute, and by 1982 a personal prelature, this latter change an extraordinary recognition of its autonomy by making it accountable only to the pope. Needless to say, not a few in the hierarchy, in the curia, and among religious-order superiors throughout the world gasped inwardly at the Pope's beneficence. Did this gesture imply a special papal approval of Opus Dei and its founder?

Undeniably, John Paul II was a man much edified by the scope, fidelity, intelligence, influence, rigorous spirituality, and traditional thinking that defined "his" prelature. An organization with many layers of commitment — ordained and non-ordained, celibate and married — with specific duties and categories (numeraries, oblates, supernumeraries, co-operators), Opus Dei is grounded in the writings of Escrivá, most particularly his series of spiritual maxims, *The Way*. Historian and lawyer John F. Coverdale identifies Escrivá's original purpose for Opus Dei in the 1930s, and by doing so identifies its current appeal and motivating force as well:

> Escrivá saw the aim of Opus Dei as promoting among Catholics of all walks of life an awareness of the fact that their baptismal vocation involves a call to personal sanctity and a desire to live out that truth in their daily lives. A sincere personal commitment to striving to model their lives on Christ's life would, Escrivá foresaw, lead the members of Opus Dei, and others who lived its spirit, to try to make their society more just and harmonious, more in keeping with Christ's teaching. Their active Christian presence in society would, thus, contribute to making it more Christian. This would not be the result, however, of an effort by Opus Dei to organize Catholics for political activity. Rather it would spring from the personal commitment of its individual members to putting Christ's teachings into practice in their personal lives and in their daily work and other activities, including their political activities. The idea is captured in a point of *The Way*: "A secret. An open secret: these world crises are crises of saints.— God wants a handful of men 'of his own' in every human activity. Then . . . *pax Christi in regno Christi* — the peace of Christ in the kingdom of Christ."[5]

Not so new. If anything, unchanging. Escrivá's followers celebrate the timelessness of his spirituality, its apolitical nature, its empowerment of the laity, whereas his critics see Opus Dei entrenched in a pre–Second Vatican Council mode of thinking, avowedly apolitical but in fact deeply political, and, in spite of its professedly pro-laity posture, classically clerical in structure and approach to ministry. It's not surprising, then, that Escrivá's cause was as polarizing as the man himself. Michael Walsh, a

British historian and unrelenting critic of Opus Dei, entertains no illusions regarding the makeup of the model Opus personality, nor of the larger ambitions of the prelature itself:

> Opus spirituality and structures inculcate a view of life which is socially stratified, self-confessedly committed to the bourgeois ideal, highly disciplined and over-respectful of authority.[6]

A perfectly oiled machine, as it were, ever at the ready, deferential to Rome, well positioned in a devotional and theological universe that is preconciliar in orientation and composition, a model "spirituality of creative resistance," a spirituality that is

> likely to be engaged in a recovery of that sense of the transcendent, of the numinous, that has been tragically lost following the ravaging excesses of the Council's liturgical reforms. In addition, [such a] spirituality is likely to be firmly situated within an established tradition of spirituality that is fully cognizant of the conventions and forms of piety that are historically conditioned yet desirous of their imaginative recovery or reinstatement. A spirituality with an emphasis on restoration will be characterized by a close affinity with spiritual luminaries of the past and with a visceral fidelity to the institutional church and its hierarchy.[7]

And "visceral fidelity" Escrivá demanded: not only for the church, Vatican authorities, and the papacy, but for himself and Opus Dei as well. And therein lies the rub. For many Catholics, Escrivá's reputed sanctity was a matter of supreme indifference, but when his followers were eager to advance his cause and gave evidence of expediting the process and courting papal favour to boot, a surprising phalanx of critics emerged keen on stalling or discrediting Escrivá's candidacy. Woodward was one of them:

The cause of Escrivá illustrates only too well what happens when a powerful group like Opus Dei, although it could just as easily be the Jesuits, desperately wants something to happen. They make it happen. For instance, the *petitioner* or *actor* of the cause is Opus Dei itself. Opus chooses the *postulator*, the one who has the responsibility to act on behalf of the *petitioner* and whose duties include handling all the legal, financial, and procedural matters pertaining to the cause. Naturally, an organization or body will choose as *postulator* someone who is congenial to their own outlook on life and brand of Christianity. The Escrivá *postulator* told me that he was simply a middle man. All the work had been done. Opus was fiercely intent on seeing their man sainted.

While I don't consider this process a political one in the negative sense of that adjective, in this case I think there was an inordinate amount of pressure. History may show some day that this pope owed these people a lot — something to do with *Solidarity*, perhaps. Right from the beginning there were problems in my view. No one was allowed to see the *positio*, that is the document or study that is put together on the life and virtues of the *Servant of God*, which by the way is the title that is given to the person from the moment the cause is initiated at the diocesan level. [There are three *positios* — the *positio super martyria*, the *positio super miraculo*, and the *positio super virtutibus* — which respectively document aspects of martyrdom, if such apply, investigate all alleged miracles and undertake medical authentication, and study the claims for heroicity of virtue.] Although one is not entitled to read the *positio* on virtues, the Congregation for the Causes of Saints shares this stuff. This time they were very secretive.

And then out of the blue Opus Dei itself announces that the *positio* on Escrivá's heroicity of virtue had been unanimously approved by a panel of nine judges. But in *Newsweek*

I was able to report that two of the judges — Luigi DeMagistris and Justo Fernández Alonso — had in fact rendered sharp disapproval of the *positio*. Each had independently cast a "suspended" vote, demanding that certain questions be resolved before proceeding further. One of the dissenting judges, in fact, warned that the beatification of Escrivá could cause "grave public scandal" to the church. You can say "yes," "no," or "suspended vote." It is very rare to say "no," but in registering a "suspended vote" you are saying that there is a problem that needs to be resolved. Two such dissenting votes are sufficient to halt a cause until all objections have been met and satisfactorily answered. But the objections of DeMagistris and Alonso were ignored. Why?

In fact, Cardinal Oddi told me that many bishops were "very displeased" by the unseemly push to canonize Escrivá. In addition, when I finally did get a copy of the *positio*, there was only one guy who was critical of Escrivá, and his criticisms were dismissed as irrelevant. In other words, it was hardly a balanced study.

It's not difficult to conclude that Woodward is no Escrivá votary. As he observes tartly of the Founder — or, as he is more reverentially addressed, "The Father" — with respect to his penchant for spiritual *bons mots*: "I think anybody who reads his books is going to be put off by them, with their little aphorisms that make Benjamin Franklin's Poor Richard look positively rich in thought; nor is his thought likely to become a school of spirituality. I think that the canonization of Escrivá was a low point in the process." For others, however, as the progressive Catholic British writer Annabel Miller discovered when she sought out an Opus Dei couple, Escrivá's summons to sainthood is a universal one grounded in the local and the ordinary. Each day, an Opus Dei member is expected to attend

Mass, spend an hour in mental prayer or meditation, do a quarter of an hour's "spiritual reading," go to weekly confession, and attend what are called circle meetings and monthly recollections. To find out what quite this entails, Miller arranged to meet Teresa and Philip Crabtree — parents of ten children — in St. Albans, and found herself in a very different world from what she had expected. Instead of being on "Walton's Holy Mountain," she was dead centre in the world of regular British family life.

> Teresa was brought up in a staunch Catholic family, and got to know Opus Dei when she was at university in London. A down-to-earth woman, she shows no signs of being oppressed by the demands of Opus. When I asked her how she coped with the daily spiritual requirements, she said: "If you don't manage it one day, don't worry. Maybe God wanted you to do something else then." Her husband Philip was brought up in the Church of England, but became a Catholic when he left university, and followed Teresa into Opus Dei. As a couple, they are deeply involved in their local parish of St. Alban and St. Stephen, where Teresa gives catechism classes to local children who do not go to Catholic schools. As for her own children, Teresa says: "The only thing I hope for is that they are good Catholics. I pray for them to become saints." Her reference to "sainthood" was made without irony. Josemaría Escrivá encouraged his followers to aim for sainthood and they openly admit this. Their idea of sainthood is not, however, to do with standing on a pedestal above the world; it is much more earthy than that. Philip told me, for example, about the challenges that he faces at work in trying to avoid the usual gossipy office chat. "I just walk away," he said.[8]

Although Woodward, and scores like him, find little appealing in St. Josemaría Escrivá, that is hardly grounds for opposition to his sainthood. But on matters relating to the unprecedented speed given his cause, the behind-the-scenes skulduggery, the failure to review Escrivá's close relationship with the Spanish government during the Franco years (the government archives were off limits), the willingness to suppress commentary on the Founder's ill temper and aristocratic pretensions, and the defensive posture adopted toward any and all critics — including those of a benign frame of mind — on these matters there is reason for some discomfiture, if not suspicion. Such public reservations, however, have not prevented Opus Dei authorities from now opening the cause for Escrivá's immediate successor — and major player in his own canonization — Alvaro del Portillo. It has become a holy juggernaut for Opus Dei members, another reason for Woodward to despair. But the politics of saint-making does not discourage John Allen, who acknowledges that, although some causes move with alacrity and others with holy doggedness, there are many factors over which the Vatican has little or no control. He realizes that because the Vatican is a human institution, it is therefore

political by definition. I think that we need to take a couple of steps back and remind ourselves what the theology is that underlies the system of sainting. The theology is never, never, that the Vatican or the pope makes a saint. As we know, if someone is a saint, he or she is already enjoying the Beatific Vision. They don't need a note from the pope saying so. The point of beatification and canonization is not to impart holiness, but to recognize the holiness that is already there. Everyone knows that at any given time in human history there are many more people living holy lives than we can possibly recognize. So why do we, then, recognize anyone? In theory, it's because we lift up saints as role models because there is something particularly compelling about their life stories that speaks to the universal church at any particular point in time. Given that, I don't think there is anything nefarious or off-putting about the thought that the Vatican might go slow on a particular candidacy because this person right now cannot serve as a role model — which is no judgement on their personal holiness or their qualifications as a saint, only that such pacing speaks to the cultural context in which we find ourselves.

Now, having said that, I think there are other factors at work here. One of the misconceptions about the saint-making process is that someone in the Vatican is sitting there deciding when things are going to go forward and when they are going to slow down, and when you are going to hear a lot about this candidate in the media and when you are not. The truth is that the Vatican is in many ways, until you get to the ultimate stages of the process, a largely passive player. The agents in this thing that drive a candidacy are the primary backers — a religious order, or an ecclesial movement, in the case of a founder — and it is a question of their commitment to the candidacy and of the resources needed to pour into the process that will determine how active the cause remains. And when the cause encounters an obstacle, do the agents go away or remain more resolute than ever? It depends, of course, on how committed the people are who are behind the cause.

Take, for instance, Queen Isabella, the Catholic wife of King Ferdinand of Aragon: she remains a potent symbol for conservative Catholics in Spain, and although her cause waxes and wanes, depending on the political climate, she will never go away because there is a nucleus of Spanish Catholics who are pledged to see her become a saint.

Sainting is, therefore, a matter of timing. It is also a matter of lobbying, funding, and discerning. Sarno disputes the politicizing, but acknowledges the politics.

To speak of the politics of canonization seems to me nothing more than a journalist's catchphrase. First of all, we have to be clear about one thing: it is absolutely true that the process has been streamlined as a result of the changes of 1983. But that does not mean the process's seriousness and thoroughness have been sacrificed. There have been many advances made in historical criticism, in theology, in order to both streamline and maintain the integrity of the process. To do both. Another element that has accelerated the causes of many of the candidates is the fact that a miracle is no longer a requirement for beatification, if the candidate is a bona fide martyr. In the case of a confessor, only one miracle is required prior to beatification; and in the case of both martyrs and confessors, only one miracle is required *after* beatification for canonization.

Now, the Congregation for the Causes of Saints does not, and cannot, create miracles. We cannot tell God how, when, if, where, and through whose intercession a miracle can be brought about. The Congregation basically awaits God's action. And so what happens in the end is simple: some causes go much quicker than others not because of a "political" decision, or because of a theological or ideological position on the part of church authorities, but because the Congregation only deals with what is sent to it. If a miracle is sent to us, we deal with it; if it is a matter of heroic virtues, we deal with it; or if it is a martyrdom, we deal with it.

However, there is no doubt about it — and this is not a secret or unique revelation — but there is a human reality about *how* we deal with what we have. For example, the Congregation has in excess of some 300 *positios*, or positions, on virtues or martyrdom that are awaiting discussion by the theologians. [The theological consultors have the responsibility — along with the *promotor fidei* or promotor of the faith, also known as the *prelatus theologus* or prelate theologian — to study the cause and determine the merits of the cause under review.] Now, how do you decide, humanly speaking, which of these *positios* is going to go forward for discussion every year, considering the fact that our experts — historical, theological, and canonical — are all university professors with demanding teaching schedules, dissertations to be supervised, exams to be set and marked? It is not as if we can give each scholar five or ten *positios* to review. Let me give you an example: the cause of Pope John XXIII involves a position of some nine or ten volumes consisting of thousands of pages. Now, if you give a full-time professor a *positio* like that, and he does the appropriate study, such an undertaking is going to take a long time.

Still, it is true that not all causes are the same. You can't put the cause of a John XXIII in the same category as the cause of a founder of a religious order, just as you cannot put the cause of Mother Teresa in the same situation as the cause of a lesser-known figure. There are some causes that, because of popular acclaim and indisputable devotion, deserve a certain precedence. But, let me assure you, the process is followed, strictly and completely.

In spite of Sarno's assurances, however, there are many besides Woodward who worry about the Congregation's response to effective lobbying and its own perception of saintly priorities. And indeed, there are many who find the apparatus controlling saint-making a regrettable departure from the church's early and more normative experience. One scholar who is especially critical of the Roman procedure — both pre- and post-1983 — is the feminist theologian Elizabeth Johnson of New York's Fordham University. She argues that the community should reclaim the sainting process by return[ing] to the method used by the church for the first twelve centuries. When a member of the church stands forth in such a way as to elicit from everyone the recognition that here is a way to Christ, here is a luminous person, someone through whom shines the rays of integrity and faith, then that person should be added to the list — to the canon — and the local bishop can then proceed to approve the addition. If the name and the reputation spreads, then others can add the name to their list, etc. In other words, this is a process from the grassroots up. I think this has happened in various places already — for instance, with the martyrs in El Salvador (Oscar Romero and the Jesuits at the Central American University).

Do I think that we should undo the Vatican bureaucracy and the whole canonization process? Yes, I emphatically do. Still, we must keep in mind that we are a universal church and we live in a global era and therefore there should be some kind of standard, some kind of measure. But fairly applied. I want to make the point that very few poor people are canonized. Who has the money? Also, very few lay people are canonized because it's the religious orders who can afford to release a person from other duties and send him/her to Rome to function as an advocate. There's something wrong with this system. It already prejudges who is going to be recognized, and I would prefer a more spontaneous and local dynamic.

Sarno is inclined to a different view. As an official of the Vatican dicastery, or department, that is in the saint-making industry, it should come as no surprise that he attaches high value to the Roman procedure — admitting a few changes, improvements, and directions — and is sanguine about the broadening and inclusive trends unleashed by Pope John Paul II.

The Congregation now gives a certain priority to the causes of lay men and lay women because in the past their causes were not done as frequently as the religious orders, simply because the process was so long and complicated and the orders had the wherewithal — personnel, financial, etc. — to continue the cause through its decades-long, and sometimes centuries-long, journey. You will see among those people involved in the causes of saints — the officials at both the diocesan and Roman level as well as the postulators, experts, etc. — a sensitizing on the matter of lay people that is a direct result of John Paul II. The pope has sensitized these people to the broader needs of the church. As a consequence, you will find many religious orders who are happy and willing to take on the causes of lay people. Permit me to add a parenthesis: there are very, very few causes for diocesan priests under consideration. [Sarno is, as you will recall, a priest of the Diocese of Brooklyn.] You should also know that a number of religious orders have also taken upon themselves the causes from Third World countries — particularly those who don't have any saints at the moment — without any possibility of financial reimbursement. I attribute this sensitization to the pope.

If Sarno is satisfied that progress is being made on the lay-cause front and Johnson wants to wrest from Rome the authority to add to the list, Allen sees the problem in a slightly different way.

Why aren't more lay people out there recognizing their peers as models of holiness? Why aren't lay organizations in the church sending people to become postulators, to advance the causes of these figures? Why, at the grassroots level, isn't more of that activity happening? My sense is —

and I know this is the case from talking to officials in the
Congregation — it is astonishingly rare for a cause of sainthood to move through the diocesan system and then end
up at the Congregation that has not been put forward by
either a religious order or an ecclesial movement. Even
those movements that are ostensibly lay-led tend to put
forward for consideration their founders, or guides who are
invariably clerical. If lay Catholics want more of their own
role models recognized as saints, then, by God, recognize
them as such.

It may well be that Allen is espousing an antinomian
approach, adopting an incendiary strategy as opposed to his
more customary irenic stance, because he wants to rouse the lay
beast and get some action. It is a trifle disingenuous, however, to
reprimand the laity for inaction when all the cards are stacked
up against them. When the expertise, the power, and the sheer
volumes of patience required are an essentially Roman or clerical preserve, when the religious orders of men and women have
centuries of applied practice, when the models that have been
incorporated into the canon bear little resemblance to the lives
of the ordinary folk that constitute the majority of Catholics,
and when the institutional structures are not in place to ensure
that the progress and continuity of a cause will not be depend-
ent on certain individuals only, it is difficult to see how the laity
can radically insert themselves into the current process with any
guarantee of serious success. This, in turn, makes papal interest
in married saints of more than marginal consequence. And John
Paul was, as they say, on side. He admitted in an address he
delivered at the annual Lenten meeting of the Rome clergy on
March 5, 1992, his own frustration in finding a married couple
to beatify. As he put it, "the normal inventory does not exist" —
the candidates were not in the system, even though they existed.
The Congregation for the Causes of Saints was not to blame;

rather, the Pontiff noted, it was the fault of the Christian community at large. Shades of Allen. Unlike men and women religious, the laity don't have on-site advocates and they don't have a history of experience. But we must find worthy lay persons ourselves, the Pope reasoned, because "there is no tradition in this area and thus the human mechanism is missing [that] which is necessary for the process of beatification and canonization. We have to think all this over. The Congregation for the Causes of Saints is somewhat the executive, but the people of God, the Christian community in various places, are responsible for the system, the mechanism for moving ahead."

If the Pope was making a case for enhanced lay involvement in the sainting process — and he was — and if the Pope was making the case that the laity be in the system — and he was — then every effort must be expended to draw lay people into the entire process from beginning to end. The Pope's prescriptions for a larger inclusivity, however, did not diminish or curtail the clerical involvement in the process, nor did he envision a further change in the composition and mandate of the Congregation itself. It's up to the Christian people themselves to get serious about bringing forward more of their own. As Woodward observes:

The pope wants to have married saints, and I have to smile at this because when I was writing *Making Saints*, moving along the pipeline were the parents of Ste. Thérèse de Lisieux, Louis Martin and Zélie Guérin. Now, to the extent that saints are to be models for others — and these others are the people living in the church today, and not the dead — the Martins are terrible models for saints because all their children went into the convent. They had five girls who entered either the Carmelites of Lisieux or the Visitation Sisters at Caen. Their other four children did not survive to adulthood. But the Martins are not ideal models for married saints, either: Louis himself wanted to be a priest and Zélie a nun. And when they got married they had to go to a priest to see if it was okay to have sexual intercourse. . . . Nobody's going to pay attention to these people.

It might be a bit harsh to say that "nobody's going to pay attention," but Woodward's point is well taken. The difficulty of making a credible, interesting, and relevant case for a married couple's canonization is going to involve some examination of the place that sexuality — not some etherealized notion, but the real thing — played in their married lives and in their own growth as mature individuals. And whenever sexuality is mentioned, the Roman Church bristles and balks. Although it is true that we are all sexual beings, that sexuality is at the heart of human self-definition, and that we live *in* and *through* our bodies, and although it is true that this is orthodox Catholic teaching — organic, liberating, and suffused with a special beauty — it is also true that this very teaching is controverted, misunderstood, and divisive.[9]

The tensions and contradictions that exist in Catholic teaching on sexuality, virginity, and marriage have never been more dramatically highlighted than in the contemporary period. The gender wars, the ongoing debate over artificial contraception (settled in fact, though not in theory), the shifting paradigms that define human relationships, the scandals surrounding sex abuse by clerics, and other issues, combine to make the Catholic sexual landscape a parched and desolate place. John Paul was right in trying to bring to this desert a few awe-inspiring examples of married folk who can give credible witness to the joy of an integrated, life-giving, and wholistic sexuality. But Woodward remains skeptical:

It seems you have a better chance of being canonized if you had a miserable married life. You suffered stoically — especially if you were a woman — from a spouse who beat you or maltreated you one way or another. I don't think the Roman authorities have quite figured out what to look for — in other words, how to recognize the virtues of a healthy and happy married life. I mean, part of the spirituality of Christianity — at its heart, as it were — is suffering: a dying God on the cross! Suffering and spirituality go together. If you have happily married persons who seem to be enjoying a normal sex life and who get along very well, what do you do? In fact, because such people are rare exemplars in our culture, we should be looking for more of them. . . .

I would argue that we turn the process on its head. All that the investigating celibates see are the joys of the body, but that's because they don't understand. In marriage there is a daily dying to the self, which is quite demanding: to have to live in a day-to-day relationship with someone else, to achieve harmony, balance, a true Christian life of self-donation, this complete life commitment has not been thoroughly thought through.

And one can see the consequences of promoting, as models of married life, persons who strike moderns as preciously arcane at best and as conduits of a discredited anti-body teaching at worst. The response will be cynical, if not risible, dismissal. If the Martins were problematic — and they were of a previous century — the Quattrocchis were an invitation to misunderstanding. Luigi Beltrame Quattrocchi (1880–1951) and Maria Corsini (1884–1965) were the first couple to be beatified *together*. The Pope was determined to use the beatification ceremony as an ideal occasion to celebrate the ageless wisdom of his apostolic exhortation *Familiaris consortio*, to warn against the rising tide of liberalization on matrimonial matters (the legitimacy of common-law and same-sex marriages), and to show to the world — and the president of Italy and the queen of Belgium, who were among the VIPs gathered in Rome for the penultimate step to saint-hood for the Quattrocchis — that, in the Pope's words at the beatification, "the path to holiness achieved together, as a couple, is possible, is beautiful, is extraordinarily fruitful and is funda-mental for the good of the family, the Church and society."

And there is much in the lives of Luigi and Maria to suggest that they did indeed serve as models of holiness in a domestic setting. Luigi was at one time a deputy attorney-general and Maria a professor, they were active in Catholic matters in the public arena, and they were good parents to their four children. But they were never quite the norm when it came to nurturing or exemplifying familial life in a regular environment. For instance, three of their four children became priests — it was never an option for their daughter — and after twenty years of marriage they chose mutually to forswear sex, occupied separate beds, and lived as brother and sister for the remaining twenty-six years of their life together. Knowledge of this anomaly prompted Jack Dominian, the eminent psychiatrist, marriage counsellor, and prolific author, to write:

> Whilst applauding this belated recognition of the sanctity of marriage, one has to ask what sort of signal the Pope is sending about married sexuality in the twenty-first century. The Second Vatican Council acknowledged the beauty and wonder of sexuality as a precious gift from God, and was quite clear about the union of sexual intercourse and love. At a time of widespread trivialisation of the meaning of sexuality, it is this teaching which urgently needs to be widely known for the sake of evangelisation.[10]

Dominian is not alone in marvelling at the notion that a credible celebration of the splendour and integrity of sexuality in the context of married love could be found in a relationship in which there was an intentional absence of sexual intimacy. This is not to deny that the married love expressed between Luigi and Maria was intense, authentic, and fulfilling; however, by eschewing sex for nearly three decades, the Quattrocchis underscored the message received by countless Catholics for centuries: conjugal sex may be good, it may be pleasurable, but it is never entirely free of suspicion and fear, and it is, although worthy, not as exalted a vocation as virginity. This is a teaching that now enjoys little acceptance, continues to be severely critiqued by ethicists, psychologists, anthropologists, theologians, and numberless Catholics, yet is painstakingly reiterated by the Vatican and John Paul at tiresome length. It came as no surprise then that when the beatification of the Quattrocchis was announced, media speculation centred on their non-sexual life, on the public significance of extolling the married life of spouses who lived as siblings, and whose children, with one exception, embraced clerical celibacy as a way of living.

Sarno was quick to respond to what he saw as biased journalism, a journalism focused on "the wild, the absurd, the abnormal," a journalism that has no time, place, or inclination to provide the larger historical and cultural picture:

Newspaper and magazine journalists are often incapable of giving the full, broad picture, and unfortunately in today's society we look for the different, the wild, the absurd, the abnormal, the out-of-context, the countercultural thing. The fact that the beatified couple abstained from sexual relations does not at all denigrate sexual activity in the life of a couple; it only shows that the Quattrocchis' response to the challenge of living their spiritual lives was met. The

church is not offering each and every individual moment of
the life of the beatified as if they should be imitated, but
what the church is saying is that a married couple can live
in union and respond to God and to each other in an heroic
manner. The Quattrocchis interpreted the Christian message
for themselves, responded to God's grace, and, therefore, it
is the responsibility of the church authorities to simply
provide the full picture of their lives and let the faithful
evaluate what elements they think are or are not acceptable
or workable in their own married lives. The church should
not be saying: unless you have holes in your hands and feet,
you are not holy; unless you can levitate, you are not holy;
unless you deny yourself sexual activity in marriage, you
are not holy. The saints are not all alike; they are all different individuals, living in different times, in different places,
and in different ways, all struggling to attain sanctity, and it
is incumbent on me to find out how God is offering me
grace to live my vocation in this particular way, in this
particular time, in this particular space, in this particular
sociocultural faith ambience.

At various times over the years, the cause of Jacques and
Raïssa Maritain has been mooted, if not introduced, with little
apparent success. They, too, dispensed with sexual intimacy
throughout their married lives and in effect lived as brother and
sister. Each achieved renown in their respective fields: Raïssa was
a poet, diarist, and mystic, and Jacques was a metaphysician,
aesthetician, and political philosopher. They were spiritual
giants in their day, and they mingled with the mighty and the
humble on both the secular and the ecclesiastical stages. For
many years it was anticipated that Jacques, a favourite of Pope
Paul VI, would be named a cardinal, but it wasn't to be. The
Maritains influenced a legion of intellectuals, artists, and political and religious leaders during their time (Raïssa lived from

1883–1960 and Jacques from 1882–1973) and they were genuinely extraterritorial in their reach and scope. Whereas the Quattrocchis were largely unknown in their lifetime and the Maritains bestrode the global stage, it is the obscure ones who have made it to the altars.

In Canada, the cause of Georges and Pauline Vanier has made little progress, despite the national recognition accorded both, particularly Georges. In 1998 Georges Vanier, Canada's former governor general — or queen's representative — lawyer, diplomat, war hero, and devoted parent and husband, was named by *Maclean's* magazine as the most important Canadian in history. Deeply respected and admired by all Canadians irrespective of political allegiance, ethnicity, language group, or creed, Vanier was, in the words of historian J. L. Granatstein, "Canada's moral compass as governor general, an unquestioned man of probity and honour."[11]

Claude Ryan — politician, editor, savant, and committed Catholic — should have been empowered to write the *positio* if for no other reason than because he understood implicitly the complex demands on Vanier's life of faith in the public arena:

> On questions of public life and the progress of civilization, he had lofty views which drew from the purest wellsprings of the great philosophical traditions of the West. But he was at the same time and to a very rare degree a profoundly religious man; one of the most moving aspects of his sojourn at Rideau Hall [official Ottawa residence of the queen's representative] was without doubt the royal liberty which he granted himself at every circumstance to bear witness to his faith in God.
>
> In an environment where by weakness more than by malice one tends to confine all too willingly one's religious values to one's private life alone, Mr. Vanier never hesitated to testify frankly and publicly to his convictions. Never,

however, did he do so in a way designed to hurt other people. . . . Wherever he found himself, in the military life, in diplomacy, in political life, Mr. Vanier loved others very much indeed.[12]

If love isn't the final measure or arbiter of holiness, then what is? But married love is more than a puzzler for the Roman overseers; it's a theological conundrum. How do you persuasively talk about the joys, fruits, grace, and plenitude of married love *without* talking about pleasure, *without* taking seriously the simple physicality, the happy carnality of it all? In other words, talking about married bliss without celebrating the ways in which such love finds open, guilt-free, and generous sex smacks of doublethink. It is not as if, however, there were never any married saints — or indeed, married couples. In *Married Saints and Blesseds Through the Centuries* (Ignatius Press, 2002), German theologian and priest Ferdinand Holbock has determined that almost a hundred married couples — in which one or both spouses were either beatified or canonized by the church — can be culled from both ancient and modern sources. Holbock acknowledges the difficulties involved in advancing the causes of the marrieds — costs, the centuries-acquired expertise of religious congregations, the considerable expenditure of time and research resources — but he also clings to the traditional notion that virginity disposes one to holiness in ways that cannot be offered by the married state, to say nothing of an active sex life. He boldly claims what remains accepted wisdom in many official circles: "the chances of living a life of Christian perfection are greater in the cloister than in the hectic confusion of the world." It is simply easier to become holy in a state of consecrated virginity than it is as a person publicly pledged to mutual love with a lifelong partner.

But if married love poses a general problem, women pose a particular problem of rising proportions. Elizabeth Johnson:

Canonization has not been good for women. Fully 75 percent of the canonized saints in the Roman Catholic Church today are men, leaving women at 25 percent. I always ask my students: "Does this mean that men are holier than women? Does it mean, rather, that men have had the power of naming in the church?" Apart from canonization, we do have the wonderful doctrine of the *communion of saints* — a doctrine, I might add, that does not distinguish among all the various peoples according to gender, race, age, class, sexual orientation . . . anything really. The point is that it's a community of people baptized in Christ, filled with the Spirit of God, and even though sinners, participating in the holiness of God. Such a community or communion stretches across all the earth, is all-inclusive, and is non-discriminatory. We see this most clearly on November 1, the Feast of All Saints. This communion is in our very midst and in the creed we confess it. For women today who are seeking an equal place in the church — or for any of the many groups that have been dispossessed — the communion of saints is an affirmation of the mystery at the heart of the church, a mystery that can subvert an institutional structure that says otherwise.

Feminist research in the last few decades has done a marvellous job in retrieving the lives of holy women in the Bible and throughout all the various historical periods of the church who have been widely overlooked. The communion of saints simply subverts canonization because it says the church is distributing honours according to some worldly norm and not in accordance with the fundamental themes and standards of the genuinely inclusive communion of saints. This doctrine — the *communio sanctorum* — has a lot of potential to encourage lay people, married people, women, people who are sexually active, and yet you hardly have any of these people being canonized. There

has been no happily married woman who has been canonized unless she was a queen, nun, or widow. What does this
say to the majority of women in the church?

Although the general — though it must be said, not exhaus-
tive — exclusion of happily married women from the rosters of
the officially holy has recently been changed with the canonization of Gianna Beretta Molla, of which more later, the comparative
absence of women is deplorable. Whether the preponderance
of men in the canon is a result of entrenched patriarchy, Roman
hostility or incomprehension, an exclusivistic reading of the
ancient doctrine of the communion of saints, a lamentable deficiency in the collective imagination, or a combination of all of
the above, the fact remains that women — and in particular,
certain kinds of women — are absent from the list. But one
special kind of woman has commanded Roman attention for
some time, and the reasons for that very attention can be both
intriguing and disturbing. Take St. Maria Goretti, for example.
She was born near Ancona, Italy, in 1890 to poor parents, and
her father died while she was quite young. In 1902, Alessandro,
an adolescent neighbour, made sexual advances, and when she
resisted an attempted rape, he stabbed her numerous times and
she died the following day, forgiving him beforehand "for the
love of Jesus." Her murderer served a sentence of thirty years,
repented, and along with many of her surviving family —
including her mother — was at her canonization ceremony as a
martyr to chastity in 1950. By refusing to accede to Alessandro's
demands, Maria paid the price of her life. Although the cult of
Maria Goretti flourished for decades, she is now seen in a
different light by many, especially by young feminist women.
The politics of her canonization was at the heart of Giordano
Bruno Guerri's inflammatory 1985 critique *Poor Assassin, Poor
Saint: The True Story of Maria Goretti*, a work that provoked a
nasty debate in Italy among anticlericals, the devout, historians,

investigative reporters, polemicists from the ecclesiastical right and left, feminists, and a smattering of libel lawyers. At the end of it all, her sainthood remains intact. Still, her popularity has waned considerably among many, including Italian youth, and Kathleen Norris, the American poet and spiritual writer, has concluded that Goretti has been given short shrift by a sex-saturated culture that finds the particular ingredients of her witness unsavoury.

> I don't find it hard to believe that Maria Goretti is a martyr in the classic sense, that she died for her faith, after all. To say anything less is, I believe, to continue to relegate her to the status of a cipher. In our age, virginity seems little enough to make a fuss over; many girls see it as a burden to be shed as soon as possible. It is difficult for us to conceive of a girl refusing to allow a violation of what she surely saw as her God-given bodily integrity, even though it cost her life. Why should Maria Goretti be so hard for us to understand, and accept?[13]

Persuaded that Goretti's witness to her bodily integrity is exactly what we need in our age of easy disparagement, Manichean contempt for the body, and the commodification of sex, Norris draws a deeply unsettling parallel with the barbarous death of the Canadian Catholic secondary-school student Kristen French. In spite of being subjected to numerous acts of indignity and sexual degradation, of being mercilessly threatened and forced to watch the videotaped death and dismemberment of Leslie Mahaffy, another hapless teenage victim of the pathological duo of Paul Bernardo and Karla Homolka, French refused to perform a particular sex act and observed to her murderers that "some things are worth dying for." This is not to suggest that Kristen "is better off 'pure' and dead than raped and alive. . . . If one dares to say to her attacker, 'Some things are worth dying for,' there is nothing joyful about it, except possibly within, some inner defiance, some inner purity and strength that defies the sadist, and the power of his weapons. The mystery of holiness infuses such defiance."[14] Although some might be outraged by the comparison of French with Goretti, Norris is right in seeing congruences in their death and witness that transcend personal background and societal formation.

Goretti's Italian peasant makeup and the Catholic sensibility prevalent in fin-de-siècle Italy during her short life, coupled with the traditional familial emphases that flourished during the Fascist period, combine to make her the most popular saint of the century. She came to eclipse that other virginal worthy, Gemma Galgani. Rutgers University historian Rudolph M. Bell, author of numerous works including *Holy Anorexia*, insists that a sharp distinction be made between these saints, although they were contemporaries:

Gemma Galgani was born in 1878, and her mother dies when she is seven years old. She is then raised by her very secular brothers and sisters and her desperate father ever scrambling to keep his pharmacy business alive. Although from a bourgeois rather than peasant family like the Gorettis, the family fortunes are in decline. Gemma's father dies of throat cancer when she is seventeen and she falls under the care of a paternal aunt, begins to experience intense spiritual epiphenomena, is desperately unhappy at home, and finds herself increasingly misunderstood. She then decides to move out of the house — there is considerable resistance to this idea from the Galgani household — and into the Giannini family, a much better-off bourgeois candlemaker's operation. While living among the Gianninis, five of whom become nuns — obviously a very devout family — Gemma's religious experiences are more regularly recorded. Gemma eventually contracts tuberculosis in her

early twenties and dies at twenty-five, one year after the
death of Maria Goretti and right before the feast of Easter.

In Bell's view, "Galgani is a compelling saint in so many
ways: confident, grandiose, manipulative, childish, abandoned,
loved, complicated, simple-minded, admired, forgotten. She is
a modern saint, at least in the narrowly chronological sense,
since she is the first person who lived in the twentieth century to
receive the Catholic Church's highest honors, beatification in
1933 and canonization just seven years later on May 20, 1940.
Yet she is also a timeless saint."[15] Bell sees her timelessness, or
transhistorical quality, in certain features of her character that
identify her as part of a tradition of female virgin saints, the
most perfect exemplar being Catherine of Siena: mystic, stigmatic, visionary, reformer, a holy anorexic — emaciated and
self-destructive. Gemma, like Catherine, is a "deeply introspec-
tive, passion-oriented, Christ-obsessed" young woman who is a
"learn-to-live-with-God kind of saint." In fact, in a dialogue she
has with Jesus that she records and dates March of 1901, she is
told explicitly that "It is I, Jesus, who speaks with you . . . in a
few years by my doing you will be a saint. You will perform
miracles and you will receive the highest honours of the altar."
It doesn't get much clearer than that.

But what is it about Gemma, who did not have the genius,
psychological penetration, or charisma of that fourteenth-century
Doctor of the Church, Catherine of Siena, that nonetheless
allowed her cause, her cult, and her sainthood to achieve a
commendable level of popularity before being eclipsed by Maria
Goretti? For Bell,

> she represented in practical and political terms certain
> female heroic qualities — innocence, simplicity of life,
> domesticity, interiority — that the Vatican was keen on
> highlighting at the time it was negotiating with Mussolini's

government to sign a concordat ensuring Catholic rights and prerogatives in the Fascist state.

Although such qualities as submissiveness, introverted behaviour, and passionate colloquies with the Divinity might suggest a limited appeal worldwide, Bell notes that, in spite of being a self-closeted loner in many ways, Galgani became a model who transported rather well. She became an inspiration to shopgirls in Ireland, to mill girls in England, as well as to young women in Portugal, China, Korea, and Brazil. But she was especially important for the Passionists — and here comes the politics — because they were more than a little annoyed that, outside of their founder, Paul of the Cross (Paolo Francesco Danei), they didn't have any saints. The Discalced Clerks of the Most Holy Cross and Passion of Our Lord Jesus Christ, more manageably abbreviated to the Congregation of the Passion, was approved in 1741 by Pope Benedict XIV and concentrated specifically on reclaiming lapsed Catholics, ministering to the sick and dying, and preaching retreats for the benefit of persistent sinners. The Passionists had wide appeal throughout Italy, and the two most influential figures in Galgani's spiritual development were Passionists — the aggressive saint-maker and spiritual confessor to Galgani, Father Germano Ruoppolo di San Stanislao, and St. Gemma's female role model, Mother Maria Giuseppa del Sacro Cuore. In addition to the urgency attached by members of the order to finding some saints (although Gemma is not technically a Passionist saint, having been declined admission to the convent), the church in Italy was increasingly distressed by "modernist" tendencies that encouraged degrees of female emancipation that made the Roman authorities uncomfortable. The Vatican of Pope Pius XI (1922–1939) was looking for a saint-protector and role model who could go some way to offset the appeal of working women, smoking women, Charleston-loving women, and sexually liberal women. A tall order, admittedly, but Gemma fit the bill.

For Gemma, in the words of poet Catherine Sasanov, "suffering's the currency that counts."[16] Gemma represents a type of saint that is more illustrative of a mystical ascesis — of a self-negating intensity — than the criteria for modern heroism would allow, and that is viewed with deep suspicion not only by society at large, but also within the church. Young women claiming a special and fervid relationship with Jesus have often posed a threat to the arbiters of orthodoxy. How do you deal with impressionable young women given to romantic notions, to irrational — if not hysterical — fantasies? Gemma and her ilk, Bell argues,

> strive to achieve a *spiritual* unity with Jesus in varying forms, from carrying the infant Jesus through to Jesus as husband, culminating with Jesus as the crucified one. They generate disbelief, suspicion and outright hostility from male clerics. These uniquely female saints — and I would include Francis of Assisi among them, because he is often thought of outside the category of gender and possessed many qualities traditionally identified as feminine — faced general incomprehension from ecclesiastical authorities. But even Francis, with his occasional struggles with the hierarchy, never encountered the kind of suspicion about his holiness that his female counterparts do. If Gemma had been a do-gooder, a teacher engaged in the active apostolate, she would not have engendered such suspicion, but her deeply private and personal relationship with Jesus, her *kenosis*, or self-emptying, becoming in fact a *joining* of self with Jesus, that posed a danger.

This danger — a special relationship with Jesus that is extra-doctrinal, outside the canons of regular and observable religious behaviour, and unmediated by clerics — is frequently contained by the church by being allocated to the realm of subjectivity. Novelist Hilary Mantel sees the church's canonization of Gemma as a

weaselly accommodation with her career history, recognizing the sanctity of her life but not the supernatural
manifestations which surrounded her: manifestations which
are so dangerously impressive to lay people, who are always
looking for a sign they can understand — even an illiterate
woman could have read the marks on Gemma's body. So
Gemma got her reward for being downtrodden, humble,
abject — not for being a living testimony to Christ's
Passion. Her bodily sufferings and her visions were not
part of her claim to sainthood. The Church recognized
that Gemma had actually felt certain pains and sincerely
believed that heaven had sent them, but they were consigned
to the subjective realm. Within the Church, pain can
become productive, suffering can be put to work. But
outside the Church suffering loses its meaning, degener-
ates into physical squalor.[17]

Gemma's suffering is indeed the "currency that counts," but
within prescribed limits. Holy anorexics are, after all, a troublesome lot.

If Maria Goretti, the child virgin and martyr, and Gemma
Galgani, the virgin mystic, are the two dominant Italian saints
of the twentieth century, the twenty-first century may well
augur change. On May 16, 2004, John Paul II canonized
Gianna Beretta Molla — wife, mother, and pediatrician — "the
first married saint of the modern era, and though women with
children have been canonized over the centuries, their role as
mother has been peripheral to their saintly virtues. But in the
story of Gianna's life, her motherhood is central."[18] From
virgin to mother, from mystical daughter to pediatrician —
quite a shift.

Molla's canonization, predictably, has not been without its
controversies. But her life itself is uncomplicated and straight-
forward. Born in Magenta in 1922, she was one of many children,

earned degrees in medicine and surgery at the University of Pavia, opened a medical clinic, subsequently specialized in pediatrics at the University of Milan, married an engineer, and in 1956 had the first of her four children. In the words of her Canadian advocate, Basilian Father Thomas Rosica, "she met the demands of mother, wife, doctor and her passion for life with simplicity and great balance."[19] Her passion for life — at least for her own life — was, however, not to prove supreme. Faced with a tumour in her uterus during her fourth pregnancy, Molla was confronted with some stark options: she could undergo a hysterectomy — thereby removing the life-threatening tumour, but in the process terminating the pregnancy — or she could choose an alternate surgery that would, sadly and predictably, create serious complications at the time of birth but considerably augment the chances of survival for the child. She chose the latter option, and given that she was a pediatrician was fully cognizant of the risks involved, particularly for herself. She reminded her husband that "If you have to choose between me and the baby, save it, I insist." The baby was born, healthy and thriving, in April of 1962, but Molla perished, a week after the birth, from septic peritonitis. Her choice was exceptional, heroic, and an extraordinary act of love, but as the prominent Catholic Dr. Helen Watt, Director of the Linacre Centre for Healthcare Ethics in London, England, carefully observes:

> In refusing a hysterectomy, Gianna Molla was going beyond the call of duty — in much the same way as St. Maximilian Kolbe did in offering his life in place of his fellow prisoner. Intervening harmfully on the body of an unborn child by having an abortion is something quite different from intervening on your own body, foreseeing but not intending that your child will die or miscarry as a result. Refusing surgery to which you're entitled is heroic, but not morally required.[20]

In other words, a loving, caring, and responsible mother faced with Molla's dilemma could have chosen otherwise. This is not to minimize Molla's sacrifice but only to avoid disparaging women who have acted differently when faced with similar choices. Molla's holiness, her heroic self-giving, and the very fact that the child she refused in any way to imperil, Gianna Emanuela Molla, has herself become a physician, have contributed to the sometimes nasty debates — mostly intra-Catholic — surrounding the emblematic or political significance of her canonization. Clearly, for many in the Vatican, in the Congregation for the Causes of Saints, and among the countless numbers who invoke her intercession, Gianna Beretta Molla has become the patron saint of motherhood, a counter-sign to all those women who have elected abortion irrespective of the reason. This concatenation of circumstances — a modern Catholic woman, a medical doctor, a devoted spouse, an educated Italian, a plummeting birth rate in Italy, wide public acceptance of abortion, a fiercely pro-life pontiff — easily explains the division of opinion following the canonization. Although many, including St. Gianna's postulator, the Capuchin Paolino Rossi, deplore the politicization of Gianna's sainting, the simplistic conflation of her life of witness to *one* act of heroism, and her co-optation by various single-issue groups in the church, the fact remains that there are several critics who see a transparent manipulation of St. Gianna to serve a "papal agenda."

Vatican critics, such as Toronto author and activist Joanna Manning, do not dispute St. Gianna's holiness. "She is obviously a good woman, but this is one of the pope's means of advancing (the pope's) agenda. Gianna fits into that — the canonization of women who are holy because they die for the sake of their babies. The message is, their lives at all times count for less. . . . They put the life of the unborn or just born over the life of the mother — and that's often to the detriment of the family, leaving other children bereft of a mother and a husband bereft of a partner. The pope doesn't allow for other choices that may be right for women."[21]

Rosica laments the polarizing strategies that obscure, if not jettison, the comprehensive and indiscriminate holiness that defined Molla:

> He insists John Paul II's decision to canonize Dr. Molla is not a papal arrow aimed at abortion, which the Roman Catholic Church says is the immoral killing of unborn human beings. Father Rosica says Dr. Molla would have been a candidate for sainthood even if she hadn't died rather than submit to an abortion. "To reduce her life to the final moments and try to declare her as the anti-abortion saint would do great injustice to everything she stands for," Father Rosica said.[22]

It is entirely reasonable to conclude, however, that she has become the "anti-abortion saint," when one considers that the two miracles required for the sainting process involved cures — both, incidentally, in Brazil — that were related to pregnancy. In one instance, it involved the miraculous healing of a seriously infected woman following a Caesarean section, and in the other a woman who successfully persisted with her pregnancy despite the absence of amniotic fluid, and against the advice of the medical authorities. Furthermore, Molla has been invoked as a patron by people struggling to provide alternatives to abortion. Reducing her life's significance to the final moments prior to death — moments during which she repeatedly cried out in severe pain, "Jesus, I love you. Jesus, I love you," is indeed, however, a "great injustice." Molla is more than her death, more than her heroic choice, more, even, than a mother and a wife.

The difficulty associated with identifying women as saints is especially highlighted by the Molla affair, but it is British scholar and writer Kathleen Jones who directly homes in on the gender imbalance among the saintly crowd:

> Traditionally, women saints have been classified as virgins, matrons and widows — that is, by family status rather than by their own achievements. Yet we do not write of "St. Jerome, bachelor," or "St. Peter, married man," and if a male saint became a widower, we assume that the loss was his private affair, not a description of his personality. Women have been treated by ascription, men by achievement; but a holy life is essentially a matter of achievement. Women do not become saints by being somebody's wife, somebody's daughter, or somebody's mother. They become saints by the way in which they deal with the problems of living.[23]

By such a reckoning, Molla would be seen less in terms of her marital status and the manner of her dying and more — much more — in terms of her life of service and self-donation, her career as a pediatrician, and in terms of the sheer joy and "passion for life" that she brought to all that she did. In other words, Molla the mother and spouse will also be Molla the whole person, her value reduced neither to one single moment nor to one specific role or social function. Then she might be seen for who she was, rather than for what she represented, and only then would the unseemly skirmishes over her reputation dissipate.

The Molla canonization also raised what is for some a tedious canard, yet which remains for others a continuing obstacle in the way of promoting more causes among the laity: filthy lucre. John Allen:

Most estimates come in at a million dollars from the beginning of the process through to its conclusion. Not everyone has that kind of money sitting around. You're talking about several years to move through the diocesan phase, then the efforts involved securing the decree of heroic virtue, the authentication of the miracle, the costs attendant on the beatification ceremony, the acquisition of the second miracle, the larger costs associated with the canonization ceremony — this is a long, arduous, complicated process, and the simple truth is that most people will give up long before they see the fruits of their labours.

Allen's concerns are seen by Woodward, however, as trivial and irritating.

It bugs me no end to have people repeat how expensive it is. "Isn't it too costly?" you sometimes hear Catholic Worker types say — not only about their founder, Dorothy Day, but about anything. Well, it's not expensive; it's labour-intensive. The little old nuns and priests, as well as those not so old, get very little pay for their work, and their diocese or order suffers the loss of their employment for other apostolates. It really is very inexpensive, especially if you eliminate some of the expenses attached to the ceremonies. All considered, the research, the travels, the tribunals, etc., don't involve much financing. If it takes fifty years, plus seven or eight fluctuating currencies, and you factor in the cheap labour, it's not very expensive at all. It's a red herring to say it is. After all, everything costs at least something.

Recent estimates generated by the Vatican have concluded that, compared to a presidential inauguration, a coronation, a royal wedding, or even an impeachment, becoming an official saint is a lot cheaper. Archbishop Edward Nowak of the Congregation for the Causes of Saints calculates an average saintly expense of some fifteen thousand dollars. For those prepared to invest in the process, one could see such a cost as a bargain, but for those skeptical about the whole enterprise, like Robert Mickens, it is a waste of money.

Most people don't really care about canonizing saints. There's only a small minority in the church who really care about championing the cause of unknown and unsung heroes. I don't believe it is, or should be, a priority. Quite frankly, most people look at the sainting process with curiosity and wonderment. For instance, before they beatified Pope John XXIII, they trotted him out in his mummified state and displayed him in St. Peter's Basilica. People lined up for hours, and for some it was an opportunity to see a pope they knew and loved, but for others it was simply a chance to see a dressed-up papal corpse. But most Catholics, liberal or conservative, are not going to invest the time and money into the saint business. Of all the offices in the Vatican government, the one that is least helpful and should be shut down is the Congregation for Saints. Can you imagine an institutional body telling us who is and who is not in heaven, who is close to God and can intercede on our behalf? Such stuff is silly. Let's acclaim our heroes as they did in the early church. The procedures we have — the whole saint-making apparatus — is simply overdone in an ecumenical age. And the saint business can be a dangerous business: Pius XII, a great pope if you take away the whole thing with the Jews, and John XXIII, whose cause had a wrench thrown in the works at some early juncture because there were so many in the Vatican who didn't like him. Of course we need our heroes, those who inspire us — look at Aristotle — but we don't need to declare them saints.

Mickens's radical surgery — never mind the occasional amputation, just toss the body live and kicking — is not likely to carry any clout either in official church structures or among a sizeable number of the laity, but his frustration with the process — the politicking, the antiquated honours system, and the commodified spirituality — does strike a chord among many Catholics. Paul Mariani, literary biographer, essayist, poet, and scholar, puts it baldly. Ruminating on the emptiness of most human achievement, and on the unsettling truth that he is a "poet-dabbler, a scribbler, most of whose work will no doubt shortly be forgotten" and who would rather watch television than assess his true measure, says, after all is said and done:

> how many saints have I ever seen anyway? Mother Teresa at a distance in the UMass football stadium? On the other hand, I may actually have seen hundreds, none of them officially recognized, of course, but saints for all that. Priests, nuns, rabbis, doctors, nurses, mothers, several of my best teachers, people who gave without counting the cost.[24]

Both Mickens and Mariani recognize implicitly the special role of saints — the need for heroes — but have more than a little discomfiture with the whole process. Their querying throws into stark relief the theological and ecclesial imperative to rethink the notion of sainthood, the criteria employed to judge the conditions of holiness, and what we mean in our postmodern era when we talk about the communion of saints. Elizabeth Johnson has researched extensively on the *communio sanctorum*:

We have in the Catholic community a sacramental imagination, whereby others can be bearers of the holy to us. For many years I was on the Lutheran–Roman Catholic Dialogue in the United States, and we had a whole round on Mary and the saints. It became obvious to me that what we were trying to do objectively — theologically, if you like — was really a matter of spirituality. Catholics believe that a holy person does not prevent us from encountering Christ, but can rather mediate Christ. For Protestants, in particular, if it's not Christ alone, then you challenge or overshadow the Gospel.

Let me tell you my own attitude about saints. I had a traditional pre–Vatican II Irish Brooklyn girlhood, and as you can appreciate, the saints were everywhere. After the Second Vatican Council I lost that for a while, largely because of the return to the Eucharist, the rediscovery of the Scriptures, etc., but when I began my work on the communion of saints — *Friends of God and Prophets* — I reopened my connection with the saints.

There are two patterns, I think, two models of approach to the saints. The first is the one I grew up with, the one that flourished during the whole second millennium of the church: the patron-petitioner or patronage model, wherein you sought out the saints to help you when you were up the creek, from whom you wanted to extract favours. The other model — companions of the faith — is a much more appealing model spiritually. As in the Letter to the Hebrews, the saints are a great cloud of witnesses who, in the words of St. Augustine, give us lessons of encouragement on how to be faithful, who walk with us during our lifetime. I find this companionship model much richer for me now. To give you an example: if I have to give a lecture to a large crowd and I'm nervous, I'll call on the saints to walk with me — not out of neediness but out of a sense of collegiality. I draw strength from their memory, inspiration from their stories.

Needless to say, the many stories of women who confronted the institutional church inspire feminists all over the place. We call on the saints to be *presente*, to come with us as we go forward. They, the saints, are our ancestors in the faith, the witnesses who have gone before us. This model is very empowering. I am a friend of God and the prophets. If we don't begin by recognizing our own holiness, the saints become esoteric people who are not like us. We have to start with a common basis, with the awareness that holy wisdom enters into souls and makes them friends of God and prophets. I think that the notion of the communion of saints has huge potential for the reform and replenishment of community so necessary in our postmodern world.

Although Johnson, as a self-declared feminist, draws continuing inspiration from the numerous female witnesses of the past, writers and critics of the stature of the British columnist Mary Kenny, who are inclined to be skittish about such a designation, are nonetheless eager to claim the likes of Cecilia, the two Teresas (Avila and Lisieux), Bernadette Soubirous, the many Catherines (Siena, Genoa, Parc-aux-Dames, Soiron, etc.), the Brigids (Ireland and Sweden), and many others as role models. Feminist or not, post–Vatican II Catholics can find in Johnson's reconceptualization of the *communio sanctorum* a bold new/old way of seeing the saints as approachable and as our friends:

To sum up: a foundational shift in the theological interpretation of the communion of saints results from the rediscovery of this company as an inclusive community of friends and prophets in contrast to a spiritual hierarchy of patrons and petitioners. From this flow several other key interpretive changes: from emphasis on the dead alone to the whole living community as all saints; from emphasis on heroic virtue and the miraculous to everyday struggle and creative fidelity; from canonized saints alone to the whole community of the dead, embraced in the life of God and accessed through memory and hope; from paradigmatic figures as elite practitioners of virtue to these same persons as comrades cherished for their witness and the encouragement it gives; and from a purely anthropocentric circle to a community of the whole natural world imbued with God's blessing.[25]

Johnson's professedly feminist interpretation of the communion of saints — egalitarian, gender-blind, indifferent to official procedures of identification and ratification, and flamboyantly inclusive — is not likely to be received hospitably by the Vatican functionaries staffing the Congregation for the Causes of Saints. They are in the serious business of making saints. And their way of going about it is not likely to be stayed by an alternate model of conceptualizing what it means to be a saint. After all, as Hilary Mantel puts it, during John Paul II's pontificate, "saints are fast-tracked to the top and there are beatifications by the bucket-load." Somebody has to do the work.

Chapter Two

THE CAUSES AND
THE CONTROVERSIES

AND TO DO the work, you first of all need a postulator, the
primary co-ordinator of the cause. Wieslaw Spiewak is precisely
such a creature. A priest of the Congregation of the
Resurrection, trained in both Poland and Italy, and assigned by
the superior-general of his religious community to promote the
canonization of the founder of the Resurrectionists, Spiewak
has a daunting task. His predecessor, who worked on the
founder's cause for decades, was unsuccessful, and new blood
has therefore been injected into the endeavour. Spiewak appreciates the time-sensitive nature of his job: the founder and his
associates were Poles, John Paul II was a Pole and naturally
sympathetic, and Benedict XVI has yet to indicate the same
passion for saint-making as his predecessor. To make matters
more interesting, historians argue over whether there was one
founder or three, and the lives of these three — Bogdan Janski,
Peter Semenenko and Jerome Kajsiewicz — read like a nineteenth-
century romantic potboiler.

Unquestionably, the foremost of the three was Janski.
Spiewak observes:

> Bogdan Janski was born in 1807 in Lisowo, near Warsaw.
> Following his studies in Warsaw, he won a government-
> sponsored scholarship to Paris when, just prior to leaving,
> he got married. This was a surprise to everyone. What was
> even more of a surprise is that after their wedding night
> and his prompt departure for France, he never saw his wife
> again. His dissolute ways as a Warsaw university student

were initially unchanged by his Paris experience. He had ceased to practise as a Catholic for some time, loved to party, drank wine from human skulls [not typical behaviour of lapsed Catholics], and was revolutionary in his politics and economics, to say nothing of his morals.

France enhanced his revolutionary credentials. He became a devout advocate of the philosophy of the Saint-Simonists [the thinking of Claude-Henri de Rouvroy, Comte de Saint-Simon, called for the radical reorganization of society along industrial and scientific lines], incorporated much of Utopian Socialism in his own thinking, travelled abroad to learn from James Mill, and prepared himself to return to Poland to share his new ideas when an insurrection by freedom-loving Poles against their Russian overlords prompted the new revolutionary government to ask Janski to stay in Paris to represent them. He did so. With passion and no little indiscretion, he wrote extensively pro-Polish and anti-Tsarist articles and tracts that prevented his return to Poland after the thorough squashing of the revolutionary government one year later.

At the same time that he was helping Polish émigrés adjust to France, he was becoming increasingly disillusioned with Saint-Simonism, and more and more moved to reacquaint himself with his forsaken Catholicism. Although he became an advocate of the rights of the Polish expatriates — writing special petitions and requests for permits, translating, etc. — he also came under the sway of such prominent Roman Catholic preachers and thinkers as Lacordaire and Lamenais. His conversion had begun. At first intellectual, and then moral, like St. Augustine. Although he came to affirm the truths of the Catholic faith, changing his moral conduct was a greater and not-so-welcome challenge. His diaries are incredible — his frankness, his sincerity, his frequent liaisons with prostitutes.

Janski's "make me chaste, O Lord, but not yet" approach to conversion (after all, he had no less a model than Augustine himself) worked for a while. He continued his intellectual investigations, his apostolic labours with Polish immigrants, and he explored possible collaborations with like-minded expats to establish a structured religious community to serve the needs of the broader society. And, in time, he accepted the full consequences of conversion with a grand, romantic gesture that involved a confession that took place in numerous stages over several months. His conversion was unquestionably serious and genuine, and his mercurial temperament, intellectual proclivities, and passionate affections finally found some secure rooting. With fellow revolutionaries Semenenko and Kajsiewicz, and under the influence of the brilliant French moralist and preacher Montelambert and the Polish poet and moral reformer Mickiewicz, Janski rented a house on the Rue Nôtre-Dame-des-Champs, where the three expatriate Poles took up residence on Ash Wednesday, 1836. Thus the beginning, but only the beginning, of the Congregation of the Resurrection. It would be another six years before two of the original founding members would make their first vows in the catacombs of St. Sebastian in Rome.

Janski would not be one of them. He died in 1840 of tuberculosis. Spiewak sees in Janski the greatest possibility for canonization.

Even though he died in Rome, I believe, and Father General concurs, we should open his cause in Poland at the diocesan level. I will gather all the literature, for the *positio* on the heroicity of virtue as well as all the documentation related to supposed miracles, the cult, the devotions, the graces, the historical material, the biographical information — and I will make my case to the ordinary, or bishop of the diocese. Thus, the cause begins. In the end, however, if I conclude that Janski's canonization is simply to ensure that "our man," our founder, is a saint like the founders of other orders and congregations, then it is not worth it. My main target should not be to make Janski a saint, but to show to my fellow Resurrectionists that Janski's spirituality has something to propose to us on our own individual paths to holiness. If I can convince one, or two, or five members of the Congregation of the Resurrection that Janski's life can teach us all something about personal conversion, spiritual resurrection, then — and only then — would I consider my work successful.

Although Spiewak has built on the foundations set by his predecessor as postulator, and although he has availed himself of the spadework of contemporary Resurrectionist historians and archivists, he knows that in the end various factors outside his control — the emergence of a cult, the authentication of alleged miracles, the absence of a saint-making Polish pontiff — could result in several years of tireless work resulting in no tangible outcome. He could be sent packing to the windswept, dank, frigid, neo-Gothic shrine of Our Lady of Mentorella in the mountains south of Rome, he could be assigned parish duties in one of the industrial wastelands of Poland, or he could be sent for a bout of near-interminable studies at the Biblicum, if his labours on behalf of Janski and the others proves fruitless.

But Spiewak is not the only postulator plying his trade. Other harried, resigned, ambitious, and plodding clerics and laity around the world are busily labouring in the vineyard of holiness trying to collect the data, muster the troops, persuade the doubting if not downright incredulous, and position their candidate ahead of the other worthies on the list of future venerables, *beati* or canonized saints. Just a glance at other ongoing causes could reduce the resolve of most ordinary postulators, relators, and promotors to dust. Following are just a few causes in various states of evolution.

There is Queen Isabella of Spain (1451–1504), Her Most Catholic Majesty, *La Catolica*, who was first proposed by *El Caudillo*, Francisco Franco, in the 1950s but who has not had a happy time of it. Isabella was a tertiary member of the Order of St. Dominic, a reforming and zealous advocate of the Catholic Church who could boast a theological titan such as Jimenez de Cisneros as her personal confessor, a strenuous critic of slavery, a key promoter of the principles of Christian humanism under the guidance and protection of the Spanish *imperium*, and, with her husband, King Ferdinand, a passionate evangelizer of the New World. Despite all this, Isabella's cause was not well served by having Franco as a backer. After Franco's death in 1975, things appeared to improve a mite, and efforts were made to promote her cause for sainthood coincident with the five-hundredth anniversary in 1992 of Christopher Columbus's discovery of the Americas. However, given the new awareness of the monstrous villainy of the *conquistadores*, the growing discontent among the aboriginal peoples in Spanish America with the forces that have sought either to marginalize or to liquidate them, the outrage expressed by the worldwide Jewish and Muslim communities over the cause of a woman who presided over their ruthless expulsion from a united Spain, and the sad record of the Spanish Inquisition (an institution with which she was closely associated), the political timing wasn't the best, to say the least. The cause was stillborn.

But never say die when it comes to saint promotion. The Archdiocese of Valladolid, along with a high-placed Colombian ecclesiastic in the Vatican named Dario Cardinal Castrillón Hoyos and the enthusiastic support and generous funding of the conservative ecclesial movement Miles Jesu, have combined to put Her Majesty back in action.

The seventeenth-century Danish scientist Niels Stensen (1638–1686) was variously a geologist, a perceptive student of philosophy, a medical doctor and researcher (he of the Stensen duct), a convert, priest, and eventually Bishop of Hanover; but it was his love of poverty — both spiritual and material — his infectious joy and his solicitous care for his flock that moved John Paul II to beatify him in 1988. John Paul's personal interest in the Pontifical Academy of Sciences, in the dialogue between science and faith, and in the need to provide role models for those Christians who have given their lives to the study of the physical sciences, make the cause of sainthood for this far-from-melancholy Dane a priority for the Pontiff and his Danish bishops.

The push for the last Austrian emperor and Hungarian king, Charles I (Karl von Habsburg, 1887–1922), received a mighty boost with John Paul's declaration of Charles as Venerable on April 12, 2003, in the presence of Otto von Habsburg, Archduke of Austria and Charles' son. Charles had the great misfortune to succeed his father, the legendary Franz Josef I, in the very midst of the Great War. He ruled from 1916 to 1919, when Austria was declared a republic, but, not one to abdicate his royal prerogative or indeed to take the temperature of the time with accuracy, Charles left with his family for a life of exile in Switzerland. It was short-lived, however, as he made two abortive attempts to regain the throne and was sent to Madeira for his efforts. The family wasn't happy, but Charles, of a genuinely jolly disposition, was resolved to make the best of it. He rented a modest house, the Quinta do Monte, which he invited the royal household's resident priest, a Father Zsamboki, to bless, straitened conditions and all. Things weren't looking up; still, he persisted in rallying the family with the cry that they were "undeservedly happy." One can excuse the other exiled royals from sharing the ex-emperor's effervescence, but there is ample ground for seeing why they adored this joyful *pater famil-*

ias. Gerard Noel, biographer and distant friend of the Austrian royals, records Charles' dying days with manifest sympathy:

> Despite a bad cold and inclement weather, he set out from his frugal residence high above Funchal to buy toys for his young family. As a result of this, his cold got worse and he caught a bad chill. The seriousness of this was not fully appreciated at first, but his health suddenly deteriorated alarmingly and pneumonia set in. He was in great pain but never complained and told his family: "I must suffer like this so my people will come together again." Charles died on April 1, 1922, holding a cross in his hands. His last words were: "Thy will be done. As you will it, Jesus." He was only 34 years old.[1]

Like those other saintly monarchs — the Anglican Charles I and the Russian Orthodox Nicholas II — Habsburg's dying was much remarked upon for its dignity, although the Stuart public beheading and the Romanov death by fusillade seem more dramatic and poignant by a yard than death by the common cold. Still, the last emperor of Austria displayed throughout his life a "moral rectitude and a firm faith," worked hard, if unsuccessfully, to bring peace to his war-riven land, and proved to be an exemplary husband and father.

Efforts to canonize Charles I began shortly after his death — in 1925, to be precise. By 1949 he had his own Karl von Habsburg prayer league, and the official beatification process itself commenced in 1954. Unfortunately for Charles, Austrian Catholics are largely divided over the cause for his sainthood; many of his principal supporters are Austrian monarchists — including, alas, two disgraced Catholic prelates: Bishop Kurt Krenn of Sankt Pölten (required to retire from his episcopal office because of his failure to exercise appropriate oversight over the sex scandals at the local diocesan seminary) and Hans

Hermann Cardinal Groer of Vienna (forced to retire because of persistent allegations of sex abuse of minor seminarians when he was a Benedictine abbot). His critics, meanwhile, have not forgotten that he was the one who approved the use of poison gas during the First World War,[2] although postulator Andrea Ambrosi argues that Charles was strongly opposed to the use of all indiscriminate means of mass destruction. At his beatification on October 3, 2004, the liturgy, in a clear effort to distance the emperor from the hostilities that left the old Europe drenched in blood, underscored Charles' support of the peace initiatives of Pope Benedict XV during the Great War.

A less divisive cause is that of the already beatified Damien of Molokai (1840–1889), the leper missioner of Hawaii and Belgian priest of the Congregation of the Sacred Hearts of Jesus and Mary and of Perpetual Adoration. His heroic life has been celebrated in scores of books, pamphlets, museums, and films, including the Australian Paul Cox's *Molokai*. Damien was beatified by John Paul II in Brussels in 1995.

Damien's cause is progressing reasonably well, given the near-universal range of his cult and the undoubted heroicity of his work with the victims of Hansen's disease on Molokai, to say nothing of the effective marketing of his holy reputation by his religious congregation — and Tourism Hawaii.

Edward Cardinal Egan, Archbishop of New York, took on a more uphill challenge with the daughter of U.S. author Nathaniel Hawthorne. Rose Hawthorne founded the Dominican Sisters, Servants of Relief for Incurable Cancer, while working in the slums of Manhattan with those who had cancer. A widow, mother, and founder, Hawthorne conforms to a pattern — to name but two, Margaret D'Youville (1701–1771), founder of the Grey Nuns and the first native-born Canadian saint, and Elizabeth Ann Seton (1774–1821), like Hawthorne a convert and founder of the American Daughters of Charity — and she represents a form of feisty originality that has undoubted appeal. However, we live in an age that is looking for other models of female Christian witness and leadership, and we have just emerged from a papacy marked both by the relentless sainting of obscure founders of religious communities and by serious doubts regarding the Pontiff's appreciation of the liberating effects of feminism. Hawthorne's cause may yet secure the backing, but still fall short of the wider appeal.

Appeal, however, is not something lacking in the cause of Archbishop Fulton Sheen (1895–1979), the prelate of the airwaves, the communications star who, at his height in the 1950s, commanded a radio and television audience of some 30 million, who co-authored a series of popular books with the famed photographer, the Armenian-Canadian Yousuf Karsh, and whose convert-generating skills were on a par with England's Martin D'Arcy and Ronald Knox. A naturally gifted orator and teacher, although inclined to the histrionic and the superficial, Sheen was the public face of the Catholic Church in the United States as apologist and as *magister*. He was a fierce competitor with a piece of chalk and a swirling episcopal cape. But his career as a bishop was lacklustre: he did not fare well as one of New York's auxiliary bishops to the formidable Francis Cardinal Spellman (there was room in New York for only one ecclesiastical prima donna), and his years as the Archbishop of Rochester were short and turbulent. He was not a modern Catholic thinker, but he understood earlier than most — and in this he was stunningly prescient — that the media mattered greatly. John Paul would find Sheen's media savvy, his traditional piety, and his orthodox teaching a handsome blend, and one not too far from his own potent mixture. Although controversy around his relationship with Spellman — part venomous speculation and part reasonable surmise — could seriously hobble Sheen's candidacy for sainthood, the fact that he has the Sheen Foundation and Chicago's respected Francis Cardinal George as major boosters, that actor Martin Sheen has publicly acknowledged that he took his last name as a tribute to the bishop, and that he was one of the first voices to speak out against Hitler on his NBC radio show, *Catholic Hour*, work strongly in his favour.

And when it comes to both encouraging and advancing the causes of public and controversial figures — and particularly those of artists — the late pontiff showed remarkable originality and chutzpah. It was John Paul who beatified the masterly Fra Angelico some half a millennium after his death, and it was the same pope who welcomed the cause of, in the words of art critic and author John Bentley Mays, the "immensely original Catalan architect" Antoni Gaudi, master builder of the Barcelona masterpiece, the Sagrada Familia cathedral. In a time when architects have become celebrities, shapers of the contemporary sensibility, and public figures capable of making moral statements — think of such names as Wright, Le Corbusier, Gehry, and Libeskind — adding Gaudi to the canon would be Rome's way of inserting its presence in the litany of twentieth-century giants of architecture.

On the matter of inserting its presence in the social justice scene of the last century, Rome has few rivals, but one of its most compelling prospects is manifestly against the idea — Dorothy Day.

Day (1897–1980) was an authentic radical: anarchist, pacifist, Christian. She had little truck with compromise, half-measures, laboured diplomacy, behind-the-scenes jockeying, or empty exhortations, but she was a loyal "daughter of the church" withal. Born in New York and reared in San Francisco and Chicago, she was variously an atheist, college dropout, bohemian, suffragist, writer for such socialist organs as *The Call* and *The Masses*, passionate lover (Lionel Moise, Barkeley Toby, Forster Batterham, and playwright Eugene O'Neill), abandoned mother, and full-time protester. She tried most things, including having an abortion. The perfect radical.

But by her own admission she grew tired of simply "following the devices of her own heart," and as she reveals in her autobiography *The Long Loneliness*, she longed to love the "Church for Christ made visible. Not for itself, because it was so often a scandal to me." With this breathtakingly honest assessment of the church she both loved and deplored, she converted to Roman Catholicism in December of 1927. This was not a decision without cost: the anti-Catholic father of her child, named Tamar Teresa, abandoned Day, as did many of her left-leaning friends. But five years later she met the French peasant-philosopher Peter Maurin, a vagabond of the spirit and the heart — a man, she acknowledged, whose ideas and spirit "would dominate the rest of my life. He was the saint." Maurin introduced her to many of the seminal Catholic thinkers of the time, encouraged her to found a paper designed to espouse their shared ideas — *The Catholic Worker* — and collaborated with her in the establishment of the Catholic Worker houses of hospitality and farm communes that were an institutional expression of their radical Gospel-driven commitment to poverty and community. Day's "new social order" was not, in her view, based on a political or ideological foundation. Rather, as Geoffrey Gneuhs, a former chaplain of the Catholic Worker house in New York, observes,

> her seeking of community in this century [twentieth], which has so destroyed community, was nourished by the Eucharist as life-giving life, so that we may nourish others. She was committed to daily Mass, reading the psalms, praying vespers, weekly confession, fasting, regular retreats, and voluntary poverty. The latter kept her honest; when she spoke she was authentic.[3]

She was indeed authentic; she was also traditional in her devotional life, orthodox in her doctrinal life, and fully observant in her moral life. A church prize. Various New York cardinals, who could be accused neither of pacifism nor of being indifferent to U.S. partisan politics, always had time for Day. In fact, it was John Cardinal O'Connor who introduced her cause (although it was first mooted by Tom McGrath of Claretian Publications in 1983), and O'Connor, a rear-admiral and close pal of New York's movers and shakers, proposed that she be dubbed the "Saint of the Lonely." Although it is far from surprising that Day would never self-identify as a saint, that she continued to insist after Maurin's death in 1949 that he was the *real* saint, and that she would argue repeatedly in her writings that "we are all called to be saints, and we might as well get over our bourgeois fear of it," the opposition to Day's formal sainting comes not from her detractors — those who have never forgiven her for having an abortion, for opposing all wars, and for advocating anarchism, the most un-American of political options — but from her disciples. Patrick Jordan of New York's *Commonweal* summarizes the core arguments of their opposition:

Their hesitancy is well grounded, and flows not from any doubt concerning the grace-filled, indeed remarkable, gifts that Day showed. Rather, it springs from a fear that her human breadth and prophetic Christian witness might somehow be diminished for the Church if made to conform to some predetermined ecclesiastical mould.[4]

The man who first proposed her canonization, Tom McGrath, appreciates the reservations many of the Catholic Worker people have with officialdom's interest in a formal ratification of Day's spiritual exceptionality. She then becomes theirs. He remains persuaded, however, that sainthood will neither "pretty her up" nor tame her, but in fact may well encourage the Roman bureaucrats and local bishops to realize that saints have a lot of wildness in them. Maybe. But the authorities don't feel too comfortable with the wildness aspect, especially when it has the potential to collide with orthodox teaching and behaviour. For instance, following the September 11, 2001, assault on the World Trade Center and *The New York Times'* laudable undertaking over the ensuing months to chronicle the lives of all the victims/heroes of that dark day, many were struck by the outstanding bravery of a Franciscan fire chaplain whose informal cult has flourished spontaneously, unaided by archdiocesan or Franciscan endorsement or encouragement. Friar Mychal Judge was one of the first to die on the site of the disaster in his valiant efforts to save lives and accompany his fire fighters into the very core of the fiery maelstrom. Cures are alleged to have occurred as a consequence of his intercession — a mentally challenged child in Rhode Island began to speak almost immediately; a hole in the heart of a Colorado baby was healed — his tomb has become a place of pilgrimage, his relics are sought after, and both the first hagiography and a web site have appeared to campaign on his behalf. However, given his self-declared homosexuality, interest in gay rights, struggles with alcoholism, and combative — although deeply affectionate — nature, church figures are less proactive on behalf of a priest who, in the words of his own order, although a good friar "who respected his vows," should not be put on a pedestal.

The populist dimension of the Judge cause hearkens back to the pre-regularization days of the early church, those days when sainthood by popular acclamation was possible, and this surely conforms with the wishes of John Paul II, determined as he was to rouse local Catholics to identify and promote their own cloud of witnesses. But there is an odour of wildness about Mychal Judge that triggers the official church's instinct for caution, an instinct that is not on display over the cause of Anne Catherine Emmerich, the nineteenth-century German stigmatic, nun, mystic, and author of the graphic, imaginative, and extra-biblical Passion narrative that served as a central influence on the theological and cinematic imagination of filmmaker Mel Gibson. Her beatification followed less than a year after the premiere of Gibson's *The Passion of the Christ* in March 2004, and although the German bishop of Münster had indicated that she was to be beatified for her virtuous life and not because her blood-soaked and arrestingly visual account of Jesus' sufferings inspired the most controversial and successful depiction of Christ's life yet filmed, few were convinced that this was all a matter of divine coincidence.

Irrespective of the nasty barbs, allegations of anti-Semitism, and outpouring of opposition from many Catholic progressives, the church easily weathered the Emmerich controversy because the German *beata* was demonstrably orthodox — eccentric and intense perhaps, but possessed of a *controllable* wildness.

Other causes, either at the early stages or well progressed, that reflect an uncanny timeliness include: George Spencer, convert from Anglicanism, Passionist priest with the name of Father Ignatius of St. Paul, tireless preacher of "little missions," spiritual dean of students, cricket maniac, humble traveller of British Rail or its nineteenth-century equivalent ("I travel third class on the railway because there is no fourth"), and the great-great-grand uncle of Diana, Princess of Wales; Blessed Esther Blondin, also known as Mother Marie-Anne, Canadian founder of the Sisters of St. Anne, a stubborn, honest, humble woman who began by teaching the illiterate and then went on to establish coeducational schools at a time when they were considered a radical, if not dangerous, innovation; the "Patron Saint of Hunks," Blessed Pier Giorgio Frassati, who was born into an economically secure and socially prominent Turin family, displayed an uncommonly keen sense of social justice (John Paul II dubbed him "The Man of the Eight Beatitudes"), was admired by his peers for both his athletic prowess and his activist commitments, and who, having successfully divined the menace of the still-incipient Fascism that would shortly put its invidious stamp on Italy, died from the polio his physicians believe he contracted from the sick he faithfully attended; and Robert Schuman, the Father of Europe, the "intellectual architect" of the European Union and its first president, one of the post–Second World War planners — Adenauer, de Gasperi, and de Gaulle being the others — who planned for a half-century of European peace, a man, according to his postulator, whose "life shows that political activity is compatible with fidelity to Christian values."

In short, we have a relative of a modern secular saint, fashion idol, and troubled beauty (Princess Diana); a forthright woman educator of liberal insight who managed to live out her life in holy obedience; a political and social activist who enthusiastically and publicly embraced the church's teachings on sexuality (Frassati's notebooks, journals, and letters, which record his struggles for purity, make for surprisingly dull reading); and a politician who handsomely exemplifies faithful Christian practice in the public arena and who fully appreciated Europe's Christian origins. As I say, timely.

The timeliness of the causes of Popes Pius IX (Giovanni Maria Mastai-Ferretti) and John XXIII (Angelo Giuseppe Roncalli) is, by contrast, more difficult to ascertain. John Paul II chose to beatify both men on September 3, 2000, the feast day of one of the towering leaders among pontiffs, Pope Gregory the Great. In doing so — in terms of the choice of date as well as the choice of candidates — John Paul was, in part at least, finishing a process begun much earlier. Theologian Joseph A. Komonchak sets the context:

> If Roncalli had died as patriarch of Venice, he certainly would not be widely remembered today. In the aftermath of Vatican II, however, the nearly universal grief that followed his death led to proposals that the council canonize him by acclamation. Pope Paul VI refused. His reasons

were threefold: the problem of departing from the ordinary process; he was also being besieged with requests for the canonization of Pius XII; and, it seems, because some of the proposals subtly implied a contrast between what was taken to be John XXIII's vision of the council and the orientations his successor was thought to be giving it. Instead, on November 18, 1965, Paul VI announced that he was authorizing the introduction of the causes of both John XXIII and Pius XII and that the process would follow the normal procedures. The failure of the canonization effort at the council, especially the linkage with Pius XII, deeply disappointed some people who saw it as emblematic of the failure of Vatican II to live up to the goals of John XXIII.[5]

But it wasn't the linkage with Pius XII that would prove the problem for John Paul II — he uncoupled the back-to-back popes for reasons that will become clear in the later chapter on Pius XII — but rather for the new, and for many inscrutable, linkage between Papa Roncalli and Pio Nono. Pius IX's cause has been around for some time, but in bringing together two distinctly different popes with two quite dissimilar popularity ratings, John Paul had adroitly deployed this *mysterium coniunctionis* of cause and intention to detonate what he saw as one of the enduring and more damaging of liberal myths: the ultraconservative pontificate of Pius IX, draped in its triumphalist and antimodern pretensions, pitted against the progressive pontificate of John XXIII, robed in humility and open to the world. Undoubtedly, John Paul was eager to eradicate what he saw as a false antinomy because he viewed both popes in a continuous line of orthodox teaching, and because he personally shared characteristics of both pontiffs and respected the markedly different historical periods that shaped their leadership. But this was an ambitious gamble.

Pius IX has few supporters outside the most intransigent of curialists, Catholic conservatives deeply suspicious of the legacy of the Second Vatican Council, and political and religious reactionaries who recall the indignities of the 1789 and 1848 revolutions as if they had just happened and who entertain serious doubts over the legitimacy of the Italian Republic, formed as it was of disparate kingdoms and sovereign territories — including, most prominently, the Papal States. It is difficult to see any appeal in the pontificate of Pio Nono, as he was commonly known, at least to Christians of the twenty-first century. He was a notorious defender of the *ancien régime* (in fairness, he had tried his hand with the new European liberalism, only to be scorched); he opposed every meaningful manifestation of the new spirit of democracy, religious tolerance, free speech, etc.; he became embroiled in the ugly Edgardo Mortara case (Edgardo was the son of a Jewish family in Bologna whose nurse baptized him in secret, and because Bologna was at the time part of the Papal City States he was taken from his parents, reared in Rome, adopted by Pius, and in due course became a priest himself); and in the end he turned his pontificate into one grand repudiation of modernity. As the Cambridge University historian Eamon Duffy sees it,

He was a pious and impetuous idealist, badly educated and prone to panic, caught in a political and moral earthquake, surrounded by advisers who told him he was God's trumpeter against the apostasy of the age and urged him on to extremes. . . . Whatever his limitations, Pio Nono has deep faith, zeal, courage, and a warm heart. In an age in which belief in divine revelation was increasingly rejected, he bore insistent witness to its reality. His beatification is perhaps a reminder that Christian sanctity takes many forms, is compatible with making a mess of things, and was not invented in the 1960s.[6]

If it is true, as Duffy argues, that beatification "is compatible with making a mess of things" — and I believe he is right — and if it is true that John Paul beatified Pius IX not in order to "celebrate particular historical choices" but because of Mastai-Ferretti's virtues, then the larger question looming must be addressed: does pontifical holiness deserve public recognition, irrespective of bad judgement, poor leadership, catastrophic decision-making, and a legacy of polarization? Does making a mess of things mean something different when you apply the criteria of holiness to the successors of St. Peter? Few question the native goodness of Giuseppe Melchior Sarto, known to history as Pope St. Pius X (the last pope to have been canonized and whose rule from 1903–1914 was marked by a stern, if benevolent, authoritarianism), and yet few historians and informed Catholics are unaware of the sad culture of delation, intellectual timidity, and ecclesial insularity that defined his pontificate.

John XXIII's beatification has nothing of the acrimony, divided opinion, fierce partisanship, or ecclesiastical nastiness of Pius IX's. The reasons why each pontiff has proceeded differently through the stages of sainthood include timing as well as personality. It is also a matter of theological perspective, papal anxiety over historical discontinuity in a post-conciliar church, and ingrained curial suspicion over the innovators (John XXIII) as opposed to the conservors (Pius IX).

Certainly, the pope who called the Second Vatican Council (although his immediate predecessor, Pius XII, also played with the idea of summoning a council) was a man of deep personal piety, traditional spirituality — as even a cursory glance at his *Journal of a Soul* indicates — a cautious and learned church historian, and an able and brave diplomat (Roncalli had been apostolic delegate to Bulgaria, Greece, and Turkey as well as papal nuncio to France). He was loved as a pastor, an administrator, and a loyal son of the church; but precisely because he discerned the spirit of the times, was prepared to listen to a world aching for liberation, and did not feel constrained by tradition, he was prepared to act boldly. As the eminent Council historian Giuseppe Alberigo of the University of Bologna correctly observes:

> The most important act of John XXIII's pontificate, one that was the most absorbing for the Catholic Church at the time, was the speech he gave at the opening of Vatican II Council. Historic research confirms that it was personally written by the pope, as shown in the manuscript of the text. It did not set a program for the council, which should be — according to the Pontiff — up to the assembly to establish; rather he defined Christian behaviour for the contemporary era . . . by the choice of an attitude of mercy and not of condemnation, and by the rejection of "prophets of doom . . . who see our time as only corruption and ruin."[7]

Unabashedly and refreshingly open to the world, inspired by the inherent goodness of nature and culture, unafraid of dialogue with humankind — irrespective of ethnicity, creed, political ideology, or gender — John XXIII was a breath of fresh air coursing through the dusty corridors of Vatican thinking. He had little time for the naysayers, for the pessimists who wanted to hobble the human spirit, and for all his fellow Catholics who looked upon the world as a fearsome place to be more anathematized than nurtured. But in the end, it was the man, not the office, not the accomplishments, and not the daring that defined him as a saint for multitudes throughout the world — Catholic and non-Catholic, Christian and non-Christian alike.

The almost universal admiration and affection felt for Roncalli throughout his pontificate was handsomely demonstrated at the time of his death by an outpouring of grief that took even the most hardened anti-popery types by surprise. Pio Nono never had it half as good. In neither case, however, did the issue of martyrdom surface, although at the time of the reunification of Italy, there were serious threats to the life of Pius IX. Not being a martyr is not in and of itself an impediment to canonization, but John Paul II had a particular hankering for martyrs, and their respective causes for canonization moved more swiftly through the process on his watch.

In John Paul's philosophical encyclical *Veritatis splendor* (1993), he bore witness to his abiding conviction that "the martyrs stir in us a profound trust because they give voice to what we already feel and they declare what we would like to have the strength to express."

There is no question that the martyrs continue to arouse interest. It has always been thus. Consider the *Martyrologium Romanum*, the comprehensive official compilation of the martyrs before the reforms ushered in by Pope Paul VI in the 1960s. As the great Jesuit hagiologist Herbert Thurston observed in his introduction to the revised edition to Alban Butler's magisterial twelve-volume *Lives of the Saints*, it would often include "phantom saints, some of them due to the strange blunders of medieval copyists, others representing nothing more than prehistoric sagas which have been embellished and transformed by a Christian colouring." In other words, there has always been a thirst — one not easily sated — for the extravagant acts of heroism, sanctity, madness, bravery, and human (though not divine) folly to be found at the heart of a martyr's calling. The lives of the martyrs make for great stories. Period.

Perhaps it is the often-outrageous acts of human self-sacrifice that appeal to us: so removed, so compelling, so haunting. As Canadian Jesuit Michael Czerny, formerly of the Justice Secretariat at Jesuit headquarters in Rome, a social ethicist by training and co-ordinator of the African Jesuit AIDS Network, succinctly puts it:

the martyrs are Christian life writ large and writ deep. They are like other people — they're not different — but in the light of their death their very lives take on a kind of illuminating significance and they become an encouragement to those who carry on with the struggle, allowing those left behind to know that it is all worthwhile and that God is with them.

Traditionally, the rubric of martyr was reserved exclusively for those who perished as a consequence of *odium fidei*, or hatred of the faith. One quite simply had to die; there was no compromise on this point. But things are always more complicated, as the British historian and authority on spirituality Donald Nicholl noted when he invoked the memory of Alphege to show that the definition of martyr has been broader than most would allow. Nicholl tells the story of a camp of incarcerated Christians who were prevented by their Communist jailers from celebrating the Eucharist, but who had managed to secure some bread and lacked only the wine. The man working in the camp store offered to bring them the wine they needed, even though he knew that if he were caught he would be summarily executed. He was discovered and he was killed.

Should the nameless Communist be regarded as a martyr? He certainly should be if we allow the criteria invoked 900 years ago by St. Anselm when he was arguing that one of his predecessors, Alphege, was a martyr. Alphege had been kidnapped by the invading Danes who killed him because he refused to countenance a ransom being paid for him to be exacted from the poor peasants on the Canterbury estates. According to certain ecclesiastics of the day he could not be hailed as a martyr because it was not for the

faith that he had died. But Anselm controverted their arguments by affirming that "he who would die for a smaller
matter would certainly die for a larger." And so St. Alphege
is honoured in the Church's calendar as a martyr.[8]

And during the pontificate of John Paul, the definition of
martyr broadened further, as Robert Sarno outlines:

> One can and must speak of martyrdom when a Christian,
> because of his or her faith, refused to transgress a command-
> ment — e.g., against justice or against chastity, or lived in
> its fullness a Christian virtue and for that reason is killed.
>
> While on the part of the Christian the determining
> element is that the person, for the love of God and conscious
> of the consequences, does not want to do anything contrary
> to the faith; on the part of the one inflicting death, it is not
> necessary that the individual act directly and formally out
> of hatred for God, against the person of Christ, His
> doctrine or His Church. It is sufficient that the person, for
> ideological reasons or for other motives, wants to force the
> Christian to commit acts which the person cannot do
> without sinning. If, in this context, we speak of *odium fidei*
> (hatred of the faith) on the part of the one killing the
> Christian, this term means *the attitude of hostility toward
> Christianity insofar as this impedes the attainment of the goal
> proposed by the persecutor.*
>
> It is not always easy to discover all the elements of a
> martyrdom. Often, and especially today, Christians who do
> not want to succumb to the demands of a dictator are not
> officially persecuted because they are Christians, but they
> are accused of common crimes, and, in particular, are
> branded as traitors or subversives of public order. Often
> there is no regular process, but they are eliminated in a
> secret manner. It often happens that they are not killed

directly, but — as it frequently happened in antiquity with those condemned to forced labour in the mines — they are put in such conditions that they die because of the trials and deprivations suffered.

We must not forget that today there are means and methods that make it possible to destroy an individual's personality without taking the person's life. Finally, the discerning of martyrdom is made more difficult because as a rule Christians are not given a choice between apostasy [a complete and public repudiation of the faith] and death; but they are simply killed because by their lives they have shown themselves to be so firm in their faith that the persecutor despairs of making them renounce it.[9]

John Paul's liberal use of the definition of martyr — embracing those who valiantly resisted regimes and ideologies that deploy a systematic loathing of the human person per se and not necessarily involving an explicit hatred for the dogmas of the church — allowed the pontiff to include under the umbrella of martyr not just the ninety-nine Angers Catholics killed during the French Revolution, whom he beatified in 1984, nor the 233 he beatified in 2001 who suffered death during the Spanish Civil War, but also the likes of the Croatian national hero Alojzije Cardinal Stepinac. The cardinal died from a rare blood disease, polycythemia, and was beatified in 1998 against a backdrop of serious opposition from various Jewish groups, Serbian Orthodox church leaders and faithful, and an international smattering of Catholics disturbed not by Stepinac's resistance to Tito's communism but rather by the perception that he was tolerant, if not sympathetic, when it came to the policies of the pro-Nazi Ustashi leader of Croatia, Ante Pavelic. John Paul was able to claim Stepinac as a martyr using the criteria outlined by Sarno, and undoubtedly similar prelates caught in the vortex of Communist tyranny — Cardinals Josef Beran of Prague, Jozsef

Mindszenty of Esztergom-Budapest, Josyf Slipyi of Lviv, all of whom suffered considerably under their respective Communist governments but none of whom was directly executed for professing the Christian faith — could be future martyrs. In fact, the Pope recognized that the common experience of martyrdom in the twentieth-century concentration camps and gulags provides, in the words of the prefect emeritus of the Congregation of Saints, José Saraiva Martins, an "ecumenism of holiness."

The more fluid definition of martyr does have its critics. Czerny, for one, would prefer a more restrictive use of the term:

> I don't think that it is necessary to use the word "martyr" for anybody who just suffers for what they believe in, or who does a good job at the work they're doing. Martyrdom, for me, means a death that communicates and continues the meaning of life in a dramatic way. I think that it should be reserved for people who have died violently for their faith, for their belief in human rights, for justice, for others. Reserve the word "witness" for those who have lived a life of enormous meaning and value but have not been signalled with a violent death.

And one such figure who *has* died a classic martyr's death, lived a boldly Christian life, bore ample testimony to the liberating power of the gospels, and has a following numbered in the millions and is yet to be sainted is the former Archbishop of San Salvador, Oscar Arnufo Romero, a man the Dominican educator and spiritual director Suzannah Malarky of the Santa Sabina Center at the Dominican University of California identifies as

> a holy person seized by God, a person seized by the truth, one who did not so much seek out the truth as he was seized by it, who gave himself to holiness, was grasped by it, and who lived his life in such a way that his holiness shone

through his very person — his actions and his words — and who in the end was recognized as real, true and holy.

Quite an accolade. But he wasn't always the icon of holiness that progressive Catholics like to fashion. He was a "reluctant convert" to the cause of social justice in his own country, El Salvador. He was not disposed temperamentally to rock the boat; he was accustomed to working with the political and ecclesiastical status quo, and he was only drawn into a more direct and confrontational stance with the government and its U.S. allies when the Jesuit Rutilio Grande was murdered (along with an elderly layman and a young boy) and no official inquiry was made into their deaths. Grande was a sharp critic of the regime, a passionate social-justice priest, and his death marked a more brazen direction by the authorities to bring troublesome priests to heel. Romero began to publicly decry the abuses of the government and the armed forces, to chronicle the assassinations, disappearances, and human rights abuses that were growing daily in the country, to defend the poor over against the wealthy, and to prevail on his brother bishops and Rome to act decisively in favour of the poor. Then, three years to the month after Grande had been killed, Romero was himself assassinated while celebrating Mass in the chapel of the hospital where he lived. The date was March 24, 1980, and it marked the birth into heaven of the newest, most popular, and most revered saint of the Americas — unofficially, that is.

For reasons that range from the political to the strategic, from the pastoral to the canonical, Rome, and more important still, the Archdiocese of San Salvador, have to satisfy themselves that the Romero cause will not be hijacked by dissident Catholics, Liberation theologians, political factions keen on claiming the murdered archbishop as their local version of a Che Guevara or Camillo Torres, or ideological enemies of the government determined to score a moral victory over the party that "sanctioned" his death. However, it is more than caution or suspicion that explains the tardiness demonstrated by both local and Roman authorities on the Romero cause. The Archbishop of San Salvador is an Opus Dei bishop with little sympathy for the groups that claim "Saint" Oscar Romero as their own; Romero's continent-wide popularity among the poor, the radical religious, and progressive lay leaders is disturbing to Vatican officials leery over the aftershocks of the "preferential option for the poor"; and such a democratic and populist acclamation of sainthood — spontaneous in origin, authentic in intention, and as dismissive of process as you can get — is a little too Protestant and egalitarian for the traditional ecclesiastical mandarins who usually preside over these matters.

Michael Czerny, who served for a period as a professor replacement for one of the Jesuits assassinated at the Universidad Centroamericana José Simeón Cañas (UCA) on November 18, 1989, is prepared to wait:

> There is no doubt that for the people, Romero was a genuine saint. I have no hesitation in saying that. In fact, I remember that soon after he died I met a Salvadoran woman with her baby, and I asked, as one always does, "What is the name of your son?" And she looked at me as if it was some sort of a dumb question and said, "Well . . . Oscar. Every family has their own Oscar, you know." That was her way of saying that a boy is going to be named Oscar because he *has* to be. There was no doubt in her mind, and for many of the people that I met as well, that this is the way it should be. I do believe, however, that the time it is taking for his beatification and canonization is also a sign of the depth and complexity of his sanctity, of his sainthood. He wasn't a saint in a monastery, a quiet parish or on a desert island. He was a saint who became a saint in the midst of political turmoil, and twenty-five years is not

enough for that turmoil to settle down and for people of very strong feelings over the civil strife to move beyond the social conflict and seek reconciliation. I think it will take a little while yet — not because he is any less a saint, but because the church in El Salvador has to *want* him as their saint.

They also have to want the martyred Jesuits as their saints, the very Jesuits Czerny was so close to and whose death so inspired him to continue their work in the war-ravaged land named after the Saviour. Long feared for its work in social and political analysis, its careful chronicling of human-rights abuses, its commitment to educating for justice, its advocacy of non-violence, and its sympathy for the cause of the Frente Farabundo Martí para la Liberación Nacional (Farabundo Martí National Liberation Front, or FMLN) — although hardly neutral on the matter of guerrilla atrocities — the Jesuit university in San Salvador (UCA) and its brave leadership faced their day of reckoning with dignity. The Jesuit martyrs of El Salvador are: Ignacio Ellacuría, theologian and rector of UCA; Ignacio Martin-Baró, psychologist and vice-rector of UCA; Juan Ramón Moreno, preacher and assistant director of the Oscar Romero Centre; Amando López, theologian and former rector of the Managua, Nicaragua, campus of UCA; Segundo Montes, sociologist and superior of the university community; and Joaquin López y López, catechist and director of the *Fe y Alegria* (Faith and Joy) Movement. Elba and Celina Ramos, mother and daughter, innocents, were also killed. The survivor of the brutal gunning was Jon Sobrino, the premier Liberationist in the land, the most feared thinker in the community (his international reputation and wide publishing record made him known throughout the Catholic world) and, next to Ellacuría, the most loathed by the government and its military thugs.

Sobrino, like many of the Jesuits who work in El Salvador and like many of those who have perished defending human dignity, is not native born. While reflecting on the deaths of his fellow Jesuits, he found meaning in the larger context of their struggles and collective death: they had become authentic Salvadorans at last.

> Tragically, but fortunately, the Jesuits are not alone in this blood. Which means that maybe for the first time in years, as far as the Salvadoran Jesuits go, we can call ourselves truly Salvadoran. Some people have the impression, and I think rightly so, that somehow Jesuits are people different from other people. Well, maybe that is the way it is — it's not the way I would like it to be. . . . When we participate in the same destiny as the majority of the Salvadorans, that means that we have become Salvadoran, and that for me is one of the most important challenges and one of the greatest joys we can have: to be real human beings in a country.[10]

These "real human beings," these Jesuit martyrs, paid the cost of *odium fidei*, and they paid it at the hands of elite soldiers who did not hate their faith (they were themselves Catholics, after all), but who hated the things they represented, the ideas they sought to foster, their very defiance of the state and its army. They are genuine martyrs whose blood, according to Tertullian, is the seed of the church. But in spite of the heroic nature of their final witness, the Jesuits are still not officially the UCA Martyrs. That, as Czerny insists, will also take time:

> Popular devotion is an important measure of sanctity, and it is an interesting measure for us today, simply because one of the things that happened since the Second Vatican Council is its decline or shift in importance. If you measure, for instance, the number of people who have come to the Jesuit tombs, or the number of prayer cards distributed on

their behalf or the number of holy cards sold invoking their intercession, then you will have to conclude that their popular support is not all that great. I was struck by that when I visited Mother Teresa's home in Calcutta, less than a year after her death, and there was a whole slew of salesmen on the streets around her house, purveyors of holy trinkets, etc. You don't find that outside the tombs of the Jesuits. I know that it is not India, but I also know that the difference is more than of passing significance: the church is not going to canonize people who haven't caught the religious imagination of the people. And I don't know if the martyrs of UCA have caught it. Keep in mind, as well, that just as Romero died in the midst of enormous social conflict in 1980, so too did the Jesuits in 1989, and it will take a while for things to sort themselves out.

And it is the sorting out that the church waits for — the right time, the right circumstances, the right confluence of cause, need, and advocates.

The sainting process is more than an institutional hurdle; it is an historical unfolding. Stalking the holy involves more than intellectual curiosity, more than the plodding reconstruction of a life, the detailed calibration of fact with argument. It involves an openness to the unnerving task of following the lineaments and contours of holiness, not only in the "other," but in oneself as mirrored in the "other." These "others," the ones we are going to stalk in the next three chapters, are those Leonard Cohen, in his novel *Beautiful Losers*, calls the "balancing monsters of love."

Chapter Three

PADRE PIO:
SAINT AND STIGMATIC

ON MAY 2, 1999, *I Frati Minori Cappuccini della Provincia di S. Angelo-Foggia* were delighted to invite the world to the Solemn Beatification of Padre Pio da Pietrelcina, their brother in Christ, fellow Capuchin, and Italian legend, and untold numbers took up the offer. The mayor of the city of Rome encouraged the inhabitants of his own city to leave on holiday; schools cancelled their classes on Monday (the day after the beatification); the *Metropolitana* (subway) was closed down; and 350,000 of the pious and the curious crammed the Piazza San Pietro for hours. All the arteries feeding the Vatican were filled to capacity by throngs of the simple devout, holiday-makers, fierce partisans of the cult of Padre Pio, regular pilgrims swept up by the ritual and excitement, tourists bored with the customary pastiche of classical and sacred Rome on offer by the Eternal City's practised masters of the quick spin, and the usual company of historians, anthropologists, and media commentators whose job it is to track the process and divine the message of these rites and spectacles that seem so "disjoint and out of frame" with the time.

After the beatification ceremony, an official concert was held in honour of the Blessed Padre Pio at the Vatican's spacious Aula Paolo VI. It was attended by the select few — some 10,000 in all. The Italian composer Sergio Rendine's *Missa da Beatificatione*, with orchestra, choir, vocal octet, several distinguished soloists, and premier star tenor José Carreras, provided an alternating rousing and sublime consummation to the day's sacred proceedings.

What's a simple Capuchin to think?

Just over three years later, on June 16, 2002, Padre Pio was canonized. An even larger crowd than the one that gathered for the beatification was expected, but a number of factors — the scorching heat (40 degrees Celsius), the natural confusion that befalls civil Rome when a sainting of this calibre is organized, and the sense by the faithful that the real threshold had been successfully crossed with the beatification and that the canonization was an assured thing — combined to bring in a crowd considerably smaller than had been anticipated. Still, clocking in at some 300,000 on-site pilgrims, a television audience of some 5 million, and a media blitz of impressive magnitude, the canonization was hardly an understated affair.

John Paul made Padre Pio number 457 on his list of canonized personalities. He also went one step further than he usually did, establishing the feast day of Saint Padre Pio, September 23, as obligatory for universal and not local celebration. Saints Adamnan, Linus, and Thecla of Iconium now have a holy partner with whom to share the day. More than likely, given his wide popularity, Padre Pio will easily eclipse his comparatively obscure companions.

The Pope was adamant in affirming the Capuchin's gift for spiritual survival in trying circumstances: "the life and mission of Padre Pio prove that difficulties and sorrows, if accepted out of love, are transformed into a privileged way of holiness that leads to an even greater good known only to the Lord." Some speculate that these words are a formal exoneration of the allegations made against the new saint that he was a charlatan inclined to take sexual liberties with female penitents, a power-hungry friar more like Rasputin than Jesus, a Franciscan fraud. Although the Vatican had censored him, twice investigated the charges against him, imposed canonical sanctions, and subjected him to prolonged juridical processes, Padre Pio neither railed against the Roman authorities nor denounced his detractors.

He suffered quietly and waited for vindication. John Paul was his final and conclusive vindicator.

And John Paul had more than a passing interest in this saint. While studying in Rome as a young priest, Wojtyla made the trip to San Giovanni Rotondo, Padre Pio's home for the majority of his life, to ask the stigmatic to hear his confession. There have been few who, having confessed to Padre Pio, have remained unmoved by his insight, compassion, rigour, and forthrightness. The future pope also sought out Padre Pio to intercede on behalf of a Polish Catholic, Dr. Wanda Poltawaska, who was diagnosed with malignant throat cancer. Just a few days after his request, the then Bishop Wojtyla wrote to inform Padre Pio that Poltawaska's tumour had disappeared. Not surprisingly, she was one of many recipients of Padre Pio's successful intercessions who thronged St. Peter's for the canonization. Also present was Matteo Colella, a young boy whose extraordinary recovery from meningitis was attributed to Padre Pio and whose "cure" was declared the final and necessary miracle required to shore up Padre Pio's cause for sainthood.

Also numbered among the devout and curious were a goodly number of members of the planetwide Padre Pio Prayer Groups, hucksters trading in the usual pious gadgets (T-shirts, statues, key chains, scapulars, rosaries, etc.), media celebrities, politicians with an eye to respectability, and superstars like Sophia Loren.

Padre Pio's appeal is far-ranging, eclectic, blind to distinctions of class and education, and anything but evanescent. Long before his death in 1968 and his canonization in 2002, the poor brother from Pietrelcina had commanded the loyalty of millions throughout both the Catholic and non-Catholic world. Not unlike the Shroud of Turin, Padre Pio's capacity to touch the soul and the imagination seems limitless.

Certainly, one of the great examples of an eminence — in this case literary — attracted to the Padre Pio mystique is the novelist, essayist, and short-story writer Graham Greene. In a staggeringly honest interview with writer John Cornwell conducted for *The Tablet* two years before his death, Greene, the author of many works of exquisite religious torment, struggle, and aspiration, including *The Power and the Glory*, *The Heart of the Matter*, *The End of the Affair*, *A Burnt-Out Case*, *The Honorary Consul*, and *Monsignor Quixote*, recalled the long-lasting effect that Padre Pio had on him:

> In 1949 I went to attend Padre Pio's Mass, in Italy, in the Gargano Peninsula. I went out of curiosity. I'd heard about his stigmata. The Vatican didn't like him. A monsignor who came to have a drink with me in Rome said, "Oh, that holy fraud!" But he'd been examined by doctors of every faith — Jewish, Protestant, Catholic — and no faith. He had these wounds on his hands and feet, the size of a twenty-pence piece, and because he was not allowed to wear gloves saying Mass he pulled his sleeves up to try and hide them. He'd got a very nice peasant-like face, a little bit on the heavy side. I was warned that his was a very long Mass; so I went with my woman friend of that period to the Mass at 5:30 in the morning. He said it in Latin, and I thought that 35 minutes had passed. Then when I got outside the church I looked at my watch and it had been an hour and a half, or two hours, and I couldn't work out where the lost time had gone. I mean, there's always the moment of meditation after he takes the host, but he didn't seem to spend an abnormal length of time on that. And this is where I came to a small faith in a mystery. Because that *did* seem an extraordinary thing. . . . Padre Pio had asked for a hospital to be built, which seemed to me a remarkable request for a man who could heal people miraculously. He had a doctor friend who had come there to look after the hospital project, and that is where I stayed. It was through this doctor that I was invited to go and see Padre Pio for a

personal interview in the monastery. And I refused, because I said I didn't wish to change my life. . . . Padre Pio had strange powers. There was one famous case I knew of: a boy of about 16 who was in great pain with cancer. The mother went to see Padre Pio and he told her that he would take the pain on himself. The boy's pain immediately departed and during that period I heard from my friend who often visited there that at intervals during the Mass Padre Pio looked as if he was convulsed with agony. The boy eventually died, but without pain. These were stories by people who knew him and were on the spot.[1]

Greene was not a credulous or deferential character. He abominated certitude, wavered constantly in his own attachment to Catholic principles of morality, played fast and loose with dogma, was often an unsparing critic of church foibles, and identified himself as a "Catholic agnostic." And yet Padre Pio, the simple Capuchin friar, haunted him. He carried photographs of Padre Pio in his wallet, feared confessing to him because he knew Padre Pio's absolution and penance would require him to give up his mistress (the wealthy and beautiful American Catherine Walston), and acknowledged in his conversation with Cornwell that although his belief is not strong, it was very possible that without Padre Pio he would have lost it completely.

Greene is not the only person, eminent or otherwise, to have been captivated by Padre Pio in life or in myth. Jesuit Michael Czerny concedes, in the wake of Padre Pio's canonization, that there is much that mystifies him about the whole process, but he is prepared to see a larger design in the exercise:

When I live through a canonization here at the Borgo Santo Spirito [the street on which the world headquarters of the Jesuit order can be found] and four to five thousand people cram my neighbourhood, I have to admit that I don't understand what motivates them, what they're coming for, what they find, or what they take home. But I have to admire that fact that they come, as they have clearly done with Padre Pio's canonization. I have to admire their way of being present. And I have to believe that God is at work. I wouldn't make too strong a distinction between what you might call a real saint and the plastic saint, or the authentic saint and the holy card saint, because I don't think it is up to us — the theologians, intellectuals, and religious authorities — to make that distinction. It would be sad if we got too sophisticated or banned the forms of devotion that we don't think tell the real story. After all, a hundred years from now the real story will be different again, for we always rewrite the stories of the saints. I suppose that we rewrite them every time we think we have a new culture. That doesn't mean that the old one was totally false or that the new one is entirely right. We can't limit how God communicates, and if God uses Padre Pio — and obviously God has — that's fine. If we're totally cynical, we might find, as some people are surprised to see, that Padre Pio speaks more to many agnostics and skeptics in Italy than an authentic reading of the gospel of St. Mark or the latest encyclical. That's the way it is.

But who is this Padre Pio?

He began life on May 25, 1887, in the village of Pietrelcina in the Archdiocese of Benevento, the son of Grazio Forgione and Maria Giuseppa De Nunzio. On January 6, 1903, he entered the novitiate of the Capuchin friars at Morcone where, two weeks later, he took the Franciscan habit and the name of Brother Pio. Ordained on August 10, 1910, he moved home for six years for reasons of health and then was sent to the friary of

San Giovanni Rotondo, where he remained until his death on September 23, 1968, at the age of eighty-one.

This is the bare chronology. He didn't aspire to high office, he rarely moved outside the confines of the friary, he spent the majority of his time in the confessional (his reputation as a confessor was legendary), he practised various forms of physical and spiritual mortification, he cultivated the virtues to a high degree, he worked tirelessly to ease the pain and suffering of countless numbers (principally through the establishment of the House for the Relief of Suffering in 1956), and he prayed with greater and greater intensity. The image of Christ was also implanted on his very flesh when he received the stigmata. The exact date is recorded: September 20, 1918.

He recounts his "crucifixion":

It was the morning of the 20th of this month [September] and I was alone in choir after celebrating Mass, when I was overtaken by a repose similar to a sweet sleep. All my external and internal senses and all the faculties of my soul were in an indescribable quiet. During this time there was absolute silence around me and within me. There then followed a great peace and abandonment to total privation of everything. . . . This all happened in an instant.

While all this was happening, I saw in front of me a mysterious person, similar to the one I had seen on August 5, except that now his hands and feet and side were dripping in blood. His countenance terrified me. I don't know how to tell you how I felt at the instant. I felt that I was dying, and I would have died had the Lord not intervened and sustained my heart, which felt as if it would burst from my chest. The countenance of the mysterious figure disappeared and I noticed that my hands and feet and side were pierced and oozing blood.[2]

The earlier experience that Padre Pio alluded to, which occurred on August 5, he chronicled himself in a letter to a brother Capuchin:

> I was hearing the confessions of our boys at five o'clock in the afternoon when all of a sudden I was filled with extreme terror at the sight of a heavenly being who presented himself to the eye of my intellect. He held some kind of weapon in his hand, like a long metal lance with a sharp point at the end, and it looked as if fire were shooting out of it. At the very moment that I saw all this, the heavenly being thrust the weapon into my soul with all his might. It was only with the greatest difficulty that I refrained from crying out, for it felt as if I were dying. I told the boy to leave the confessional because I felt ill and did not have the strength to continue.
>
> This agony continued without ceasing until the morning of August 7. I can't tell you how much I suffered during this period. Even my internal organs felt torn and ruptured by the metal weapon. . . . Since that day, I am mortally wounded. It feels as if there is a wound in the center of my being that is always open and it causes constant pain.[3]

This adumbration, or prefiguring, of the stigmata that occurred on September 20 is traditionally called a *transverbera-tion*, a technical term used in classical mystical theology to describe a phenomenon that involves a spiritual being piercing the heart or side of an individual with either a lance or sword. The great Carmelite saint Teresa of Avila recounts such an experience in her autobiography. Clearly, Padre Pio linked the transverberation to the stigmatization, but the *meaning* of these dream/trance/vision experiences confounded him. What he did know was how unwelcome these intense experiences were for him, how searing the shame, how real the blood loss, how incalculable the sense of isolation. He wrote in a letter to his provincial, Padre Benedetto:

> Just imagine the anguish that I felt then and I still experience practically every day. The wound in the heart bleeds copiously, especially from Thursday night until Saturday [the Passion Triduum — Holy Thursday, Good Friday, Holy Saturday]. Father, I am dying of sorrow for the mortification and confusion caused by what I am suffering in my soul. I fear that I shall die from loss of blood if the Lord does not heed the cries of my poor heart and take this affliction from me. Will Jesus, who is so good, grant me this grace? Will he at least take away this confusion that these external signs cause in me? I will raise my voice and will not cease to beg him until, in his mercy, he removes, not the agony or the pain (which is impossible because I want to be inebriated with suffering), but these external marks are an indescribable and unbearable humiliation.[4]

Padre Pio is not imploring God to remove the suffering — he gives every indication of actually *welcoming* it — but of excising the very public shame that accompanies the life of a stigmatic. He seems to invite the pain of the crucifixion — after all, his participation in the supreme sacrifice of Jesus provides him with an extraordinary opportunity to make amends for the sins of others — but the very marks that single him out for this unique participation are the ongoing source of his soul-crushing humiliation.

The presence of the stigmata, then, is not a guarantee of divine warrant; it is not sought after, it is not gloried in; it is more often a mark of division and contention than a sign of unity and harmony. Not insignificantly, much has been made of the fact that Padre Pio was a friar in the Franciscan family and that the founder of this most popular of Roman Catholic orders —

Francesco Bernardone (1182–1226) — is inarguably the greatest of stigmatics.

Two years before his death, Francis took to the rugged terrain known as Mount La Verna in the Apennines for forty days — in the manner of Moses, Elijah, and Jesus — to discover the deeper truth of his life and mission. His dream-vision, clothed in the language of Revelations, clearly served as the consummate epiphany of God's will for him. None of his biographers quite capture the romantic aura, otherworldly shimmer, and noble quirkiness of this revelatory moment as well as Gilbert Keith Chesterton:

> It would seem that St. Francis beheld the heavens above him occupied by a vast winged being like a seraph spread out like a cross. There seems some mystery about whether the winged figure was itself crucified or in the posture of crucifixion, or whether it merely enclosed in its frame of wings some colossal crucifix. But it seems clear that there was some question of the former impression; for St. Bonaventura [Franciscan theologian and official biographer of St. Francis] distinctly says that St. Francis doubted how a seraph could be crucified, since those awful and ancient principalities were without the infirmity of the Passion. St. Bonaventura suggests that the seeming contradiction may have meant that St. Francis was to be crucified as a spirit since he could not be crucified as a man; but whatever the meaning of the vision, the general idea of it is very vivid and overwhelming. St. Francis saw above him, filling the whole heavens, some vast immemorial unthinkable power, ancient like the Ancient of Days, whose calm men had conceived under the forms of winged bulls or monstrous cherubim, and all that winged wonder was in pain liked a wounded bird. This seraphic suffering, it is said, pierced his soul with a sword of grief and pity; it may

be inferred that some sort of mounting agony accompanied the ecstasy. Finally after some fashion the apocalypse faded from the sky and the agony within subsided; and silence and the natural air filled the morning twilight and settled slowly in the purple chasms and cleft abysses of the Apennines.

The head of the solitary sank, amid all that relaxation and quiet in which time can drift by with the sense of something ended and complete; and as he stared downwards, he saw the marks of nails in his own hands.[5]

Ever the lyrical novelist, with a romantic's love of the narrative of the inner landscape, Chesterton skilfully paints a portrait of majesty and wonder. Whether it is factual or not is largely irrelevant. Something happened — something wondrous and strange, something that changed the world. Out of this consummation, this visionary moment when all coalesced with piercing clarity, Francis understood that his radical response to God's call would entail a conformity to the way of Christ that would be utter, entire, relentless, unforgiving. Biographer and theologian Donald Spoto draws the right conclusion from the Mount La Verna vision:

All his life, he had prayed to know who God was. The answer came in the dream vision: his God was the God of the abandoned, dying Jesus — and he, Francis, was now united in the dying of Jesus, to whom he had given his life. . . . now, in his decline and death, in his frustrations and failures, he would follow the path all the way to the cross.[6]

Spoto is skeptical about the physical stigmata, notes the shaky historical evidence regarding the physical marks of the cross on the person of Francis (after all, his body was already covered with the scars of ulceration, the signs of emaciation, and the wounds of leprosy), and makes much of the disbelief of several of Francis's associates and the omission of any reference to the stigmata in the proclamation of Francis's canonization by Pope Gregory IX in 1228.

Debates about the significance of the stigmata in the context of Francis's particular psychological life continue unabated. Clearly, Franciscan iconography, hagiography, the history of intra-order squabbling, and the politics of saint-making have all attached high importance to the actuality, if not the meaning, of the stigmata — its timing, purpose in focussing the uniqueness of Franciscan spirituality, and teleology. And, in turn, Padre Pio's stigmata should be situated within the larger context of the ascetical tradition that shaped him.

Padre Pio was a Capuchin. John Corriveau, the general minister of the Capuchins at the time of Padre Pio's canonization, explains the order's history:

> To get to our origins you must really go back to the period immediately following the death of St. Francis when his followers, the Order of the Friars Minor (Lesser Brothers), evolved from a predominantly lay brotherhood into a community of educated clerics and went in directions that occasioned serious divisions within the Franciscan movement. In time, two factions appeared: one, the *Osservanti*, insisted on a more primitive form of Franciscan life; the other, the *Conventuale*, resisted this trend. Tensions grew, and by the sixteenth century new reform groups emerged — including the Capuchins, arguably the descendants of the Spirituals [Franciscans whose purist reading of Bernardone's will, rule, and testament put them at odds with the Holy See, resulting in their eventual condemnation]. But the Capuchins did not incur papal wrath. Quite the contrary: their leader, Matteo di Bassi, secured approval from the Pope to live the Rule of St. Francis more strictly and to wear a habit with a pointed hood, the *cappuccino*. Friaries

sprouted up all over Italy, and the Capuchins now constitute the second-largest congregation within the Franciscan
family.

The Capuchin emphasis on strict poverty, the gathering of
alms, the radical simplicity of Francis himself with his willing
submission to the sundering demands of the gospel, appealed
enormously to Padre Pio. Father Corriveau:

> Both Pio and Francis had a tremendous devotion to Christ,
> and particularly, the Cross. In fact, for Francis the two key
> mysteries in the life of Jesus that touched him deeply were
> the Crib and the Cross. They were interconnected reali-
> ties. Francis preached that the Word of the Most High
> God took flesh in the womb of the Virgin Mary, and yet he
> does not see the Incarnation as a Christological event so
> much as a manifestation of the humility of God the Creator.
> Humility is at the heart of everything that you touch in
> Francis. The power to change the world resides in humil-
> ity, and for that reason, when he gave his identity to his
> order, he said that he wanted them to be called the Lesser
> Brothers the powerless brothers — because in their very
> powerlessness they could change the world. He said that
> the brothers should exercise no power among themselves,
> that they should hold no position of authority in either the
> church or in society, because the only authentic instrument
> of change in the world can be discovered in the powerless-
> ness of God, the humility of God, which the Lesser
> Brothers must emulate.

So it is with Pio. He reminds us that, like Francis, we
must go back to our roots and discover how it is possible to
serve *without* power. Pio is an *interpretation* of the life of
Francis for our time. Pio never held a position of authority
in the Capuchin order, not even as a local superior or vicar

of a house. He stands as a sign of contradiction in a world dedicated to control. Interestingly, he received the stigmata in the final year of the Great War: in the very midst of acts of great and deadly and futile arrogance, with nations seeking to impose their will on others, there emerged this figure of humility, this figure who bore the sign of the Cross — the sign of Divine Humility itself — on his very person.

A sophisticated reading of the life of Pio will certainly situate his "meaning" within his relationship to the original Franciscan. In what sense then is Pio a Francis for our time? The matchless affection for Francis over the centuries, his appeal for those outside traditional religious boundaries, his iconic and cultic status among the romantic and conventional alike, his contemporary currency as the proto-saint of ecology and the environment, his skill as a poet of ordinary mysticism, and his reputation as a man who loved generously and freely (a troubadour of the soul), make Francis in many ways a very different kind of saint from Padre Pio. The Francis of Italian filmmaker Franco Zeffirelli's imagination — *Brother Sun and Sister Moon* — is the Francis of mass appeal: handsome, lithe, charismatic, a natural lover (his relationship with St. Clare, although chaste, is charged with passion), and a spiritual pathfinder of breathtaking originality. This is not Padre Pio.

Where Padre Pio and St. Francis most align is, according to John Corriveau, in the mystery that is holiness itself:

> With Pio's canonization, the Church takes possession of him. And I don't mean the official or hierarchical church, but the people themselves. The people define who he is — certainly who he is to them. The vast numbers in St. Peter's Square at the time of his beatification and his canonization see him in no small part as a modern miracle worker. There are verifiable facts about his extraordinary powers of inter-

cession that confirm his image as a miracle maker. How do you work with that?

Let me say something about my brothers at San Giovanni Rotondo. They deal with Pio's reputation as the miracle man of Italy reasonably well. For example, every year on the Feast of Padre Pio, the 23rd of September, I preside at the Eucharist at midnight, although there are people in the huge square of San Giovanni from noon until 2:30 in the morning and they sit there in prayer for fourteen hours. Fourteen hours!! I listen and watch, as a critical North American, the whole unfolding. In fact, the first time I went I spent a long time on the roof just listening to my fellow Capuchins talking not about Pio but about Jesus Christ. Indeed, they start off by talking about Moses and the burning bush in Exodus 3, the bush that burned but was not consumed. Moses saw that it was a marvellous thing, and when he went over to examine the bush he became conscious that it was a sign of the holiness of God. In the same way, people are attracted to the holiness of Pio. But Franciscans must insist that, once drawn to the holiness that is Pio, the people must be led to the *source* of that holiness: Jesus. Pio offers us an opportunity to evangelize.

I don't care why people come to Pio, only that they come; and that by doing so we can lead them to the deeper understanding that it was Christ who made Pio who he is and that he can also be the way, and truth, and the light for them as well.

Corriveau's practical grasp of the evangelizing possibilities inherent in the pilgrimages to the shrine that is San Giovanni — that as the people come to the "home" of St. Pio to pay homage, to ask for favours, to participate in something greater than being just part of the aggregate of humanity gathered in the square, the friars can bring them from a single manifestation of the holy to the source of that holiness — speaks volumes about the pragmatic and missionary impulse at the heart of the Franciscan movement itself. Corriveau attaches special significance to shrines in this regard:

> Look at the great shrines in Canada: St. Anne de Beaupré, St. Joseph's Oratory, Martyrs' Shrine in Midland. It's not only seniors who go to these places. There are a lot of young people who go to these shrines. Why? They are not attracted by the same things that attract their grandmothers, although it is not uncommon that their interest is first sparked by listening to their grandmothers talking about these pilgrimages as strong faith moments in their lives. San Giovanni attracts 7 million pilgrims a year. A good number of them, at least half, are the young — drawn, I believe, by the mystery of holiness, even if they don't know what this means. I suppose we could "package" Pio for youth, but I think that is an impossibility given that we didn't even do a particularly good job of packaging him during the run-up to his canonization. He's a spontaneous event.

Trekking off, then, to San Giovanni Rotondo can be a salutary experience for the young, exploring the outer perimeter of holiness, a place where the burning bush can be approached with wonder, curiosity, and fear. After all, faith is not exclusively, or even primarily, a cerebral affair. This is where saints, shrines, and stigmata come in, as Corriveau knows well:

> Knowing God does not begin as an intellectual process. Faith moves from the heart to the head, and these places — shrines — engage the heart. Now, for me, if I go on pilgrimage, I always go to Assisi. Why, you might ask? Basically because Francis appeals to me on all levels — emotionally, intellectually, spiritually. He engages me in a

way that Pio does not, at least at the present time. But what attracts in the end is the mystery of holiness. And the stigmata — an experience shared by both Francis and his disciple Pio — tells us something as well about this mystery of holiness. Francis started with his devotion to the crucified, but he received the stigmata near the end of his life. By contrast, Pio received the stigmata near the beginning of his active life as a friar, and it disappeared at the time of his death. But in both cases this tangible, lived identification with the suffering Christ reminds us of the terrible truth that identification and union with God is a real possibility and we are attracted at the same time as we are daunted by such a prospect.

The general minister of the Capuchins is not given to pious revels, nor to cynicism. He is cognizant of the many reasons behind Padre Pio's wide appeal, is fully aware of the numerous stories and claims revolving around Pio's paranormal activities (his aptitude for bilocation and his predilection for levitation, among other things), and appreciates the fact that for most people the lure of the holy will not be responded to — at least in the first instance — by the intellect.

The appeal of St. Pio cannot be found in his systematic teaching, for there isn't any; it cannot be found in the wild heroics of a missionary's witness, for he never left Italy for hostile shores (or for any shores, for that matter); it cannot be found in bold strategies of reform, for he initiated none; it cannot be found in his influence in the chambers of power, for even the Vatican marginalized him for a time; and it cannot be found in his bracing contemporaneity, for his devotional life and ecclesiological perspective remained rooted in an earlier time. The appeal lies elsewhere.

Pio's piety is simple and unadorned. Like Thérèse de Lisieux with her "little way" spirituality (which she described as an attitude of inexhaustible hope in the rich mercy of Divine love), Pio offers a homespun spirituality that is accessible, non-threatening, non-elitist, marked by its populism and its non-esoteric regimen for spiritual enlightenment. Rustic, humble, and simple, it is, like Pio himself, a rural Italian invention fully consonant with the Franciscan tradition and unabashedly visceral.

Many fellow Capuchins found Pio's spirituality unattractive, too unsophisticated, too earthy, and too raw for their more refined Franciscan — yes, Franciscan — palettes. But to get to know the real Pio was to entail a re-evaluation of the friar's life and faith. This was especially true of the man charged with the responsibility of shepherding the cause of Francesco Forgione (Padre Pio, that is) through to its conclusion: Florio Tessari, general postulator of the order.

I never met him personally and didn't care much for his spirituality, at least in the way it was transmitted to me by people who were devoted to him. Quite frankly, I didn't like his spirituality at all, as I understood it. But when I took over the office of general postulator I got to know him better. I think that what changed my thinking involved "reading" Pio's personality in a different light from the way I had been. Of course, there is a medieval approach — the bilocations, ecstasies, the odour of sanctity, the alleged cures — and then there is the approach that assesses him under the rubric of how he has helped me live my Capuchin life, my Capuchin charism, with greater fidelity, stripped to the essentials, exacting ever-greater acts of self-surrender. For those of us not Capuchins, Pio represents a rock of security in a sea of accelerated change. In our technological society, with its comprehensive pleasure-seeking impulse and with all the anxiety that this generates for many people, Pio, by means of his very strong direct personal experience of God, offers people hope. He offers them a kind of certainty.

Yearning for certainty is not, of course, a quality particular to the rural inhabitants of Italy. The cult of Padre Pio is widespread and has flourished with few checks. Brother Florio is not alone in having initial misgivings over Pio's spirituality. Several of his confreres shared his discomfort. But one who manifestly did not is Gerardo di Fiumeri, the vice-postulator for the cause of Padre Pio, and a friar who knew Pio for many years. Brother Gerardo first met Pio at San Giovanni Rotondo in 1946, and during the early '60s he lived with him, served as his superior and proculator, witnessed on numerous occasions his stigmata, confessed to him, and asked Pio if he could be his spiritual son:

> Living with Padre Pio was very, very, very nice for all the friars. He had an impressive memory. He recalled the birthday of each friar — the name day, or feast day, as we call it. He would tell each friar the day before the commemoration that he would say Mass on the feast. For me, of course, named after Gerard Majella [a Redemptorist lay brother, eighteenth-century wonder worker, and patron saint of expectant mothers], the feast day is in October. It was his habit to pray with the people every day from eleven o'clock to noon, and he would stop at my door on his way back from the church, but I didn't see him. Then I heard a rustle at the door, and when I got up to open it, there was Padre Pio with a flower in his hand for me. It was my feast day and it was a very kind and simple thing to do. I still have that flower with me as a souvenir.

Brother Gerardo was entrusted with the task of promoting Pio's cause in 1970, and he laboured in that capacity for thirty-

two years. It was with considerable relief that he saw the culmi-
nation of his efforts with the canonization, and he entertains no
doubts — none — on the matter of Pio's sanctity:

> The perfume, the bilocations, the ecstasies — these are
> mystical gifts, but they are not the true essentials of sanc-
> tity. The essentials are the virtues. It is also important to
> keep in mind the things that Padre Pio taught us, the most
> significant of which is that Jesus crucified is the only
> Saviour. In the poor, we see Jesus, and in the sick, we touch
> Jesus. We are twice blessed when we encounter the sick
> who are also poor, argued Padre Pio. I am now seventy-
> three years old, and I have worked on the cause of Padre
> Pio for nearly half my life. It is time to rest and it is time to
> move beyond chronicling the life to observing the teach-
> ings of Pio. This is very important.

Although Brother Gerardo makes it sound as if promoting
the cause was simply a matter of tenacity and of personal
survival, it was in truth more than a matter of devoted persist-
ence, personal longevity, and benign trust in the process. There
were the controversies to be faced.

And controversies there were aplenty. In fact, Vaticanologist
and author John L. Allen Jr. has dubbed the Capuchin "St.
Padre Pio of the Holy Rehabilitation."[7] Allen marvels at the
speed with which Pio has moved from being a clerical pariah to
being a saint. He cannot think of any historical parallel. It is not
unusual that a future saint, whether a visionary, mystic, or
doctor of the church, would find him or herself subject to
scrutiny by church authorities. It is not at all uncommon, in
fact, for the most vigorous resistance to emanate from precisely
those authorities that will be critical in the end for the approval
of a cause. The Vatican is more inclined to be suspicious than
supportive of anything or anyone who challenges the bound-

aries of orthodoxy or established practice. But, it takes time. Think of the long rehabilitation process involving Joan of Arc or Meister Eckhart or Girolamo Savonarola — matters of centuries — and you get a closer approximation to the norm. Pio was exonerated within a few years of his death and sainted three decades later.

The controversies began almost at the beginning of his priestly ministry. He would often collapse into a trancelike state (his "ecstasies") while celebrating Mass, thereby prolonging the liturgy interminably. Although the long-suffering devout found Mass punctuated with an ecstasy a spiritual bonus, many others — including Pio's Capuchin brothers — complained, and he was instructed by his superiors to limit himself to the customary half-hour celebration. Minor complaints at best. But once the stigmata appeared, the complaints, delations, and calumnies began in earnest. Popes Benedict XV and Pius XI both ordered inquests into the authenticity of the stigmata. Physicians and archbishops were dispatched to do their work. Efforts by the Vatican to move Pio from San Giovanni Rotondo were unsuccessful because the local citizenry threatened a riot — and not for the first time.

In 1922, Agostino Gemelli, a theologian, physician, and internationally respected specialist on stigmata cases, judged Pio an hysteric, determined that his wounds were kept open by carbolic acid, and concluded that the stigmata was of psychological and not spiritual origin. According to Pio biographer Luigi Peroni, there was no surprise in Gemelli's assessment: of all stigmatics, only Francis of Assisi and Catherine of Siena escaped his censure.[8]

After the Gemelli report, there were investigations by the Holy Office of the Inquisition and in 1923 a warning, or *monitum*, was issued cautioning Catholics to keep their distance from the emerging Pio cult. Subsequent *monita* were issued in 1924, 1926, and 1931. Talk of moving him once again provoked threats of violence. The Vatican's patience was being increasingly tried. In the early 1930s he was forbidden to entertain visitors, hear confessions, or celebrate Mass in public. These restrictions were subsequently lifted, and from 1933 until just after the Second World War, Pio's travails with the Vatican and Italian episcopacy were muted — if not tabled for another time.

Trouble and mischief started up again in the 1950s, at the time of the building of the Casa Sollievo della Sofferenza (House for the Relief of Suffering), a hospital for which Pio had secured the funding after Pope Pius XII had released him from his vow of poverty. The Italian anticlericals, both within and outside the government, were keen on mocking the "poor" friar who successfully raised the billions of lira needed and who, not long ago, had been a victim of Vatican harassment rather than their new-found fiscal *wunderkind*.

And the Vatican repeatedly had difficulties with Padre Pio, none of which were ameliorated by his stunning success as a fundraiser. Although Pio was never implicated in allegations of fiscal mismanagement, dodgy investment schemes, money laundering, or insider trading, in the early 1960s he once again found himself the subject of an official Vatican investigation conducted by the yet-to-be-appointed Archbishop of Ancona, Carlo Maccari — at the time a consultor of the Sacred Congregation of the Council.

Maccari's report, the contents of which have never been made public, was highly critical of Padre Pio. He appears to have taken seriously charges of sexual impropriety on the Capuchin's behalf (one accusation, much discussed in the Italian press of the time, involves Pio having sex with female penitents twice a week). Rumours abound of his confessional being bugged in order to substantiate the charges. Pio's biographers and advocates have argued strenuously that the calumnies were the result of malignant gossip, envious friars, sexually frustrated village women, hysterical zealots keen on achieving fiscal and spiritual profit (parts of Pio's Capuchin habit and his cushion were lifted by the devout), and jealous disciples fearful of competing affections. In the end, Maccari's report was not acted upon; he is reputed to have recanted his anti-Pio sentiments and indeed invoked Pio on his deathbed (pious apocrypha, perhaps). By the time of Pio's own death, the Vatican had moved from what Luigi Peroni calls a fifty-year persecution to full rehabilitation. No small part of that rehabilitation was engineered by John Paul II.

Not surprisingly, the papal exorcism that appears to have expelled all doubt and reservation over the authenticity of Pio's sanctity has not been successful in all quarters. The American Atheists is one such body:

> the beatification and canonization of Padre Pio — and the tacit acceptance of the miraculous, paranormal events associated with the controversial friar — come at a time when the Vatican finds itself in competition with energetic Pentecostal and evangelical Protestants. Pio's paranormal accomplishments appear at times to have more in common with "signs and wonders" fundamentalism and tent revivalism than restrained Roman Catholicism. The "saint factory" strategy of canonizing a record number of personalities for church veneration is proving to be a media savvy move that encourages and supports growing public credulity.[9]

Catholics are divided over the Pio legacy. He is not the founder of a new religious body; he did not hold high ecclesiastical office; he did not suffer martyrdom at the hands of persecutors of the church; he did not establish a new system of theological or philosophical thought; and he did not contribute a major body of spiritual reflection to the community. He lived simply, bled amply, counselled untold numbers in the confessional (at one point, people were required to take numbered tickets and could wait up to two months before their confessional time slot), read into the deepest recesses of the soul, reputedly engaged in paranormal activities with the greatest of reluctance, withstood relentless personal assaults on his integrity from critics and detractors in his order and from without, and died a beloved legend. He was nothing exceptional, and yet he captured the imagination and the heart of huge numbers of both the devout and the cynical. Conservatives, in particular, were drawn to him, and they came from across the denominational divide. Pio biographer and Lutheran cleric C. Bernard Ruffin starkly proclaims Padre Pio of Pietrelcina

> one of the most significant figures in Christian history, a man of prophetic stature who, through great personal holiness and wisdom and through a ministry in many aspects inexplicable to science, tended to confirm the truth of the Gospels and the veracity of historical Christianity to an indifferent, unbelieving age . . . an evangelist who never conducted a crusade and who, though he never travelled more than a mile or two from his monastery walls in fifty years, yet seemed capable of transforming lives to a degree unimagined by Billy Graham or Oral Roberts.[10]

At the same time that he is compared favourably with American televangelists, the darling of Pentecostals and Charismatics, he becomes a rallying point for increasingly disaffected Catholics, distraught by postconciliar directions that seem to them threatening to the church's holiness of doctrine and practice. Capuchin Brother Jean of the Monastery of St. Francis in Morgon, France, has drawn succour from Pio's personal resistance to the many changes ushered in by the Council and has used Pio's fidelity to the old order as a tool to admonish modernizers. A strong defender of traditional morality (Pio wrote to Pope Paul VI shortly before his own death thanking him for *Humanae vitae*, the 1968 papal encyclical that reaffirmed the ban against all forms of artificial birth regulation), and a strong defender of the centuries-old rules of the Franciscan order, Pio was especially appalled by the revolutionary liturgical changes promulgated by the Council and introduced — in often scattered and irreverent ways — in churches across the world.

Even before the end of the Council, in February 1965, someone announced to him that soon he would have to celebrate the Mass according to a new rite, *ad experimentum*, in the vernacular. . . . immediately, even before seeing the text, he wrote to Paul VI to ask him to be dispensed from the liturgical experiment, and to be able to continue to celebrate the Mass of St. Pius V. When Cardinal Bacci came to see him in order to bring the authorization, Padre Pio let a complaint escape in the presence of the Pope's messenger: "For pity sake, end the Council quickly."[11]

It is neither alarming nor surprising that a friar like Pio would be attached to the traditional way of celebrating the liturgy and that he would find the new order of things distressful. Nor is it surprising, given his popularity throughout Italy, that he would be emboldened to seek dispensation from the Roman authorities. Padre Pio *was* tradition.

An examination of his spiritual teachings reveals an earnest body of fervent, uncomplicated, traditional maxims and exhortations that have for centuries constituted the core of popular Catholic piety: put your trust in Christ as your personal Saviour; know that you have no righteousness of your own; remember that good works come only through Christ; recognize that the devil is a *real* individual, bent on destroying you, but do not fear him; always pray to God and say, in every circumstance, "Thy will be done"; love the cross; offer every action up to God; never worry; aspire to the heavenly prize; rejoice in the Lord; confess to a priest weekly; receive Communion daily; be faithful in spiritual reading; and examine your conscience frequently. Nothing suspect in this.

Although his emphasis on a personal relationship with his Saviour might hint at a Protestant stratagem of bypassing the church in the interests of salvation, nothing Pio did was outside his structured, visceral, and all-embracing Catholic world. His struggling, rugged, no-holds-barred Christianity appealed to John Paul II long before his election to the papacy. Perhaps it was Pio's deep sense of victimhood and expiation, his utter trust in Providence, his willingness to withstand persecution at the hands of uncomprehending authorities, and his steadfast focus on the unalterable truths of Catholicism that secured the Pope's attraction to the cult of Pio. Undoubtedly, John Paul II entertained none of the reservations about Padre Pio held by all his predecessors save John Paul I (Benedict XV, Pius XI, Pius XII, John XXIII, and Paul VI), reservations that either brimmed over into deep distrust or remained mildly niggling suspicions. Only John Paul II gave him a completely clean bill of health and provided him with the kind of pontifical endorsement that has seen him move through rehabilitation to sainthood at warp speed.

Leonard Cohen's description of a saint as a "monster of love" certainly applies to Pio of Pietrelcina, especially when you consider the etymology of monster — *monstrum* in Latin — which combines divine portent or warning with the marvellous. The marvel is to be found not only in the paranormal — least of all in the paranormal — and more in the excess of love. And the warning? A beacon in the tumult, argue some Capuchins; a judgement on the corruption of power ecclesiastical and secular, argue other Capuchins. Pio himself saw things differently. For him it was a simple matter of shepherding:

I belong entirely to everyone. Everyone can say, "Padre Pio is mine." I deeply love [all humanity]. I love my spiritual children as much as my own soul and even more. I have regenerated them to Jesus through suffering and love. I can forget myself but not my spiritual children. Indeed, I can assure you that when the Lord calls me, I will say to him: "Lord, I will stand at the gates of heaven until I see all my spiritual children have entered." (Archives of Padre Pio)[12]

In an age quickly unnerved by religious leaders and spiritual mentors hellbent on bringing their followers to the doors of heaven, such language as this can be disquieting. The genius of Pio's pastorship, however, is to be found in his abjuring of power, his suffering at the hands of power, his steady conviction that he is a conduit of God's love. In the end, he was a holy subversive.

Chapter Four

TERESA OF CALCUTTA:
GOD'S PENCIL

THE ALBANIAN ARTIST Ilir Fico knows something of the turmoil that accompanies civil disorder. Having suffered for years under totalitarian rule and then under the chaos of war as his country fell prey to the political and social disruptions of the 1990s in the Balkans, he finally managed, accompanied by his family, to flee his native country for Canada. Aware that when in Albania he could be jailed for a decade for painting abstract images, he now revels in his new freedom as if under the influence of an intoxicating drug. His most ambitious work to date is the series of forty-seven paintings that feature fellow Albanian Agnes Gonxha Bojaxhiu, better known to history as Mother Teresa of Calcutta. Fico's devotion to Mother Teresa is "as inexplicable as love," and as enduring as the joy he now feels at being free: "Mother Teresa is an inexhaustible source of inspiration and beauty. . . . Mother Teresa is the holy water to dilute the spirit of civil war."[1]

Although the civil war that Fico is talking about is the one that ravaged his country — a war that saw province pitted against province, religion against religion, ethnicity against ethnicity — Mother Teresa has been herself at the centre of a civil war. Indeed, some would argue she is the *cause* of a civil war, with Catholic pitted against Catholic in a clash of ideologies that sadly demonstrates the sometimes wrenching legacy of the Second Vatican Council and the pontificate of John Paul II.

How is it possible that this "monster of love" whose compassion is universally recognized and whose name is synonymous with service has become so wildly controverted a figure?

Manifestly, Mother Teresa has had a deeply transformative influence on legions of people dispersed throughout the planet, from different walks of life, from various professions, and of all ages. One who was so influenced by Mother Teresa was Donald Nicholl, scholar, peace activist, former rector of the Ecumenical Institute for Theological Research at Tantur, Israel, and author of *Holiness, The Beatitude of Truth: Reflections of a Lifetime*, and *The Testing of Hearts: A Pilgrim's Journey*. In an article exploring the significance of *metanoia* (a Greek term that means "change of heart" and is often spoken of in the context of a religious conversion), Nicholl observed that the term "means recognizing that it would be death to the spirit to continue in the old way." Because Nicholl respected the importance of autobiography and story when speaking of the high and often ineffable truths of the spiritual life, he spoke of the dramatic movement of the spirit that he and his wife experienced when they first met Mother Teresa:

We were on the eve of that stage in life when the last of the children to leave home would soon be departing, and we both had a sense that this might be the moment for us to start living the Gospel in a more radical fashion. That might, we thought, require us to abandon our present position and go live amongst the poor in the Third World. So we went to London to speak with Mother Teresa and to seek her help in discerning what the Holy Spirit was asking of us.

In the event I have to say that we were somewhat surprised — almost disappointed — by her reaction. She showed herself so concerned because we seemed over anxious that we were not doing enough to spread the Gospel. She could not have been more gentle, nor more affirming of what we were already doing — though it must be reported that our meeting with her turned our world upside down in ways that we had not foreseen — but gently turned upside down.

However, it so happened that we were not the only people seeking her counsel that day. There came a young woman, a university student, to tell Mother Teresa she wanted to join the Missionaries of Charity and to serve in the home for the dying in Calcutta. But, the student explained, since she was approaching her final year at the university she would wait until she had taken her degree before joining the Sisters. "You mean," said Mother Teresa, "that you would deprive the poor of India of a year of your service?" What a steely response to give a youngster only twenty years old! And yet it came from the same source as the gentle response to us.

The explanation for the seeming disparity, I take it, is that although every one of us is in a different position from everyone else and therefore each one's *metanoia* will follow a different path, nevertheless for each one of us the desire of the Holy Spirit is the same. It is that each of us should stop centring our lives around our false self, that which is infected with death, and become open to the exceeding great promises recorded in the Second Letter of Peter — that we should begin to share in the divine nature, which is life itself, untouched by death.[2]

For Nicholl and his wife, the encounter with Mother Teresa was both inspiring and upsetting. The fragile nun from Albania was not the sensitive religious the Nicholls naturally assumed she was when it came to assessing the young woman's priorities. She immediately, perhaps aggressively, demanded to know why the poor must wait. No nuancing, wavering, or gentle discerning with Mother Teresa. Her no-holds-barred approach admitted little in the way of prolonged deliberation, tentative probing, or Ignatian weighing of the pros and cons. She was a force to reckon with on first encounter, no matter one's status, age, or gender.

Kathryn Spink, author of *Mother Teresa: A Complete Authorized Biography*, recalls her first encounter with Mother Teresa:

My very first meeting was actually rather indirect in that I had been requested by a publishing company to produce anything that I could on Mother Teresa. So I wrote to Malcolm Muggeridge [the broadcaster and author who had written the influential profile of Mother Teresa, *Something Beautiful for God*], who was then leading a great British campaign on her behalf in those days, and he, in turn, referred me to someone living just south of London who had been one of the co-workers of Mother Teresa, a lay helper in Calcutta. I was invited to her house and she took me to her loft and revealed an old tin trunk such as missionaries took out to India in those days. It was full of miscellaneous scraps of paper, bits of old newspapers, cuttings, that sort of thing, and truly constituted the unofficial archives of Mother Teresa. The helper said to me that if I rung up Mother Teresa and got her permission I could then use this trunk of materials for the biography.

So, I sat up for three nights on the trot, waiting to connect with Mother Teresa. On the third night, in the early hours of the morning, she actually answered the phone herself — as she always did, in fact — and I asked her permission to write something about her work. And she said, characteristically, "Oh, no, no, no. There's been Malcolm's book and there's no need for anything else." But I, with all the irritability of one who had lost three nights' sleep and with the arrogance of youth, presumed to argue. So she said, in the end — not wanting to be unkind, I think — she would meet with me the next time she came to London and we would then see. Two or three weeks later she arrived at the Missionaries of Charity house in London and we met.

What struck me most at this first encounter is simply her understated presence. Let me explain. I was kneeling for about twenty minutes in the front room of the house — it served as their chapel — when I realized that she was practically beside me. There was something about the sheer smallness of her presence that underlined for me what she always maintained: she is just an instrument of God. After our prayer, we spoke and I then realized that she had a very strong will and was adamant that what was God's will cannot be tampered with and that she knew what was God's will most of the time.

She gave me permission to write about her work in Europe. She didn't want it concentrated on Calcutta, but rather on the spiritual poverty of the West. And she said so in no uncertain terms. And so I wrote my first book on her some twenty years ago now, and then in 1991 I approached her again, this time to get her permission to write her biography.

Over the years I became quite close to her. I worked with her, and there were plenty of jolts. The first surprise for me was the time she put a tiny baby into my arms, a baby that was destined to die in a few hours, and instructed me to "Love that child until it dies." I had had at that point no previous experience of working in a slum and suddenly I was confronted with a child that I had to love and sing to until the child died. I have come to believe that it is only with a direct experience of this kind that you can begin to understand Mother Teresa. It was certainly a shock at the time. I then understood that the sanctity-of-life doctrine wasn't essentially a rational understanding for Mother Teresa. You had to touch the poor, touch the dying, dive into life.

A life lived with no half measures is an exhausting and perhaps inhuman life. But for Mother Teresa it became the only kind of life, although there was little indication at the beginning that her life's trajectory would become as radical an adventure as it in time became.

Born to Kolle Bojaxhiu and Drana Bernaj on August 16, 1910, in Skopje, capital of the then Albanian republic of Macedonia, the future Teresa (at the time known as Gonxha) was the third of three children. Her father was a moderately successful co-owner of a construction business and a local politico with growing ambitions. Following a meeting in Belgrade in 1919 he was killed — some argue poisoned by Serbian police — and the family's fortunes were imperilled by Bojaxhiu's business colleague, who took over full ownership of the firm. Drana reinvented herself as an entrepreneur by establishing an embroidery business. Thus the family's survival was assured, and by all accounts the children appear to have had an uneventful and mostly happy childhood — and this during the ravages visited upon the Austro-Hungarian Empire throughout the First World War, and its ruthless dismemberment after the 1919 Treaty of Versailles.

Gonxha was a preternaturally religious child given to increasingly longer sojourns in church. She pored over missionary magazines with a pious romantic's dreaminess and holy zeal for souls. By the age of twelve, according to biographer Spink, she first felt the rumblings of a vocation, and just seven years later she made the decision to enter religious life.

During a pilgrimage to the Marian shrine of Letnice, not far from Skopje, her vocation became more defined: she herself would become a missionary. "I remember," she said, "it was the evening of the Feast of the Ascension. I held in my hands a lighted candle. I was praying, I was singing, joy overflowing within me. That day, I decided I would consecrate myself totally to God in religious life."[3]

It is important that the decision to commit herself to God was fine-tuned at a Marian shrine. The role of Mary in her life, her spirituality, her sense of mission, her personal friendship with Pope John Paul II, and her leadership of her order cannot be gainsaid.

For John Paul II, Mary proved instrumental in all that he did and was. Similarly, Mary enjoyed a position of unique reverence for Mother Teresa, who invoked her intercession at the time she was contemplating a religious vocation — in fact, she attributes to the Patroness of Skopje the very discovery of her vocation. And when she branched out on her own in 1948, the white sari she wore as a substitute for her traditional religious habit had a blue border symbolizing her resolve to model her life and ministry on that of Mary.

Not surprisingly, then, when she chose a religious congregation, it was the aptly named Sisters of Our Lady of Loreto. She travelled to the order's motherhouse in Dublin, spent a couple of months learning English, embarked for India, spent two years as a novice in Darjeeling professing temporary vows and changing her name from Gonxha to Teresa — "it wasn't the name of the great Teresa of Avila. I chose the name of Teresa of the Little Flower, Thérèse of Lisieux" — lived in Calcutta teaching geography and history at St. Mary's of Entally School, professed her final vows in 1937, and assumed the responsibility of director of studies at the school. In many ways it was the natural and largely uneventful progress of an obedient nun's life of service. She says of these years: "I was the happiest nun at Loreto. I dedicated myself to teaching. That job, carried out for the love of God, was a true apostolate. I liked it very much."[4]

But her religious life was soon to be seriously disrupted. On a train to Darjeeling on September 10, 1946, at a time when British India — the Raj — was itself in great turmoil, Mahatma Gandhi was leading a non-violent movement for independence, and the scars of the Second World War were still sore in those territories that constituted the Pacific Theatre of war, Teresa heard what she dubbed "the call within the call," her "day of inspiration," when she understood that she was to take the irreversible step of leaving her order to commit herself to a life of complete service to the poor.

> She would later say, "the call of God to be a Missionary of Charity is the hidden treasure for me, for which I have sold all to purchase it. You remember in the gospel, what the man did when he found the hidden treasure — he hid it. This is what I want to do for God." The call was clear: "I was to leave the convent and help the poor while living among them. It was an order. To fail it would have been to break the faith." Answering this call meant leaving her community, even though she was very happy there. It meant getting the necessary authorizations, which would not be easy.[5]

And indeed they were not. For a nun to leave her order, to be exclaustrated, to transfer to another order, to be dispensed of her vows — whatever the request — required both local and Roman permission, and all the proper channels would have to be doggedly pursued. They were. On April 12, 1948, Pope Pius XII gave approval for the then Sister Teresa to live as an independent religious. Within a short time she opened her first "school" in the Motijhil quarter of Calcutta, begged successfully for funding for a dispensary, expanded the number of students, and at first refused and then accepted young women eager on sharing her life and vocation (the Missionaries of Charity was legally established by the church as a congregation under the canonical jurisdiction of the local bishop in 1950 — fittingly, Rome's authorization was sealed on the Feast of Our Lady of the Rosary).

The new congregation, as the Roman decree indicated, requires of those who would commit themselves to the community that they not only take the three traditional vows associated with religious life — poverty, chastity, and obedience — but that they take a fourth vow as well, one that requires them to dedicate their lives to the "poorest of the poor." They are enjoined to "spend themselves unremittingly in seeking out, in towns and villages, even amid squalid surroundings, the poorer, the abandoned, the sick, the infirm, [and] the dying."

At the time of the "founding," Sister Teresa became Mother Teresa. A new order was born. But what of the old one? Although the Sisters of Loreto provided her with support for many years after she left their community, and although she professed to have been the "happiest nun at Loreto," according to biographer and theologian Paul Williams, what she publicly stated as true was at odds with what was in fact the case:

> She described her life as a nun in the Loreto convent as one of perfect peace and contentment. "To leave Loreto," she said, "was my greatest sacrifice, the most difficult thing I have ever done. It was more difficult than to leave my family and my country to enter religious life. Loreto, my spiritual training, my work there, meant everything to me.' But the truth of the matter is that Mother Teresa came to detest the Order after she had been demoted as headmistress and sought ecclesiastical release from her solemn vows so that she could become a secular social worker.[6]

It is not uncommon to view the same experience differently through the combined lens of maturity and reflection. It is also not uncommon to rewrite, to revise, in the light of changed circumstances. Whether Mother Teresa left the Loreto nuns disgruntled over her treatment by her superiors or as the result of a summons to deepen her commitment to the poor, the fact remains that she received continued material support from her former congregation and that there is no record of a lingering estrangement on either side.

By 1952 there were some thirty women in the order, and a home, Nirmal Hriday, for dying destitutes was opened on the

Feast of Mary Immaculate (August 22). A year later, the sisters opened self-sufficient rehabilitation centres for lepers, at Titagarh and Shanti Nagar, and established their central head-quarters at 54 Lower Circular Road, Calcutta. They had arrived with a vengeance. India was their home, and Mother Teresa belonged to India. In fact, in 1962 she received the first of what would amount in the coming decades to a veritable deluge of awards and honours: the Padmashri, or Order of the Lotus, Award, bestowed by the government of India. Shortly there-after, she received the Magsaysay Award from the SEATO nations of southeastern Asia.

In 1965, during the third year of the pontificate of Paul VI, the Missionaries of Charity became a Society of Pontifical Right. By now, the order boasted more than three hundred sisters and thirty homes, and received an invitation from the Archbishop of Barquisimeto, Venezuela, to open a house in Cocorote — Mother Teresa had now established her first base outside India. Growth proceeded exponentially. By 1971 the Missionaries of Charity had homes in England, Australia, Tanzania, and in Rome itself. In fact, as a sign of pontifical favour, Mother Teresa was granted Vatican citizenship. She also opened her first operation in the United States and was awarded the Pope John XXIII Peace Prize, the Good Samaritan Award, and the Templeton Award for Progress in Religion.

By the time she received the ultimate international distinc-tion, the Nobel Peace Prize, in 1979, her order had acquired several approved branches, including the Co-Workers of the Missionaries of Charity, the Missionaries of Charity Brothers, and the Contemplative Sisters of the Word. Following the Nobel Prize, the rate of expansion for recruits and for new homes became meteoric.

As her accomplishments accumulated, so, too, did her numer-ous awards and accolades. Increasingly, the media became obsessed with her — and she with them. This unique relationship — and there was no more sophisticated nor adroit a manipulator of the media in the annals of saintdom than Mother Teresa — was by turns adulatory, mutually beneficial, hypercritical, and deconstructionist. She was both the darling and the demon. As time unfolded, the media became less her monkey in the cage and more the monkey on her back.

Throughout the 1980s, the Missionaries opened new homes throughout the world — including, for the first time, Communist states (most still officially atheistic), as well as numerous war-torn countries including Ethiopia, Southern Yemen, Nicaragua, and Lebanon. The order benefitted from the *glasnost* and *perestroika* of Mikhail Gorbachev by opening a home in Moscow itself. Not to be outdone, Gorbachev's fellow Slav Karol Wojtyla invited Mother Teresa to open a shelter for the homeless in the Vatican. Naturally, given that it was designed to commemorate the Marian Year, it was named A Gift from Mary.

Mother Teresa's unqualified support for traditional Catholic teaching on all matters relating to sexuality — premarital sex, abortion, homosexuality, artificial means of birth regulation — became more strident, singularly focused, and indeed ubiquitous in the last two decades of her life. She became a reliable barometer of Vatican anxiety and a major component of a "culture of life" strategy conceived and organized by the Pope himself. They were partners in a mission that they saw as staunching the flow of the "culture of death" into the very arteries of humanity.

By 1990 Mother Teresa was eighty years old; her health having become increasingly precarious, she retired from the leadership of the Missionaries of Charity, only to find herself re-elected once again at the order's chapter in September 1990. She broke three ribs in Rome, succumbed to malaria in Delhi, broke her collarbone, developed a lung infection, was hospitalized regularly for various heart-related problems, and still managed to appeal to presidents George Bush and Saddam

Hussein in a doomed effort to avert the first Gulf War. She also travelled to Beijing, exhorted the U.S. presidential and vice-presidential families — in the presence of thousands of guests at a National Prayer Breakfast in Washington — to commit to saving life at every stage of development, received the Congressional Gold Medal of Honor a few years later, and then, weakened by her progressively deteriorating condition, died in her Calcutta home on September 5, 1997. All the world went into mourning — again. It had been barely a week since the world was convulsed by the death of her friend, Princess Diana of Wales. She was given a funeral on a par with those accorded Mahatma Gandhi and Jawaharlal Nehru, the great shapers of modern India. Human society had lost one of its great souls.

And now the controversies were to begin in earnest.

But first, Lucinda Vardey, occasional consort of Mother Teresa, author and publisher, assesses her spirituality and work:

It's about going into the gutters and spreading love around where needed and it's doing it one person at a time.

Mother has been criticized for being an opportunist, but I think she was just good at her job in helping — to be more specific still, in serving the poorest of the poor. While researching and writing about her and her "simple path," I realized that the sisters and brothers of her order are all Mother Teresas, that they are extraordinary givers, every day without respite serving the poor. And the poor, predominantly, are quite ungrateful. Because you are poor doesn't mean that you have good manners. Very often if someone gives you something, you're not going to say thank you because they are going to give it to you anyway.

I was in a homeless shelter for men in Rome, peeling potatoes. I had to choose between peeling and cleaning the toilets, and because I prefer cleaning the toilets and I am not particularly good at making food I decided I'd do the potatoes. The man I worked with peels potatoes in this Rome shelter every Wednesday. He lost his wife two years previous and this is what he does to get out of his apartment. He used to run a restaurant, and he peeled potatoes as if it were a five-star activity. My potato peeling, by contrast, was simply appalling. But something happened while we were working side by side that took me aback. Many of the men would come by and ask what they were having that day, and when I responded "potatoes," they responded, "What, again?" It took all of me to refrain from saying, "You're lucky you've got anything, any food, any shelter." But then I realized that this attitude that "we don't like the way it is done" is just human. So how do you continue to be joyful when you don't receive much back? That's the heroism I saw in Mother Teresa and her Missionaries of Charity: sure, they have the sustenance that comes from prayer, the grace to carry on, but they don't receive the kind of human nourishing we all need.

I think Mother was worn down by the lack of reciprocity. She frequently said that she was not out to change the world, to usher in a new theology, but only to bring us back to the basics of Christianity, to the fundamental message of Jesus that we love one another.

I think India understood this about Mother. The Hindus and the Indian government made her a Mahatma, someone who has surpassed all suffering, who has entered Nirvana, who has given her love selflessly to others and is completely at one with God. To watch a Catholic nun embraced by Hindus as a Mahatma is more moving to me than Mother Teresa's beatification. It is a marvellous gesture of peace-making in a world rent by religious violence.

In addition, Mother's attraction to Gandhi (she named one of her homes for lepers after him) and her abiding sensitivity to Hindu customs (the bodies of the dead were burned on pyres) prove invaluable as signs of interfaith reverence. It is about time that the institutional Roman Catholic church bows down a bit to the sacred customs and rituals of other religions. Mother was a model for us all in this regard.

Vardey, a practical businessperson with a no-nonsense spirituality, has been drawn to Mother Teresa's witness because she sees in her the integrity or congruence of action and word, as well as the transparency that mark the "saint." Such is also the case for numerous other editors, publishers, writers, activists, coreligionists, and media personnel. But not for Christopher Hitchens.

Hitchens, gadfly extraordinaire, unreconstructed secularist, apologist for atheism — or at best, in-your-face agnosticism — columnist for *Vanity Fair* and *The Nation*, critic, essayist, and scourge of the establishment, delights in controversy. He has written hard and sharp analyses of political skulduggery in the seats of power and sees as a function of his self-assigned identity as a contrarian the mandate to expose the chicanery of the mighty and the untouchable. He especially revels in the role of Voltaire's disciple screaming from the rooftops, "*Écrasez l'infame!*" And Mother Teresa is the infamy.

In Hitchens's view, most powerfully represented in his Channel Four documentary *Hell's Angel* and in his sustained polemic *The Missionary Position: Mother Teresa in Theory and Practice*, the Albanian nun is a shrewd and practised trickster, utilitarian in her motives, jesuitical in her intrigue, wholly given to God and her will (and the difference between the two is not always clear). Mother Teresa is not a pawn of the unscrupulous; she is their willing accomplice. Frequently courted by the influential, the venal, the morally unsavoury, the totalitarian, and the fanatical, in the Hitchens perspective she is no dupe. She is the neutral ally prepared to do commerce with the devil him/herself in the interests of her goal.

Agnes Bojaxhiu knows perfectly well that she is conscripted by people like Ralph Reed [onetime chairman of Pat Robertson's Christian Coalition], that she is a fund-raising icon for clerical nationalists in the Balkans, that she has furnished PR-type cover for all manner of cultists and shady businessmen (who are often the same thing), that her face is on vast highway billboards urging the state to take on responsibility of safeguarding the womb. By no word or gesture has she ever repudiated any of these connections or alliances.... It is another chapter in a millennial story which stretches back to the superstitious childhood of our species, and which depends on the exploitation of the simple and the humble by the cunning and the single-minded.[7]

One doesn't have to subscribe to Hitchens's naked Darwinism (Darwin himself was neither hostile to nor unaware of theological subtlety) to realize that his take on Mother Teresa is about more than a scathing indictment of religion per se. It is an unblinkered condemnation of religious zeal, of do-gooders hell-bent on leaving their mark on history, of moralists everywhere prepared to consign multitudes to oblivion in the interests of their creed. Mother Teresa not only gives the lie to religion's claim to wholesomeness through her connections with the murky worlds of big finance and bigger tyranny, but she also undoes the claims of Jesus of Nazareth by consorting with mammon at the expense of humanity. Not surprisingly, Hitchens has raised more than a few hackles — clerical and lay.

Hitchens's detractors are many, and I suspect that he likes it that way. Friends, fans, and even foes of Mother Teresa have found his vituperative slashings of the venerable nun of the

gutters a bit over the top, even for Washington's premier icono-
clastic expatriate Brit. But the Roman authorities are nothing if
not determined to show that no stone has been left unturned in
the pursuit of Mother Teresa's sainting. Stung by the criticism
that has accompanied the canonization of the founder of Opus
Dei — Josemaría Escrivá de Balaguer — as well as the canonization of Juan Diego of Guadalupe fame (of which more later),
the Vatican is going out of its way to appear fair and open to
persuasion on the matter of Mother Teresa's cause for sainthood.
Hence the invitation extended to Hitchens to be interviewed
about his views on Mother Teresa by a panel of three clerics in
archdiocesan headquarters in Washington. He was to be, if only
for a brief time, a reprise of that hoary and sadly undervalued
functionary, the *advocatus diaboli*. Hitchens proved as firm of
purpose as his Hell's Angel herself:

> Now, I have a sneaking regard for the Holy Father. . . . It's
> therefore slightly sad for even an unbeliever to see him end
> his days like some medieval seller of relics, bending the
> rules to allow special dispensation for a sly and worldly
> sinner. And that's why it was my pleasure and privilege to
> be the first ever to represent the Evil One pro bono.[8]

Not to be outdone, even by himself, Hitchens unleashed a
new verbal fusillade in Britain just months before her beatification in 2003. Once again he reviled her as a hypocrite, a shameless
seeker of publicity at any cost, a lackey of dictators like the
comic-barbaric Duvalier duo in Haiti, and an anti-woman, pro-
poverty spiritual virago. Hitchens argues that Mother Teresa's
indifference to real suffering, and her willingness to invalidate
the mad irrationality of another's pain in the interests of subsum-
ing all in the wilful pursuit of God's purposes, reveal a fundamental
inhumanity about her. And, to add insult to injury, in Hitchens's
view Mother Teresa appears to have avoided any of the reassess-

ment that follows the death of an icon or celebrity; she appears immune to revisionism, insulated from the regular critiques that accompany mortals. He remains resolved to stir the pot. As writer Jim Holt notes:

> Christopher Hitchens has set off a stink bomb at the shrine of Mother Teresa, making her out to be wilfully obtuse about the suffering of others. Interestingly, Dorothy Day, the heroine of the Catholic Worker Movement, has so far escaped this sort of revisionist soul-blackening. Evidently her saintliness was balanced by piquant elements left over from her bohemian-libertine past. She had redeeming vices.[9]

Mother Teresa's vices appear not to be of the redeeming kind. Day had an abortion, a goodly number of love affairs, a dangerously Communist streak, and not the easiest personality to circumvent, and yet in the minds of devotees and critics alike she remains refreshingly redeemable. Hitchens is not alone in working to snip God's pencil. Ex-convent girl, lapsed Catholic, feminist theorist, and bold "original" Germaine Greer has also had Mother Teresa in her sights. Accordingly, she released her vituperative volley within days of Mother Teresa's death:

> Compared to the aged husband I saw not long ago gently buttoning his agitated wife into her overcoat, Mother Teresa had a terrific life, jet-setting hither and yon, basking in the glow of universal approbation, rushing in where more thoughtful charity workers feared to tread, grabbing the headlines and the loot, $30 million a year.[10]

There is something deeply visceral about the criticism of Hitchens and Greer, something so feral, primitive, and pained that even when their critiques are covered with that patina of respectability and objectivity they so skilfully deploy as seasoned public intellectuals, you cannot help but be singed by the heat of their fury. Why the fury?

In one sense, Holt is right. Mother Teresa became in her lifetime a model of holiness that admitted of no redeeming vices. Fiercely obedient and fiercely demanding in obedience, driven, disinclined to nuance and compromise, contemptuous of political propriety, and prepared to fix her sail to whatever ship of disrepute floated by as long as God's forsaken were touched by love in the end, Mother Teresa is not that much different from other headstrong saints of the past, except that whereas many of the confessors, martyrs, and virtuous women of history have had their struggles with church officialdom, laboured under the shadow of disapproval, and known the bitter taste of failure and obscurity, Mother Teresa seemed to have the papal Good Housekeeping seal of approval from the outset and basked in the rays of global affirmation. She was a star in her own time. And therein lies part of the problem. In addition, she could be a prick to an uneasy conscience. While many individuals, agencies, and governments lacked either the determination or the resources to redress the egregious wrongs of society, or felt immobilized by the sheer magnitude of the task, Mother Teresa had no problem galloping in where a legion of angels dared not tread. She cajoled government officials, badgered diffident if not exhausted relief workers, prodded religious women and men to make greater sacrifices, connived with business and political leaders to get things done even as they sought to use her for some specious legitimacy, and insisted on controlling her media image. She had little time for theological and philosophical dissent, neither grasped nor indicated any desire to understand current issues like feminism, subscribed unconditionally to a traditionalist reading of the natural law theory, disregarded the determinative role of political ideologies in the shaping of systems and nations, and was passionate about only one "industry": love of the poorest of the poor.

Mother Teresa's single-mindedness strikes her critics as wilfulness and inflexibility, and her one-size-fits-all approach to begging (mendicancy being a venerable tradition in both Hinduism and Christianity) demonstrates a willingness to shake hands with the devil should it be necessary to secure the level of support required to serve society's unloved. Greer and Hitchens, among others, see Mother Teresa as a calculating, empire-building, publicity-seeking, and power-loving nun, whereas biographer Spink sees her unbending purposefulness and willingness to do commerce with the unsavoury in an entirely different light:

> She was certainly very aware of what God wanted, and if something was God's will, then there wasn't a great deal of compromise and she would go out and get it done. I think that many of the criticisms coming from Hitchens and others centre around her associations with people of power and finance who are considered of morally dubious character. She actually believed that everyone should be given the opportunity to do good and that that should be as accessible as possible. She was not manipulative, but she was certainly determined to do what she believed was the will of God. . . . She saw in every individual — regardless of whether they were prince, journalist, or pauper — the Christ whom she sought to serve. Many have accused her of pursuing publicity, so let me give you an example of how unimportant celebrity status was to her. When she received the Nobel Prize, she was given some kind of medallion, which she misplaced in the cloakroom twenty minutes after accepting it. She was indifferent to these tokens personally because all that mattered, all that was important, was the recognition these awards afforded the unacknowledged poor of the world and *their* needs.

The argument that Mother Teresa suffers all the attention she receives, all the honours she accepts, and all the praise that she is accorded because it guarantees attention to the poor and marshals support for their cause, is not likely to persuade the cynical, the jaded, or the hostile. The fact that Mother Teresa does not decline the many perks her high profile warrants in a celebrity-obsessed world doesn't help the case of her apologists that Mother is utterly detached from these perquisites and cares not a whit for her own comfort or personal prerogatives. For instance, although it is true that she flew first class, it is also true that this seating arrangement was made by the airlines in order to ensure her comfort and safety as well as to prevent the disruptions that would naturally follow once passengers in coach realized who was seated on their plane. This is a protocol employed by most airlines when they are transporting a celebrity — any celebrity — and in and of itself does not betray a sinister and hidden luxury-loving penchant deep in the heart of Mother Teresa.

Her celebrity status is, of course, the direct result of her relationship with the media, a relationship her critics dub exploitative and sophisticated in its simplicity. Others, including Gaston Roberge, the Canadian Jesuit, mass-communications scholar, and longtime resident of India, see it differently:

She wanted the media's help to make known her work, which she called God's work. She needed the media for that. . . . Did she go around focusing on life's miseries? In a sense, yes. [But] when there are millions of poor people, that's worth talking about with force and conviction. . . . Perhaps people thought that her image of poverty excluded them [but] . . . balanced pictures don't lead to action.[11]

Certainly she was selective and strategic in her use of the media, and she knew that in many ways she was their creation, but she was not enamoured of the media, did not court their favour, and knew how intrusive they are. The postulator of her cause, a priest-psychologist of her own order, the Winnipeg-born Brian Kolodiejchuk of the Ukrainian Byzantine Rite, speaks of her media savvy:

> On the one hand, I think that she understood that through the media her work would be well known, that whenever she accepted awards or gave an address she was furthering God's work with the poor, and that is why she co-operated with the many requests for interviews. In fact, I once remember an interviewer asking her why she gave him an interview, and she responded that it was her way of helping him do his job.
>
> On the other hand, as she herself acknowledged, her experience of the media was one of the greatest trials and sacrifices of her life. She even spoke of making a contract with Jesus whereby for every photo that was taken of her, one soul would spring out of purgatory. Indeed, as she wryly observed, perhaps because of her long exposure to the media, she can bypass purgatory in the next life.

Whether her symbiotic relationship with the media began, as many surmise, with the BBC documentary, *Something Beautiful for God*, that she did with Malcolm Muggeridge in 1969 (later a bestselling book) — which was itself a follow-up on an earlier thirty-minute interview — or whether, as author Dominique Lapierre argues, it began with her Nobel Prize in 1979 and its accompanying media frenzy, Mother Teresa decided to channel the media's ravenous attention to her — or as she would put it, God's — advantage. Clearly her experience with Muggeridge was formative. In her first interview with "Muggs," she not only captivated a skeptical film crew, a notoriously cynical interviewer, and a jaded production team, but she managed to grip a national audience in unanticipated ways. The BBC sought to replicate this experience with a more extensive profile of Mother Teresa, and it was then that Muggs travelled to India for *Something Beautiful for God* and their personal friendship was sealed — permanently. Stories — apocryphal, fantastical, and sober — abound about the shoot, Mother Teresa's "luminous" presence, the miracle of the lighting, the softening of hardened hearts, the limitless charm of the nun herself, and Muggs's transformation. Critic Paul Williams notes acidly that it was at this time that Mother Teresa "seemed innately to realize the first principle of mass communications: the semblance is more important than the reality."[12]

Whether it was in the late '60s or the late '70s, Mother Teresa came to negotiate her way around the shoals of media focus with commendable (at least in a "this-worldly" sense) savvy. She remained in control of her media image up to the dying years of her leadership, and although under aggressive siege from Hicthens and a formidable phalanx of feminists both Catholic and secular, she was as disciplined and proprietorial over access to — and responsibility for — her public image as her deteriorating health permitted. And then she died.

Lucinda Vardey recognizes the fierce fighter to the end:

What I saw in Mother was a very organized, open-hearted woman who had a lot of work to do and didn't have much time to do it. Even when I saw Mother at prayer, saying the rosary in the afternoon, on her knees, on concrete, in a very noisy chapel in the Calcutta motherhouse, with dogs, goats, and cows outside the window, I noticed how the human cacophony of the city penetrated the chapel but never diverted her from the rosary.

The last time I saw her was in Rome three months before she died, and she was in a wheelchair but she still managed to stand during the reading of the gospel, and she was resolved not to sit during the consecration. She had almighty strength, the strength that gets you through the desert, as St. John of the Cross calls it. When Mother died, who knows what she saw or thought in the last minutes? We need to understand that sainthood is not something supernatural, it's about being in the muck deeper than the lot of us. It is not about floating around. I heard once that a toilet cleaned by Mother Teresa was unlike a toilet cleaned by anyone else. What a punctuation point.

Two startling things have surfaced about her death, one of which is bizarre and the other ennobling: respectively, the exorcism and her "dark night of the soul." The exorcism was performed under the authority of the Archbishop of Calcutta, Henry D'Souza, who insisted that the request for this ancient and rarely used ritual — itself a subject of considerable debate among theologians, health professionals, liturgists, and canonists — came from Mother Teresa herself. She appears to have been agitated and incapable of sleep in her final days, and the archbishop concluded that an exorcism would indeed be appropriate under the circumstances. Given her deteriorating state of health and her imminent death, it is not medically surprising that she would be restless — after all, it is Mother Teresa we are talking about, endlessly eager to serve God in practical ways. Using the services of an exorcist was, at best, an irregular judgement. But it was at least at Mother Teresa's request. Was her soul deeply disturbed near the end? Was there no serenity for the good and faithful servant? Would she not go gently into that good night?

Undoubtedly, the publication prior to her beatification of several of her private letters to her spiritual directors, with excerpts appearing as well from her spiritual diaries, portray a troubled soul, frequently arid, bereft of God's love, crushed not by God's proximity but by God's seeming absence, tortured, unsure, and floundering. Father Kolodiejchuk:

Mother Teresa's dark night is to me — and I imagine for
many — the most heroic thing about her. We might have
expected, given all that she overcame and accomplished —
building her homes for the dying and the derelict, the resistance of the hostile, etc. — that she would have deservedly
enjoyed a real sense of union with God, with Jesus, whom
she so clearly loved. But now we know that that wasn't
quite the case. In fact, it was the opposite.

For instance, although she had written about darkness
before the crucial year of 1946 — the Day of Inspiration,
September 10, the day she resolved to leave the convent
and commit her life to the poor by living among them — it
was after this date that she experienced her spiritual night
most intensely. Not at first. In the months immediately
following September 10 she had what are called interior
locutions, whereby she distinctly heard the voice of Jesus
— not exteriorly, of course, but in the imagination, a real
dialogue taking place, something very different from a
meditative exercise. During this time she experienced
a tremendous union, an utter sweetness, which changed
completely once her new work began. The darkness set in.

St. John of the Cross speaks of both the dark night of
the senses and the dark night of the soul, and she experienced both, but there is a strong difference in the way she
experienced the dark night of the soul from that of most
others who have recorded their spiritual growth. The dark
night of the soul is preparatory for union with God — the
soul is emptied, selfishness eliminated, all our hidden and
deepest attachments evacuated — everything is scoured.
God takes everything out. In one letter to the archbishop
she remarks that God simply took everything. Then comes
the union. But then comes darkness again. In Mother
Teresa's case, and there have been a few like hers — for

example, St. Thérèse de Lisieux, who had eighteen months of darkness preceding her death — the experience of union is followed by a long period of desolation. As far as we know, it lasted from the very beginning of her work right up to the end. There is no evidence that this darkness ever lifted.

She decides in 1946 to love Jesus as he has never been loved before, and she contextualizes this desire with Calvary. There's Jesus with Mary at the foot of the cross, and as it says in the Gospel of John, Christ calls out, "I thirst." This scene is at the heart of Mother Teresa's inspiration and religious charism. Her union with Jesus is with the Jesus on the cross, the Jesus of Gethsemane, the abandoned Jesus, the Jesus who tasted the bitter gall of betrayal, the anguished Jesus who knew defeat and not triumph. This is *her* Jesus, the Jesus of "My God, my God, why have you forsaken me?" Her union was by not experiencing union. Ever at the foot of the cross.

Her way of darkness was to experience Jesus on the cross. Not only did she live a life of material poverty, as do all members of her order, but we now discover that she lived an interior poverty as well, in full identification or solidarity with those who know only God's absence. In her later years she would often observe that she and her sisters came to understand that the greatest poverty was to feel unloved, uncared for, unwanted, lonely, and now we know that that is precisely how she felt at her very core.

In her letters she would say that all the attention, all the awards didn't even touch the surface of her soul because all she wanted was Him, and that wasn't to be.

And yet, knowledge of this prolonged agony of yearning for union with her God and of being deprived of it eluded even her official biographer, Kathryn Spink:

I did not know that when she first went into the slums she underwent terrible doubts, a deep sense of loneliness, and a feeling of rejection by the church. I think that what is so remarkable about her is that so many people, including many far closer to her than I, had no real indication that she was in constant turmoil or agony. We saw only her joy.

And for the grand numbers who have been touched by her, directly or indirectly, it is the joy that they recall. As the saint-makers work to bring Mother Teresa to the altars, the disclosures of her personal turbulence only serve to enhance her saintliness. The die, in her case, has been well cast. And so the sainting begins.

The very same prelate who authorized the exorcism also began the official process of making Mother Teresa a saint of the church. It wasn't only D'Souza who was on her side, however: John Paul II waived the five-year waiting period between the death of a candidate and the commencement of the process.

Much like similar rules in the Hockey Hall of Fame, this waiting period was deliberately designed to let the initial rush of enthusiasm — the Princess Di effect, if you will — wind down, so that a more detached and scholarly assessment could take over. The church, after all, does not want to discover belatedly (as the halls of fame periodically do) that its heroes had feet of clay.

But just as a Wayne Gretzky emerges to confound the sports bureaucrats and make them waive the well-meant hesitation, so Mother Teresa ended up being above the rules.[13]

If Mother Teresa was scheduled to move at warp-speed courtesy of the Pope, the preparatory work still needed to be done, appropriate judgements made, data collected and assessed, personnel assigned (Kolodiejchuk was chosen by the Missionaries of Charity to be the postulator of the cause), and energies marshalled for the common project: the sainting of Agnes Gonxha Bojaxhiu of Albania.

Postulator Kolodiejchuk entertains no doubts about the efficacy and wisdom of the official process:

> For most people the process is simply a confirmation of what everyone knows to be the case. In fact, many ask why we need to go through the process at all, given that we already know that she is a saint, but I would counter that the exercise of gathering the wealth of material and examining the fruits of our research provides us with a much greater in-depth knowledge of Mother Teresa. Her reputation for holiness is authenticated, confirmed, in such a way as to give us security in our knowledge of her sainthood.
>
> For those of us who are Missionaries of Charity, the beatification and hopefully canonization of Mother Teresa validates our own individual vocations as a way to personal holiness. And it is an occasion of joy for us to see the picture of our Mother hanging in the Basilica of St. Peter's, knowing that she is an example for the whole church.
>
> It is also important to note that the attention to the process and to the end results — beatification and canonization — is another way of reminding people of the presence of the poor. You cannot quantify this kind of witness. Only God knows of all the love and service shown to the poor because of the beatification and, in time, canonization. People are inspired, and then ask themselves how they can best express their love of God in serving and loving the poor. Who is it in *my* community, in my own family, who needs thoughtful and compassionate attention, who needs my love? We are influenced by others.

As we have seen with Elizabeth Johnson and others, the model of holiness associated with Mother Teresa corresponds to a traditionalist paradigm that no longer holds appeal for many Catholics. There is no doubt that there is a core element of heroic sanctity in the work and life of Mother Teresa, and that the official criteria for sainthood may well be easily met, but the institutional approval that would seem to expedite the road to canonization may well isolate or narrow her value as a witness for large numbers of contemporary Christians — particularly women, who see in her a *type* of woman saint who serves a patriarchal culture that carefully circumscribes the role of women in society and church. Kathryn Spink disagrees.

It is true that the kind of paradigm you speak of can be used in a very negative way, but I think that Mother Teresa is actually unique and should be kept that way. If she is to be an example of heroic holiness, then I think that the important thing to do would be to identify the centrality of the poorest of the poor with her message rather than all the other issues: model for woman, anti-contraceptive posture, Vatican spokesperson, etc. In many, many countries of the world, Mother Teresa will be remembered and honoured not for her ecclesiastical usefulness but because she stepped into the slums to help the poor in the same way that St. Martin of Tours [the fourth-century monk and patron saint of France] shared his cloak with a naked beggar, whom he subsequently recognized in a dream was Christ.

The only reason — and I should emphasize that I am not a Roman Catholic — the only reason that I believe Mother Teresa should be sainted is because it places the poorest of the poor at the centre of the church again. From that point of view, it is valuable to have Mother Teresa of Calcutta an official saint.

But first she was beatified, and for that to happen — as with everything else to do with Mother Teresa — there was great controversy over the authenticity of the miracle alleged to have occurred because of her intervention. In 1998, a young and illiterate woman by the name of Monica Basra invoked the intercession of Mother Teresa while in acute pain from either an ovarian tumour or tubercular peritonitis — there was a puzzling dispute among various specialists over the nature of her life-threatening disorder, although the majority were convinced that there was a tumour. Whatever the diagnosis, she recovered "instantaneously, completely, permanently, and in a way that was scientifically inexplicable." Such was the conclusion of a five-member medical commission of the Congregation for the Causes of Saints. Appropriately, the physicians left it to the theologians to determine whether what occurred was a miracle or not. The Vatican was satisfied that it had its one authenticated miracle required for beatification. Others weren't so easily convinced. Several physicians at the West Bengal state health department asserted that the ovarian tumour or cyst was only a lump and was successfully treated with drugs. Basra's husband publicly scoffed at the notion of a miracle and attributed the cure entirely to the doctors. Christians and Hindus appeared joined in combat over the attribution of "miraculousness" to the Basra claim, although there was division even within the respective faiths. Still, the Vatican accepted the medical report of its own commission, and the last stumbling block on the way to being declared Blessed was removed.

The adherence to miracle testing as a requirement of the process for sainting may have seen its day, however. Paolo Molinari, postulator general of the Society of Jesus,

... questions the practice of pinning sainthood on scientifically assessed miracles. As knowledge of human genetics and the body's biochemical processes grows, phenomena that are unexplainable today may have demonstrable mechanisms a decade from now. Twenty years ago, researchers had little idea how cells turned cancerous; today there is a vast line-up of biochemical suspects. Might this mean that yesterday's miracles would not pass by today's scientific standards?

Father Molinari and other postulators would like to see beatification and canonization based essentially on a candidate's outstanding moral example taking into account the assistance and inspiration such moral models can provide, rather than requiring two blockbuster medical miracles.[14]

Molinari's point might appear threatening to the saint-making industry if for no other reason than the existence of the miracle-assessing apparatus meticulously put in place over the centuries. When it comes to the matter of an alleged miracle, a document, the *positio super miraculo*, must be prepared, containing the history of the facts of the supposed miracle and the results of the diocesan inquiry with all supporting documentation. If the alleged miracle is based on a physical cure, then physicians must examine all the data. At the Roman level, the panel of medical experts that assists the Congregation for the Causes of Saints is called the *consulta medica*. The doctors are not asked to state that a miracle has occurred in the particular instance under examination, but rather, if the alleged cure can be explained scientifically.

But for all the care taken to ensure that the miracles attributed to a potential saint are legitimate — the medical panel must certify that the cure was "sudden, complete, and permanent" and has no medical explanation — the procedure is not without its critics, both within and outside the church. After all, during the pontificate of John Paul II the number of causes proliferated, the rules were changed, and the quota of miracles either relaxed or, in the case of martyrdom, eliminated for beatification. Even so eminent a Vatican prelate as Tarcisio Cardinal Bertone, former secretary of the Congregation for the Doctrine of the Faith, has mooted publicly the notion that the key requirement for sainthood is a life of heroic virtue and that miracles are now anachronistic. And this is the same fellow who has taken a strong dislike to Harry Potter and his wizardly ways.

Such a life of heroic virtue, Lucinda Vardey is convinced, is neatly summed up in the following example.

Mother Teresa gave me a piece of paper she called her business card. It was a little mimeographed thing affixed to a piece of yellow cardboard. On it was listed the "fruits": the fruit of silence is prayer, the fruit of faith is love, the fruit of love is service, and the fruit of service is peace . . . these are the steps of love-in-action. This is her "simple path."

Her originality can be found in the simple fact that as a woman she got up and left a safe environment for an unsafe one. At the time she did this, India was in real turmoil, and yet she did what she had to do anyway. Her mission is all about the feminine. Not the feminine in the way it is often portrayed in traditional Catholicism — safe, virginal, removed, the feminine perfectly embodied in the mother of Christ, so holy that we cannot touch her. No, I mean feminine holiness grounded in the breastfeeding, menstruating, occasionally depressed, post-menopausal woman; holiness that is pragmatic, dirty, basic, tough, a holiness every mother can identify with. And that's Mother, as everybody called her, Mother Teresa, a down-to-earth woman who gave out of her emptiness and yet was always replenished to give more. This was Mother's motherhood, and it must not be lost in the iconography of a woman dressed in a sari.

Mother Teresa's giving, her love, was tangible, a getting-up-in-the-middle-of-the-night kind of giving, a giving to the last drop, a giving to the sick when you hardly have any strength left yourself, a giving out of one's own vulnerability because that is where one's heart gets exercise. Her motherhood was about loving day in and day out, a loving that only finishes when you die. Her teaching emphasized the Calcuttas in our own backyard, the emotional poverty we find even in our own families. This is the feminine holiness of Mother Teresa.

For others, Mother Teresa's holiness is best situated not in her tradition-saturated ecclesiology, her conventional anthropology, her indifference to politics, or her unquestioning obedience to the all-demanding mission of service to the poorest of the poor, but rather in her "authority of compassionate courage," an authority Dominican scholar Mary Catherine Hilkert argues places her in a varied crowd that includes the likes of Maya Angelou, Etty Hillesum, Helen Prejean, Dorothy Day, Jane Goodall, and Las Madres de Plaza de Mayo, an authority that

. . . emerged in part from the undeniable fact that they have known suffering — in their own bodies, in their families and countries, in the religious bodies to which they belong.[15]

Mother Teresa knew suffering — intimately. As Pope John Paul II said in his homily for her beatification,

Mother Teresa shared in the passion of the crucified Christ in a special way during long years of "inner darkness." For her that was a test, at times an agonizing one, which she accepted as a rare "gift and privilege." In the darkest hours, she clung even more tenaciously to prayer before the blessed sacrament. This harsh spiritual trial led her to identify herself more and more closely with those whom she served each day, feeling their pain and at times even their rejection. She was fond of repeating that the greatest poverty is to be unwanted, to have no one to take care of you.

A mystical reading such as this has the capacity to remove Mother Teresa from that grounded reality Vardey spoke of, the unintended etherealization of a very pragmatic, wilful, and occasionally soiled nun who made her home — literally and metaphorically — in the slums of humankind. For some, like Malcolm Muggeridge, Mother Teresa is the Holy Spirit spelled out:

> Jean-Pierre de Caussade [a French Jesuit spiritual writer who lived from 1675 to 1751] writes of how, all the time, the sequel to the New Testament is being written by saintly souls in the succession of the prophets and apostles, not in canonical books, but by continuing the history of divine purpose with their lives. So, just as great artists have painted the Incarnation, great writers described and dramatized it, great composers set it to music, great architects built it, great saints lived it, by Mother Teresa's mere presence, even just by thinking about her, the follies and confusions of our time are confuted, and once more God's Almighty Word leaps down from heaven, to live among us, full of grace and truth. This is what saints are for; you spell them out, and lo! the Holy Spirit has spoken.[16]

No hagiographer can outdo Muggeridge in his enthusiasm for Mother Teresa's cause for sainthood. His is the verbal counterweight to Hitchens's lethal polemic. They represent the polar positions on the matter of Mother Teresa of Calcutta, God's pencil. And why is this so? Is it a requirement that the universal recognition of holiness entail deep division of opinion? Is Mother Teresa a holy fraud, or the authentic thing?

Undoubtedly, she has some influential figures in her court
— John Paul II and Malcolm Muggeridge — and not a few
working their catapults outside the precincts (Germaine Greer
and Christopher Hitchens). There are those working for
her and those working against her. Like a politician — God's
politician. And there's the rub.

In a time when many are skittish about claiming God's
alliance with human projects, when the ominous theocratization
of secular politics in both democratic and non-democratic
regimes has many frightened, when the invocation of God's blessing on crusades and jihads against causes, governments, and people
judged as infidels or as apostates continues unabated, and in a
time when the proliferation of ultraconservative spokespersons
in the media and through well-funded lobbying forces seems
beyond termination, in a time such as this, Mother Teresa can
look suspect. Was she one of "them"?

Mother Teresa's certainty damns her, in the eyes of some. In
the eyes of others, she represents, either willingly or unintention-
ally, a type of woman that is pre-modern. For her admirers, and
their number is legion, and for her apologists, and their number
is markedly less, Mother Teresa is simply Mother, endlessly
giving, radically committed to Jesus, one signed with love.

In the end, the ancient argument of the rabbi — if it is of
God, it will flourish, and if not, it will die — applies conclusively
to the reputation and witness of Mother Teresa. And the odds in
her favour are impressive. Take, for instance, one Abdus Sattar
Edhi, a contemporary Islamic saint. Edhi's work on behalf of
the poor, sick, and abandoned of Karachi, Pakistan, is legendary.
According to the eastern European scholar and journalist Anatol
Lieven in his article "A Saint of Islam" for *The Tablet* (24
November 1990), Edhi, with the support of his wife Bilquis, uses
his fleet of ambulances to bury the unclaimed dead, establishes
and funds a score of orphanages, a network of free dispensaries, a
diabetes centre, and homes for physically disabled children and

abused women. And they do this in the face of institutional indifference, social hostility from their economic class, and incomprehension from the large number of people who benefit from their love and generosity. But they persist.

The highest praise accorded Mr. Edhi is the noble tag, "Pakistan's Father Teresa."

That says it all — a male, Muslim, Mother Teresa; her sainthood is assured — embedded in a legacy of universal inspiration.

Chapter Five

POPE PIUS XII: CHRIST'S EMBROILED DEPUTY

IT WAS THE radical Jesuit priest Daniel Berrigan who coined the phrase the "icebox pope" to describe Pope Pius XII. Pictured to the world as a remote, indeed august, figure of aristocratic bearing (legitimately, as it happens), looking so severe and ascetic — so saintly, that is — that Catholics throughout the world saw him as a distant approximation of divinity. Well, sort of. Pius was not a priest one easily loved. And he seemed to prefer it that way. Berrigan caught the sympathy of a generation with his phrase, and it remains for many an apt way of describing the princely Eugenio Pacelli. But should it really be?

Certainly, two decades after Berrigan first used his less-than-flattering term, the CBC radio personality Erika Ritter spoke openly and derisively of Pius, observing on her program that in her school classroom in Saskatchewan, Pius's official photograph hung on the wall like a judgement on them all. Pius, the imperious Servant of the Servants of God; Pius, the ever-watchful Roman Pontiff. This man was pope from 1939 until 1958, and for many years after his death his legacy remained largely unstained — boring, in fact — a legacy not unlike that of most modern popes: of blessed memory, sanitized, sacralized, non-controversial, and all of a piece with predecessors worthy and otherwise. Shirley Williams, the one-time cabinet minister in the Labour government of Great Britain, Harvard professor emerita, and a co-founder of the Social Democratic Party, recalls her impression of Pius, dating from her encounter with him:

In 1950, my father and I went to Rome together to celebrate the Holy Year. The great church of St. Peter was
ablaze with candles, and one could feel it emerging from the
darkness of the war years and of the Nazi period before that.
We had a private audience with the Pope, Pius XII. Refined
and frail, he seemed almost translucent in his gold and
white vestments. At that time, before controversy bruised
his reputation, he appeared almost saint-like, removed in his
spirituality from the horrors of the secular world.[1]

It didn't take long before the "horrors of the secular world"
would invade his sanctuary and significantly tarnish his reputation. For historian Istvan Deak, professor emeritus at Columbia
University and the author of many books including *Essays on
Hitler's Europe*, Pius was not exceptional as a ruler, was very
much in the mould of a particular pontifical type, and looked on
the world with more than a little reserve:

Pacelli very much belongs in the tradition of the Bishops of
Rome of the modern era. For them, modernity was a terrible problem and ushered in the withering away of the Papal
States, the arrogating to the state of the powers of marriage
and education, etc. The popes felt they were under siege
not only by all forms of totalitarianism and state atheism,
but by all the political forces and movements that circum-
scribe the prerogatives and obligations of the church in the
public arena. Accordingly, Western materialism was as
much a problem as Communism for Pius XII. And then to
this you add Nazism. The Nazis were brownshirt Bolsheviks,
in the eyes of most churchmen, and although immoral in
what they preached and practised, they weren't the only or
most immediate danger.
  In addition to trying to work his way around these
competing ideologies, Pius was vulnerable in other ways.

Since the resolution of the Roman Question in 1929 [the Lateran Treaty effectively resulted in the formal establishment of the Vatican City state as a sovereign power in its own right, independent of the Republic of Italy], Pius enjoyed considerably more jurisdictional and legal leg room than his immediate predecessors, but he was still vulnerable in some key areas. Garbage, for instance. Without the resources and facilities of the Fascist state, the Vatican had no access to water or sewage disposal. When the Nazis took over Rome in 1943, he was even more vulnerable.

One has to keep in mind that this pope, although he was no longer a prisoner of the Vatican like all his predecessors from 1870 to 1929, was nonetheless defenceless, his every move dictated by circumstances that underscored his weaknesses. Still, he was the head of an organization of hundreds of millions of people, an organization that has a longer tradition and a sphere of influence greater than any other on the planet.

Jesus would not have signed a concordat or treaty with the Nazis. You have to react to events and developments, and on the matter of the persecution of the Jews by the Nazis, the Pope was given a golden opportunity to prove his discipleship to Jesus. If Pius had done nothing else but make the bishops understand — and the church is the one truly transnational organization — that he strongly disapproved of Nazi policies with regard to the Poles, and with regard to the Jews, many Catholics would have felt that they had an obligation to something other than their nation. I know that nationalism is very strong, but there is another feeling at work among Catholics that reminds us that the church is a universal, cosmopolitan reality.

There is another voice besides nationalism that Catholics could have listened to. Catholics could say no, and nothing would have happened to them because no German was ever punished for *not* killing a Jew. The Pope could have said to Catholics: do not obey, do not participate in the killing of innocents. I really wonder what would have happened.

There are many scholars, concentration camp survivors, partisans, and others who do not share Deak's view, and there are some, like the eminent Catholic savant, author, and publisher Justus George Lawler, who are categorical in affirming Pius's proportionately modest culpability when compared to that of other major international leaders:

> it should be noted that Pius XII's relation to the actual Holocaust during the war years — even if given the worst possible interpretation — is provably slight. This stands in sharp contrast to the glorification of [Abraham] Lincoln whose relation to the slave holocaust is provably causal . . . .[2]

Non-Catholics like Sir D'Arcy Osborne, British Minister to the Holy See from 1936 to 1947, were inclined to be openly sympathetic to Pius XII, as illustrated in a letter he wrote to *The Times* of London in 1963:

> So far from being a cool (which, I suppose, implies cold-blooded and inhumane) diplomatist, Pius XII was the most warmly humane, kind, generous, sympathetic (and incidentally saintly) character that it has been my privilege to meet in the course of a long life. I know that his sensitive nature was acutely and incessantly alive to the tragic volume of human suffering caused by the war and, without the slightest doubt, he would have been ready and glad to give his life to redeem humanity from its consequences. And this quite irrespective of nationality or faith. But what could he effectively do?[3]

Historian José M. Sánchez, author of *The Spanish Civil War as a Religious Tragedy*, among other works, sees the Pius XII controversy as a desperate effort to ascribe blame for a terror too unimaginable to measure by the ordinary standards of individual and collective behaviour:

> What makes the controversy so contentious is that it deals with the most horrifying event of modern times. Who can blame a survivor of the Holocaust, such as [Saul] Friedlander, for criticizing the Vicar of Christ for not speaking out forcefully against the Nazi machine of destruction emanating from a Germany that was long one of the bastions of Christianity? For those wanting to place blame, it is tempting to overlook the fact that the Germans were the instigators of the Holocaust and to criticize the bystanders — the Allies, the neutrals, and above all the papacy — for not preventing it. What the Allies and the neutral nations lack is the single individual in charge upon whom the blame can be placed; what the papacy has is the single individual, who furthermore claimed to be the Vicar of Christ. Add to this Pius' personality and the impression he gave of omniscience, and it is easy to see why he has become a target of the critics. It is one of the great ironies of history that two persons with opposite temperaments and ideologies are paired together in this modern horror: Adolf Hitler, whom some see as the individual solely responsible for the Holocaust, and Pope Pius, singled out in similar fashion as the sole person who could have prevented or lessened its terrors.[4]

As you can see, the range of opinion and judgement on the matter of Pius XII — the question of his "silence" during the Holocaust, his personality, and politics, the simple fact that his papacy marked the apogee of a certain papal modality and monarchical style — runs the gamut. There is no shortage of critics and defenders, detractors and apologists; a veritable industry flourishes, with little possibility of diminishing in force and output in the near future. Pacelli's cause for sainthood unfolded in an atmosphere of mounting acrimony during Pope John Paul II's declining days, and the trust and cordiality that have characterized Catholic-Jewish relations over the last quarter-century have been stretched to the breaking point. How did Christ's Deputy become so embroiled in a debate that is itself a deadly microcosm of the polarizing divisions that exist in the Catholic Church at large?

To begin at the beginning: who was Eugenio Pacelli? Born into a Roman family of the lesser nobility, his father Filippo was a lawyer of the Roman Rota (the second-highest court of the Holy See) and a consistorial advocate; his mother, Virginia Graziosi, came from a family with a long history of service to the Vatican in the financial area; and his brother Francesco played a leading role in the negotiations that occurred prior to the signing of the Lateran Treaty of 1929. Educated variously at the Gregorian University in Rome, the S. Apollinaire Institute and La Sapienza, the state university in Rome, he was ordained in 1899, was very quickly picked up by the important Congregation for Extraordinary Ecclesiastical Affairs, taught public law at the Academy for Noble Ecclesiastics (the training centre for future Vatican diplomats), and by the time he reached his late twenties was a domestic prelate (*monsignore*). His rise in the corridors of power was brisk and predicted.

During the First World War he represented the Vatican in its many and doomed efforts to facilitate peace, was ordained a bishop in 1917, and appointed nuncio to Berlin, where he served for twelve years and where he developed a deep interest in and affection for German culture and Catholicism. And then, in 1929, he was both named to the College of Cardinals and appointed Secretary of State to Pope Pius XI. In 1939, he was elected to succeed Pius XI and saw the first six years of his nineteen-year pontificate dominated by the Second World War and its far-ranging consequences. Although the remaining years of his pontificate would see new missionary initiatives, the proclamation of the Assumption of the Blessed Virgin Mary into Heaven as dogma (and therefore an exercise in papal infallibility), persistent struggles with an expanding Communism, and the increasing centralization of power into the pope's hands with the subsequent subordination of the curia, it was the war years that have come to define his place in history. As Andrea Riccardi of the University of Rome and respected founder of the San Egidio Community, notes in his biographical entry on Pacelli: "the 'silence of Pius XII,' that is, his not more forcefully condemning the Holocaust and other Nazi atrocities, has been, especially since 1962, the most widely controversial aspect of his pontificate."[5]

More precisely, all came unglued in 1963, for this was the year that saw the publication and staging of the play *Der Stellvertreter*, variously translated as *The Representative* or *The Deputy*, by German playwright Rolf Hochhuth. It was the dramatic bombshell of the century. Wherever it was performed and in whatever language, fierce debate, charged feelings, protests, and even riots followed. During a run of the play at Toronto's Crest Theatre, armed police on horseback were called out to quell disturbances, and actor David Ciceri, who happened to be a Roman Catholic, agonized publicly over his performance as Pius XII. The play is arguably anti-Catholic, but it is inarguably anti-Pacelli. The pope — the deputy of the title — sacrifices principle for policy, institutional integrity for survival, compassion for expedience, truth for posterity. He turns a deaf ear to the young Jesuit priest Ricardo Fontana, who implores him to act on behalf of the Jews, and he remains implacable and steadfast in his "silence," no matter what the cost.

A play of nearly Wagnerian length, suffused with postwar German angst, polemical, in turn both historically sound and recklessly speculative, emotionally incendiary, prey to the worst features of intellectual reductionism and callow melodrama, *The Deputy* may well be, in the words of Justus George Lawler, a third-rate literary effort comparable in its impact to *Uncle Tom's Cabin*. Few individuals are involved as closely in defending the reputation of Pius XII as German Jesuit Peter Gumpel, the relator of Pacelli's cause for sainthood and a survivor of Nazi persecution himself.

I would certainly say that, after the publication of Hochhuth's scandalous play, a number of people turned on Pius XII. This is not so surprising, because the Roman Catholic Church has always had enemies, usually from the outside but from the inside as well. I have been told by many of my U.S. colleagues that there has long been a latent anti-Catholicism in various American circles. The Hochhuth attack provided them with a pretext to attack the church. But this is, of course, not the only reason.

The pontificate of Pius XII was one of the most difficult in modern times. After all, he had to make many decisions during the period of ascendancy for Nazism, Fascism, and Communism, decisions that many people in good faith can argue should have been different. This difference of opinion is normal and can be dealt with.

What I do not like is the case when people who do not have sufficient historical background, who do not know the complete circumstances, and who are unaware of the context in which Pius had to make his decisions, jump into print or go on air with, at times, really foolish observations. This, of course, obliges us to answer, and then we have a controversy.

In Hochhuth's case particularly, you have to consider that he comes from the extreme left, and he did with Pius what he did also with Winston Churchill in his play *Soldiers*. In this play he accused Churchill of having ordered the murder of Sikorski, the prime minister of the Polish government-in-exile, and here Hochhuth made a big mistake. Now it is true that Sikorski died in somewhat strange circumstances — he was killed in a plane crash after leaving Gilbraltar — and Hochhuth thought that everybody was killed and therefore there were no witnesses. But here he made a huge mistake. The pilot survived and was living in California at the time the play premiered. He understood that he was implicated — accused, indeed, of deliberately downing the plane. He proceeded juridically against Hochhuth, because in English law only the person who is the direct subject of the defamation can act legally to clear his name, and that is why Randolph Churchill was unable to act on behalf of his father.

The case came to a tribunal, and Hochhuth, wisely enough, did not show up in England. His lawyer said that he had corroborating documents, but they were deposited in a Swiss bank. The judge asked him, "What bank?" He refused to identify the bank and said that it was a classic question of life or death for the person who had given him the information, and therefore he could only publish it in fifty years. The judge didn't buy this. He dismissed the case and the matter was settled out of court. Much of the proceedings were broadcast on the BBC, but what applies in the case of a maligned politician and eminent war leader does not appear to apply in the case of the church.

Gumpel's ardent defence of Pacelli is based on his conviction that the pope was a holy man, that his stewardship as the Universal Pastor has been grossly misunderstood, that both ecclesiastical and secular politics are being waged under a cloud of ferocious deceit, and that there are many competing ecclesiological or ideological subtexts to the controversies swirling around Pius that have yet to be addressed publicly, honestly, or directly. Pacelli is at the heart of a vortex, only part of which is his doing. If anything, the situation is more tempestuous now than it was in the period immediately following the appearance of *The Deputy* on the world stage. Things are not abating. The atmosphere is more intense. The lines have been drawn. Loyalties are being stretched. And the truth, as the old saying would have it, is the first victim.

Michael Marrus, Chancellor Rose and Ray Wolfe Professor of Holocaust Studies at the University of Toronto, is one of three Jewish scholars appointed to the now-dissolved Vatican creation, the International Catholic-Jewish Historical Commission. He is also the author of numerous books on the Holocaust. He insists that the Hochhuth play must be seen in its context, in terms of the questions it raises at the beginning of the process.

I would say that the play itself is a voice of accusation. At the beginning of the 1960s there were many other voices of accusation. I can't give you the exact year of publication, but this is the same historical moment when there appeared a book on Franklin D. Roosevelt called *While Six Million Died.* This is the time when we first began to have in the general media discussions on the Holocaust itself, when the term the Holocaust became more commonly used, and when it became increasingly evident that there were insufficiencies wherever one looked: societies, governments, peoples, all failed to respond to the murder of European Jews, failed to do what seemed so evident in the 1960s, a time of political radicalism, a time of idealism, a time of growing ethnic consciousness on the part of many different peoples.

I was in the United States during this period when, for instance, the emerging black nationalism was sending shock waves through many different communities. This is the historical moment when the Holocaust is coming to be seen in a different way than had been the case hitherto. This is the time of polemics — the Eichmann Trial in Jerusalem and the publication of Raul Hilberg's magisterial book *The Destruction of the European Jews* (1961) — a time when there is a great deal of thinking about the subject.

Now the voice of Hochhuth, as I said, is a voice of accusation, a voice that takes all kinds of artistic liberties with its subject and causes shock waves throughout the Catholic world, the Jewish world; and I think to some degree the shock waves are with us to this day. I say this because — and I regret this, although it is very evident — because it is now a subject of high polemics on *both* sides of the story. In my own work I have tried to get past these high polemics, not because I am incapable of polemicizing myself on these issues, but because as an historian I have an obligation to look at the subject with the greatest degree of historical objectivity that I can bring to the subject, with a clear impartiality in order to advance our understanding of the issue.

No one, no group, no society, no nation, no institution that I know of can be said to have responded adequately to the Holocaust. We are very much in a post-Holocaust period, we are still coming to grips with the subject, and we are still second-guessing the men and women of the 1940s. And as we do so, they come up short. It remains to be seen whether we would do any better with our own manmade catastrophes. The jury's still out, but I think we have no reason to be wildly optimistic. I think it is important to bring to this subject a spirit that underscores our willingness to learn from the Holocaust rather than score points. It has taken some time for this tone to emerge in the literature, and Hochhuth should be seen at the beginning of this process.

Marrus's measured observation concerning the Hochhuth event is not shared by everyone. Although more sympathetic portraits of Pacelli have appeared since 1963 — John Newrick's drama *Pius XII* being but one of them — the film version of *The Deputy* by the celebrated Greek filmmaker Constantin Costa-Gavras, provocatively entitled *Amen* (2002), has managed to inflame matters considerably. No small part of the increasingly heated debate — very little is being done to douse the flames — revolves around the notion that Pacelli has been made a scapegoat. Michael Novak — an author, the George Frederick Jewett Chair in Religion and Public Policy at the Washington-based American Enterprise Institute, and one of the most respected conservative voices in U.S. Catholicism — has argued in "Pius XII as Scapegoat" (*First Things*, August/September 2000) that Catholic critics have sought to discredit Pius XII in order to "diminish the papacy in general" and thereby promote their liberal blueprints for ecclesial reform; that Communists and German nationalists of various hue and stripe have a lot to gain by making Pius the premier, if not only, villain; and that many Jews deeply distraught over the failure of international Jewry to do more to save their persecuted brethren have found in Pius a convenient salve to their tormented consciences. Deak is not so convinced.

Pius is not at all a scapegoat. I think he could have done much more. He should have risked his life and his papacy to do more. There were thousands and thousands of people who risked their property, their positions, their very lives, and he did not do it. This is not only a question of the Jews, for whom he could have done something concrete as in the case of the Roman Jews, but in general. It is simply not enough to say that Communism is a great enemy and that we have to be pragmatic. He already had a great enemy in the

Nazis. He knew that they were determined to wipe out the Catholic Church and that fierce conflict was inevitable.

What I find so appalling, really, is the truth that Pius did not even stand up for his own institution; he did not defend the church in Eastern Europe, and that includes the most loyal Catholics in the world: the Poles.

It is very difficult to defend Pacelli and to defend the papacy in general, because at the moment of truth he was no better than anyone else. This I see as the crisis of Europe.

The failure of Pius, in Deak's view, to be better than anyone else, to function in an heroic manner and truly provide the moral leadership clearly lacking in all other quarters — ecclesiastical, political, and social — simply cannot be gainsaid. There are no mitigating or ameliorating factors. Papal nuncios, national episcopates, Vatican leadership, and religious orders were all compromised by the church's constricted vision. Determined to protect the rights, prerogatives, and very future of the institutional church, the priests and bishops, Deak argues, prioritized in such a way as to seriously dilute their commitment to the gospel. In fact, many national hierarchies and papal ambassadors operated in a way that reflected the insularity of head office and the xenophobia of the local church. Marrus, however, is less categorical.

From the point of view of the Vatican, it was not in a position to lay down a set of policy guidelines for nuncios who found themselves in often extraordinarily difficult conditions — that is, under Nazi occupation. Local considerations had to govern the means of expression and the choice of political options.

You know, it is only in retrospect, from our current vantage point, a post-1960s vantage point, that we look to people who "spoke out," as if this is what was called for at the time of the Holocaust. For the people who found themselves in that world "speaking out," in the idiom of the '60s, was not something that their culture, their training, their style, or their immediate experience would have taught them was the right thing to do. I don't think that we should disparage their declared obligations to save as many people as possible at the same time as they sought to preserve the institutional structure of the church in a time of Nazi attack or occupation.

I think that what we can learn from this is the realization that priorities need constant examination, and that Vatican diplomacy of the 1940s was not the *summum bonum* it often thought it was. It is the job of historical investigators to enter that world — so different from our own — and to remember that when Jews and others respond to the pope's apprehension over Nazi retaliations that surely there is nothing worse than the Holocaust, we need to appreciate that this view reflects a state of mind and a knowledge of events that is ours and not theirs.

The incapacity of most political and religious bodies to comprehend the monstrous evil that confronted them should not be downplayed. In fact, it was Israeli writer Amos Oz who reminds us that believing is one thing and understanding is quite another:

The mother of the man who married my elder daughter is an unusual Holocaust survivor. She was taken from Holland with her mother and sister to Ravensbruck, a concentration camp, where the mother died. The two girls were nineteen and eighteen. At Ravensbruck, the girls heard stories about Auschwitz from detainees who had been there but were not sent to their death because they came from mixed marriages. Then something happened that I think was unique in the history of the Holocaust. The foreign ministry in Berlin gave an order saying, Send those two girls to Theresienstadt. There they were introduced to Adolf Eichmann, and he and several SS commanders interrogated them. Eichmann asked what they knew about Auschwitz. He said, "If you ever say a word about your life in Ravensbruck or what you know about Auschwitz, you, too, will go up in those chimneys." At Theresienstadt, they were given work. Twice during the war, Eichmann saw those two girls.

As it turned out, this woman grew up and was one of the witnesses at the Eichmann trial — in Jerusalem in the early nineteen-sixties. It was hard for her to testify. At the trial, Eichmann tried to say that he was just a cog in the wheel, that he hadn't even the capacity to decide on one life. I am telling you this story because, despite Eichmann's warning to the two sisters about being quiet, they did tell everyone they could in Theresienstadt. They talked about Auschwitz and the gas chambers, but not one person at Theresienstadt believed them. They were called hysterical. So: how could people in Jerusalem or New York believe something that even the inmates of Theresienstadt refused to believe? Knowing is one thing. Believing another. Understanding another.[6]

The enormous, surreal, and epic nature of the Holocaust dwarfs reason. Many did not understand. Many more stared blankly at a reality that crushed resistance. Few grasped the range, demonic methodicalness, and orderly madness of the Nazi concentration camp system. As survivor, scientist, and writer Primo Levi notes: "at no other place or time has one seen a phenomenon so unexpected and so complex: never have so many human lives been extinguished in so short a time, and with so lucid a combination of technological ingenuity, fanaticism, and cruelty."[7]

In spite of the shattering uniqueness of the Holocaust, however, the sheer scope of the malevolence, the failure of institutions to discern the menace, to consolidate the opposition, and to grasp, if not the nature of the beast, at least its *modus operandi*, cannot be explained away or exculpated. For Deak, the church's lack of nerve boils down not to its detachment from politics but its misjudgement:

> The eternal struggle between the altar and the sword, between the Church and the State, was central to the history of Western civilization. In Western Christianity there was always a tension, and often a choice between dynastic or national authorities on the one hand and the internationalist Church on the other. The Roman Church frequently served as a refuge from the increasingly aggressive demands of the state. It was the Church leaders' terrible mistake in modern times to surrender to nationalist sentiments and to bless the arms of all warring nations, including the arms of Nazi Germany. Those who want the Church to get out of politics unconditionally might recall that, for instance, in China the Catholic Church lost its autonomy and became an integral part of the bureaucracy. In Germany in 1933 the German Catholic Center Party was potentially the last bastion of defense against Hitler's dictatorship. It was abandoned by the Vatican's Concordat with the Nazi regime. In this and other cases it was not the fact of the Church's involvement in politics that was shameful but its failure to support Catholics who opposed an evil regime.[8]

Deak's castigation of the Roman Catholic Church revolves around his conviction that the church's international nature was forgotten by its myopic leaders, that their inadequacy in ensuring the church's pan-national perspective, their deficiency in invoking the church's global solicitude, seriously diminished the church's ability to withstand the assaults of Nazism and Fascism. By behaving more like regional or indigenous churches — by acting more like Protestant churches, with their strong Erastian focus — the Roman church's local hierarchies, with the tacit agreement of Rome, forswore their genuinely universal jurisdiction, depleted their reservoirs of resistance, and abandoned their ancient charism on the altar of nationalism. Well-steeped in the tradition himself, a graduate of the most prestigious Catholic school in his native Hungary, rigorously educated by the Piarist Fathers and deeply conversant with the various iterations of the Catholic fact in Eastern Europe, Deak's excoriating of the church is inspired not by animus but by disappointment — a disappointment grounded in his belief that the church, and Pius notably, squandered their not-inconsiderable strengths by acting timidly and safely rather than with confidence and with the risk born of courage.

Marrus is in agreement with Deak, to a point. He goes further, however, than Deak, linking the tepidity of the Vatican's response more to weak structures than to weak leadership. In a review of University of Rome professor Peter Godman's *Hitler and the Vatican: Inside the Secret Archives that Reveal the New Story of the Nazis and the Church*, Marrus argues that both Popes Pius — XI and XII —

preferred understatement in their dealings with Hitler; both trimmed their denunciations to preserve the concordat; both were hesitant, indecisive, and opportunistic rather than resolute in their response to threats; and both shrank from a more forthright course of action proposed in the very center of the Vatican. To be sure, both abhorred Nazism; they were simply uncertain how to contend with it. Both also understood the practical limitations of papal authority in a system that allowed contradictory initiatives and whose imperious claims to universal authority contrasted with a fragile, ramshackle structure to enforce a party line.[9]

Regardless of the shortcomings of the Vatican bureaucracy, however, the leadership that emanated from the Supreme Pontiff remains definitive. Although it is true that the Vatican Curia, the central administration of the Holy See, the various dicasteries and diplomatic services, the archivists, historians, and information gatekeepers, all have their discrete and often competing functions, the fact remains that the hierarchy is still a hierarchy, and the Roman pontiff is at the pinnacle of the pyramid. Pius could — and did — send sometimes clear and sometimes oblique messages concerning his intention, and there is little doubt in the end about how he viewed his role during the war, the Nazi occupation of Rome, and the plight of the Jews in the Third Reich. One interesting aperture throwing light on Pacelli's view of the papacy, the church, and anti-Semitism is the initiative undertaken by one of the most prominent and respected Catholic laypersons in the world: Jacques Maritain.

According to Marrus, Maritain, a Thomistic philosopher, political thinker, French ambassador to the Holy See, and a tireless advocate on behalf of the Jews both during and after the war,

in the summer of 1946, when all minds were being turned to postwar reconstruction, had the idea of getting Pius XII to issue an important statement, perhaps even an encyclical, on the subject of anti-Semitism and the Holocaust. Having presented his idea to the Pope's principal assistant, Giovanni Battista Montini, the future Pope Paul VI, the idea went nowhere. Pius indicated that he had already spoken and referred to a speech he had given [an address given on November 29, 1945, to an audience of seventy

Jewish refugees of German concentration camps], and, as well, he let it be known that the Vatican was not interested in pursuing this. Maritain, perhaps the leading Catholic layman of his day, someone who had deeply studied the issue of Catholicism and the Jews [his wife, the Russian poet Raïssa Oumansoff, was a Jewish convert to Catholicism], a man who was very friendly toward Eugenio Pacelli and a diplomat with the most positive of inclinations towards the Vatican's postwar aspirations, nevertheless emerged from this encounter with the Pope deeply disappointed.

When he stepped down as ambassador, Maritain "confided to his friend Charles Jourdan about his 'heart-rending ambivalence': a 'growing affection for the person of the pope,' on the one hand, but a 'growing disappointment with regard to his actions,' on the other."[10] The failure, or perceived failure, of Pius XII to act during — and even after — the war, or to act in a manner commensurate with his power and influence, is at the heart of the debate over his cause for sainthood.

Perhaps sensing the difficulties that would arise over Pius's cause — the ongoing post-*Deputy* acrimony, disputes over access to the Vatican's wartime archives, Catholicism's dark history of anti-Semitic behaviour, the controverted role of anti-Judaism in Christianity's foundational years, the sometimes-tortured relationship of the Vatican City state with the state of Israel, and the ongoing difficulty of getting that objective and fair assessment so essential to a balanced judgement of the time, the personalities, and the issues because the atmosphere is so polemicized — Pope John Paul II pursued a strategy of redress that is both bold and inspired.

John Paul's politics of saint-making always had a theological as well as a pastoral component, but nowhere is his institutional strategy clearer than in his addressing the troublesome legacy of the Church of Rome's sinfulness, whether it be outbursts of dangerous zeal, myopic religiosity, cruel and senseless persecution, or obstinate failure to acknowledge offence, seek forgiveness, and make reparation. No pope did as much as John Paul II, particularly by way of preparation for the third millennium ("the hermeneutical key to my pontificate"), to purify memory and seek healing. The saints were a major part of this strategy. We look to the saints to find that witness lacking in others, to find that undimmed vision of God's reign so often obscured by church politics, and to nurture faith, revivify hope, and inspire love. And John Paul II, one who lived in the shadow of the *lager* and the *gulag*, the life-denying camps of Nazi and Soviet ideology, was consequently even more interested in the special place of the martyrs, whose blood does more than a little to expiate the weakness of most.

Thus began the new litany, the modern martyrology. And the names are impressive. There is Titus Brandsma, the Dutch Carmelite, whose cause was introduced in the early 1950s but whose beatification was presided over by John Paul II in 1985. Brandsma perished in Dachau concentration camp in July of 1942 following a terminal injection, and although it is debatable whether he died technically as a martyr or not (his case was advanced under the title of confessor), there is no doubt that his *presence* in Dachau and the treatment he received there resulted in his death. An unrelenting critic of the Nazi ideology even before the occupation of Holland, he used his considerable influence as religious adviser to the Society of Catholic Journalists to encourage resistance to the Nazis. He was anything but nuanced. In his written defence submitted to the German police, he was emphatic about his reasons for opposition to the Nazi creed:

"The Church rejects Nazi ideology on account of religious conviction. In questions of principle it cannot yield, whatever the consequences. This is the official view and also my own." To his fellow journalists he had written: "The Nazi regime is imposing orders which can in no way be harmonised with fidelity to Christian principles. . . . If you want to retain the Catholic signature of your paper, you will have to refuse, even if they ban its publication. There is no other way. We have reached the point of no returns."[11]

It is no surprise that he was incarcerated. He lectured weekly at the Catholic University of Nijmegen on Nazi ideology, he protested publicly against the anti-Jewish Nuremberg laws, he denounced the Nazi Council of Information for the Dutch as "a sewer of falsehood and imposture," and when finally imprisoned by the Nazis he was esteemed by his fellow cell-mates for his personal courage, generosity in sharing food, and gift for inspiring others.

Earlier still — on October 10, 1982, to be precise — John Paul canonized the Polish Conventual Franciscan friar Maximilian Kolbe, a man whose personal bravery exacted a terrible cost. Kolbe, a hyper-industrious cleric who founded various publications and reviews to promote the cult of Mary Immaculate, worked with fevered perseverance as a missionary in Japan, built up the largest friary in the world (called Niepokalanów, or the City of the Immaculate), organized shelter for Polish refugees (most of whom were Jews) fleeing German aggression, and publicly exhorted his readers to remember that "beyond armies of occupation and the hecatombs of concentration camps, there are two irreconcilable enemies in the depth of every soul: good and evil, sin and love."[12] Kolbe understood the war external and the war internal, refused to free individuals from their personal responsibility to resist evil, and stood his ground as a friar — and as a Christian — against the godless credo of the Nazi invaders. He was arrested in February of 1941, dispatched first to Pawiak prison and then to Auschwitz, where he was subjected to especially harsh treatment. The punishment meted out to him appears to have fortified him in his determination to give his life for others.

In the summer of 1941, three prisoners escaped, and the Lagerführer announced that ten prisoners would be chosen from the blocks from which the three fugitives had escaped, and that they would be sent to the underground starvation cell known as the Bunker to die as retaliation. A noncommissioned Polish officer, Franciszek Gajowniczek, one of the ten doomed men, cried out in despair, "O my poor wife, my poor children, I shall never see them again." Kolbe, prisoner 16670, stepped forward and offered himself as a substitute for Gajowniczek. He was sent to the Bunker, where he died an agonizing death. In fact, the SS were so annoyed that he was taking such a long time to die (he was the last of the ten to do so) that they chose to give him an injection of carbolic acid to hasten the end in order to make room for a new lot condemned to execution. It was August 14, 1941, the eve of the Feast of the Assumption. Respect and love for Kolbe was widespread throughout the camp, and his reputation flourished after the war. It came as no surprise, then, that his cause was formally introduced on March 16, 1960.

Kolbe, a Pole, a cleric with a special devotion to the Blessed Virgin Mary, a man of boundless energy and formidable will, and a priest who defied tyranny to do its worst, held enormous appeal for Karol Wojtyla from the beginning of his own ministry. They are kindred spirits. Although Kolbe's Mariology was all-consuming and the Pontiff's more measured by comparison, and although Kolbe's theological acumen was less expansive than the Pope's, and whereas some critics of the canonization found traces of "benign" anti-Semitism in Kolbe's writings while the Pope's personal standing in the Jewish community is, by contrast, unparalleled, there is more that unites the two men than divides them. This was a sainting that John Paul was convinced was right, and although some reservations were registered, there was no outcry of opposition.

Not so in the case of Sister Teresa Benedicta a Cruce, better known to history as Edith Stein.

No one, argued John Paul, better illustrates the heroic witness of the martyr wedded to the fearless pursuit of the truth than this philosopher-nun. She was born in Silesia in 1891; her father died when she was quite young, and she did not share her mother's devout Jewish faith, nor her practical aptitude for survival. But she did betray an early interest in philosophy, and subsequently studied the subject at both Breslau and Göttingen universities. It was at the latter academy that she joined the Philosophical Society, a gathering of students of the great phenomenologist Edmund Husserl, and met such thinkers as Max Scheler (a considerable philosophical influence on Wojtyla) and Anne and Adolf Reinach, thinkers who appealed to Stein both intellectually and spiritually.

After Stein left Göttingen, she studied at Freiburg directly under Husserl, actually writing her dissertation under his supervision and serving as his research assistant for a few years. It was difficult for her to find full employment at the university (the times were not propitious for women lecturers), but she remained ever hopeful. The year 1921 proved to be an important one in her spiritual pilgrimage, because that was the year she discovered the autobiography of the great mystic St. Teresa of Avila while staying at the home of fellow philosophers Theodor Conrad and Hedwig Martinus. She devoured the autobiography of the sixteenth-century Carmelite nun and concluded that "the *Life* of our Holy Mother Teresa happened to fall into my hands [and the] long search for the true faith came to an end." Stein was baptized on January 1, 1922, in the parish church of St. Martin in Bergzabern, and was confirmed one month later in the private chapel of the Bishop of Speyer, Ludwig Sebastian.

Her life as a Roman Catholic commenced in a manner similar to that of most converts — with intense ardour. But with the substantial difference that she already possessed a profound interior disposition to the contemplative life with a taste for deep private meditation that struck many with its seasoned maturity.

From 1923 until 1931 she taught at St. Magdalene's in Speyer, wrote numerous works and translated many others, and became an instructor at the German Institute for Scientific Pedagogy in Münster. Then, in the fall of 1933, she entered the Carmel in Cologne, took the name in religion of Sister Teresa Benedicta a Cruce, professed first vows in 1935 and perpetual vows in 1938, at the same time writing some of her most important works, including *Finite and Eternal Being*.

At the end of 1938 she was sent to the Carmel in Echt, the Netherlands, in what turned out to be a final hope of escaping the Nazis. In 1942, after the Dutch Roman Catholic hierarchy issued a pastoral letter denouncing the roundup and deportation of Jews in Holland, Edith and her sister Rosa were arrested by the Gestapo, as were all Dutch Jewish converts to Catholicism, as a punitive act against a defiant episcopate. The Steins were deported to the assembly camps of Amersfoort and Westerbork to await final transport to Auschwitz-Birkenau, where they were both killed.

At the time of her beatification in Cologne in 1987, John Paul underscored in his homily the high regard in which he held Stein:

> The church now presents Sister Benedicta a Cruce to us as a blessed martyr, as an example of a heroic follower of Christ, for us to honour and to emulate. Let us open ourselves up for her message to us as a woman of the spirit and of the mind, who saw in the science of the cross the acme of all wisdom, as a great daughter of the Jewish

people, as a believing Christian in the midst of millions of innocent fellow men made martyrs. She saw the inexorable approach of the cross. She did not flee in fear.

Although the beatification in 1987 and her subsequent canonization in 1998 made sense to John Paul, the Jewish community was incensed. As early as the 1980s, when it was clear that the Pope was moving in the direction of Stein's sainting, opposition from Jewish groups was already coalescing around two specific concerns: the fear that the sainting of a Jewish convert to Catholicism might foster the development of organized initiatives within the church, focused on converting other Jews; and the appropriation of the Shoah, or Holocaust, by the church through the symbolic representation of a martyr like Stein. By the time she was canonized, apprehension over her designation as a martyr — the misunderstandings that can arise over the true nature of "witness" and the ugly competition between two religious traditions over the meaning of her death — had reached crisis proportions. Rabbi Dow Marmur of Toronto gave an interview to Canadian writer Myrna Kostash for her *Ideas* radio program, "The Case of Martyr Teresa Benedicta," in which he highlighted the difficulties most Jews have over the identification of Stein as a martyr:

> The problem of Edith Stein as far as Jews [are] concerned is first of all connected with the issue of the church having a need to declare someone a martyr who was a Jew originally. The church has a long history of really getting very excited each time a Jew is converted. We know why — after all, the poor pagans don't know any better. But the Jews, from whose midst Jesus came, they should really know, and if they should still persist in being Jewish, then there is something radically wrong with them — and if someone breaks away and embraces Christianity, that has to be celebrated.

To me, this whole business of Edith Stein the martyr is a throwback to that particular tradition. In addition, those who died in the Holocaust did not die as martyrs. Martyrdom means choice, but nobody had a choice. It was premeditated murder; there was no question of martyrdom. As well, Edith Stein died because she had Jewish genes, according to the Nazis, and not because she was a Christian and testified to her faith. Christians have to understand this: she was not killed because of her Christianity but because, as far as the Nazis were concerned, she was as Jewish as the rest of us, and when I say "no, she was not Jewish," it is because I refuse to allow the Nazis to define who is a Jew.

The whole question of canonization is so very strange and very peculiar and says so very little about Edith Stein as far as I am concerned, but a lot about church politics.[13]

No such scruples existed for John Paul, however. For both him and the Roman Catholic Church, Stein was like Maximilian Kolbe: together, in the Pope's words, "these two martyrs of Auschwitz . . . would lead us into the future." But not only would they lead Catholics into the future, they would help in the purification of memory, they would help expiate the sins of countless baptized Catholics who did nothing during the Holocaust, and they would go some way to redeem the church in the eyes of a cynical and hostile world. That's the strategy.

Although the Stein sainting was controversial, several other causes are progressing without incident: Franz Jägerstätter, the Austrian layman beheaded for refusing to fight in the army of the Reich; Karl Leisner, an ardent opponent of Nazism, whose health was broken in Dachau and who was ordained practically on the eve of his death; Johann Gruber, an Austrian priest-theologian who laboured valiantly in the Mauthausen-Gusen concentration camp to nurture hope and attend to the suffer-

ings of the most needy before he was kicked to death by his
jailers; Jacques Bunel — Père Jacques, the French Carmelite
friar made famous in filmmaker Louis Malle's *Au Revoir les
Enfants*, who worked tirelessly and ingeniously to protect Jewish
children from being hunted down for deportation and who died
shortly after the liberation of Mauthausen-Gusen; Blessed
Clemens August Cardinal Graf von Galen, known as the "Lion of
Münster" for his fearless denunciations of the Nazi creed; and
Conventual Franciscan friar Nicola Placido Cortese, who
perished at the hands of the Gestapo for helping Jews and
Slovenes in the Veneto region of Italy. These are only a handful.
There are many more.

But of special significance is the case of the German Jesuit
priest Rupert Mayer, the Catholic conscience of Germany, the
"Apostle of Munich," whose funeral entourage brought out
hundreds of thousands to line the streets to pay their respects to
a man whose integrity and courage was beyond reproach. Paolo
Molinari, whom I earlier identified as the postulator general of
the Society of Jesus, has carried the Mayer dossier for years and
knows his subject intimately:

> During the First World War, Mayer served as a military
> chaplain and was often found on the front line. He provided
> comfort, consolation, and the sacraments to the wounded
> and the dying, even as they fell. In fact, while hearing the
> final confession of a dying soldier, he was wounded by
> shrapnel and had to have his leg amputated. He lived for
> the rest of his life with a wooden leg.
>
> He was so admired by the officers and fellow soldiers
> that he was accorded the Iron Cross for his service as a
> chaplain, a rather significant honour from a country that is
> not predominantly Catholic. After the war, he took up resi-
> dence at the Church of St. Michael in Munich, where there
> was a small community of fellow Jesuits.

This was a very difficult time for all of Germany. The Treaty of Versailles was a rather vicious and vindictive treaty, considered by many historians and by Pope Benedict XV himself as a grave injustice. Poverty and deprivation were everywhere. As a consequence of these conditions, the Bolsheviks made considerable advances in the German cities, and in Munich in particular there was a Bolshevik regime. During this period the nuncio, Eugenio Pacelli, was actually confronted by revolver in his nunciature. He refused to leave and defied his intruders to kill him if they wished. Pacelli knew, like Mayer (in fact he knew Mayer), that the number of poor families was growing quickly and dangerously.

Mayer helped his people to rebuild: he meted out jobs so that some money could be earned and he encouraged by example and by preaching a practical charity at the level of the local church community. His whole approach to life was marked by tenderness, care, and compassion at even the simplest of levels. For instance, in ski-crazy Bavaria he would celebrate Mass in the train station for those who wished to get out of the dire conditions of the city for the nearby slopes. And he did this, not for legal reasons in order to make sure that the people met their Sunday obligation to attend Mass, but because he loved people. He said at one point, "I understand your desire to go skiing, so I will make it easier for you to do so without having a qualm of conscience." His was a very human approach to life.

In 1933, things worsened considerably. Hitler came to power. Mayer was one of the few in Germany who *really* understood Nazi ideology. He used his pulpit at St. Michael's to denounce the Nazi creed, Nazi tactics, and Nazi leaders. The Gestapo regularly monitored his homilies and he was frequently arrested. Hitler himself took a personal interest in Mayer, as they had had a private confrontation at Munich's Hofbrauhaus in 1919, at which time Mayer conceded that Hitler was a great orator but an agitator and economical with the truth. His critique would get bolder and bolder, and at one point — 1923, to be precise — he announced at a National Socialist meeting that a German Catholic can *never* be a Nazi. As you can see, his opposition to the Nazis is there from the beginning.

Eventually, he ends up in Sachsenhausen concentration camp outside Berlin in 1939, only to be released a half a year later because the Nazis were disturbed by the level of his popular appeal and by the fact that they could not afford to have him a martyr. He was sent into exile to the Benedictine monastery at Ettal, where he remained until the end of the war.

The American army of liberation returned him to Munich, and he found himself doing exactly what he had done at the end of the First World War — helping the survivors cope with the horror of the war and its devastating aftermath. But he was exhausted. He collapsed and died while reading his homily on the Feast of All Saints, November 1, 1945.

Although Mayer did not die a martyr, his life was a sustained witness to the high demands of gospel integrity, to the commitment to truth irrespective of the personal consequences, and to the fully human value of freedom exercised responsibly in society, a freedom that disposes one to serve others humbly and with love. Mayer did this in the teeth of Nazi opposition, put his life in danger of torture and death, suffered imprisonment, and was virtually put under house arrest for the duration of the war.

Another Jesuit, Alfred Delp, *would* pay the ultimate price. Like Mayer, he was a member of the same Jesuit province, they had the same provincial superior — the redoubtable Augustin Rosch — and they both served time in prison for opposing Hitler. Unlike Mayer, however, Delp was executed.

Mary Frances Coady, Canadian writer and biographer, is the author of *With Bound Hands — A Jesuit in Nazi Germany: The Life and Selected Prison Letters of Alfred Delp*, and she situates Delp within the larger resistance:

> Delp was a writer and editor for a Jesuit publication, *Stimmen der Zeit*, that was suppressed in 1941. He was interested in political systems and he was highly critical in his editorial work of both the Nazis and the Communists. He also had connections with some workers' groups that had formed part of the underground resistance.
>
> Sometime in 1942 he was invited by Rosch to join the clandestine group later known as the *Kreisauer Kreis*, or Kreisau Circle [members or friends included at some time, and in various degrees of association: aristocrats Count Helmuth James von Moltke, Baron Karl Ludwig von Guttenberg, Peter Yorck von Wartenburg, intellectuals Adam von Trott, Julius Leber, and Hans-Bernd von Haeften, Lutheran clerics Eugen Gerstenmaier and Harald Poelchau, Catholic Centre Party politicians Hans Peters and Paul van Husen, and Jesuits Rosch, Delp, and Lothar König]. The work of the Circle was to plan the rebuilding of Germany after what they knew to be the inevitable defeat of the Nazis. Of course, to even suggest defeat was considered treason and treason was punishable by death.
>
> The leaders of the Kreisau Circle had invited the Jesuits to join because they wanted to establish a link with the German bishops in the hope that the bishops would support their efforts and speak out as a collective body against the Nazi system. The Jesuits — Rosch and König in particular — had such episcopal connections.

The Nazis were anything but indifferent to the Jesuit order itself. In fact, they declared the whole order as an enemy of the Reich. They were declared unfit for military service and there was a plan to expel them all from German soil, a plan that was never enacted. But the Gestapo kept an ever-close watch on them.

The Jesuits didn't oppose the regime in any sort of uniform manner, and in truth some of them were quite slow to realize the implications of Nazi ideology. Those who did openly oppose the Nazis — like Mayer and Delp, for instance — did so mainly in their preaching and writing. And like all those critical of the Nazis they were eventually arrested and sent to concentration camps.

It was only a matter of time before the Nazi authorities would close in on the Circle. Following the doomed attempt by Count Claus Schenk von Stauffenberg to assassinate Hitler on July 20, 1944 — although the bomb deposited in Hitler's forest headquarters by Stauffenberg, chief of staff at the General Army Office in Berlin, did extensive damage and seriously wounded Hitler, the Führer survived — the fast and vicious reaction of the Nazis meant that the fate of the Jesuits was sealed. Although Delp debated with the others the right way to go about removing Hitler — Moltke was persuaded that they could not begin a new Germany with blood on their hands, while Delp leaned in the direction of the assassination — all three Jesuits were manifestly uninvolved in the actual attempt. They were in Munich, not in Berlin, and there is little evidence that they were apprised of Stauffenberg's plan of action. But they were marked for arrest: König eluded capture entirely; Rosch avoided capture for a while, but was eventually caught, although not executed; and Delp was both caught and executed.

While in prison, Delp wrote a letter, dated New Year's Night, 1944–1945, to "M" — generally identified as *Mitbrüder*, or "fellow Jesuits" — and in this letter he outlined his view regarding the failure of the Vatican, the German church, and Catholics generally in the wake of the Nazi tyranny:

> Of course it will be shown eventually that the pope did his duty and more, that he offered peace, that he explored all possibilities to bring about peace negotiations, that he proclaimed the spiritual conditions on which a just peace could be based, that he dispensed alms and was tireless in his work on behalf of prisoners of war, displaced persons, tracing missing relatives and so on — all this we know and posterity will have documentary evidence in plenty to show the full extent of the papal effort. But to a large extent, all this good work may be taken for granted and also to a large extent it leads nowhere and has no real hope of achieving anything. That is the real root of the trouble — among all the protagonists in the tragic drama of the modern world there is not one who fundamentally cares in the least what the Church says or does. We overrated the Church's political machine and let it run on long after its essential driving power had ceased to function. It makes absolutely no difference so far [as] the beneficial influence of the Church is concerned whether a state maintains diplomatic relations with the Vatican or not. The only thing that really matters is in the inherent power of the Church as a religious force in the countries concerned.
>
> This is where the mistake started: religion died, from various diseases, and humanity died with it.[14]

Many will argue with Delp's somewhat sanguine view of papal involvement, and others with his gloomy estimate of actual Vatican power and influence, but there is no denying the validity of his observation — shared in great measure by his fellow

Christian martyr, the Lutheran theologian Dietrich Bonhoeffer (who would be executed a couple of months after Delp) — that the European crisis underscores the failure of Christianity to have been deeply appropriated by the people at large. The failure of Western societies to ensure humanity's social, economic, intellectual, and religious regeneration underscores the dramatic, urgent, and compelling need for the faithful to become more dedicated and intense if the church is to be anything other than a vaguely "idealistic value."

What sustained Delp in the end, according to Mary Frances Coady, was neither a facile belief in the church nor a fanatical will to survive, but his own Ignatian spirituality.

As a Jesuit, Delp was trained in the Spiritual Exercises of St. Ignatius Loyola, the founder of the Society of Jesus. These "exercises" are a guide to deepening a person's life and service as a Christian. One of the mottoes of the Jesuits is "finding God in all things," and Delp sought to do precisely this, to see the divine in all of creation, and to avoid withdrawal from reality into a spiritual or religious ghetto.

He had no patience with sentimentalized or superficial religion. Even in prison, as he was awaiting execution, he tried to discern the divine in the things that were happening to him. At the same time, he was struggling against a mounting feeling of despair over what seemed to him to be in the end the futility and failure of his work. Strangely and powerfully, he accepted this futility and failure and made peace with it in a profound way, believing that there was a greater meaning in his situation than he himself could understand.

Clearly, he came to grasp the implications of his witness; he knew that "his" Germany was not that of the Nazis; he knew that the Jesuits were, in his own words, "feared as a reproach in the prevailing state of pathetic, immeasurable human bondage"; and he knew that his world was "no longer a world of idylls."

On February 2, 1945, the Feast of the Purification — the traditional day for Jesuits to make their vows — Delp was hanged ignominiously on a hook in Plotzensee Prison, his body burned, his ashes strewn over sewer waste.

Although his cause has not been introduced — he was not a model Jesuit in some respects, appears to have been less than scrupulously obedient to his provincial, could be wilfully argumentative, and there are suggestions in some quarters that his correspondence with his church secretary admitted of a familiarity not customary for celibate clerics of the time (any hint of sexual commerce or even of unrealized erotic passion is enough to scotch a cause in its infancy) — Delp was, in the estimation of the monk-poet Thomas Merton, a humanist, a mystic, and a prophet, a man whose struggle highlighted the tragedy of the concentration camps and of "the inhuman complacency that is *totally incapable* of seeing in itself either sin, or falsity, or absurdity, or even the slightest impropriety."[15]

Merton saw in Delp a doomed but noble refusal to be implicated in that human regression to the "climate of moral infancy" that characterized the Third Reich. Adolf Eichmann represented for Merton the quintessentially sane man who embodied the crisis of the liberal conscience and the impotence of a humane tradition in the face of the unspeakable savageries of the Nazis. Eichmann was the immaculate German officer who symbolized the corruption of obedience, the sterility of the Kantian conception of duty, and the wedding of technology with death. Eichmann's moral vacuity was accompanied by an extraordinary rectitude of manner and conviction, revealing the gaping insufficiency of a purely abstract morality at the cost of eliminating a concrete, existential respect for human reality.[16]

As Hochhuth observed, "a uniform comes to an end at the neck."[17] But where does the white cassock of the pontiff come to an end?

If Delp is not "canonizable," why is Pope Pius XII?

For Michael Marrus, this is not the right time to be advancing the case for Pacelli's sainthood.

I think that any discussion of this possibility must begin with reference to Pope John XXIII and to the great changes ushered in by the Second Vatican Council of 1962–1965. This Council began a process which I believe is irreversible, but a process than nonetheless is going to take time. You cannot turn around the culture or the disposition of a church with one billion members — international in scope, with many different national points of departure, culturally, intellectually, and so forth. You simply can't turn around views in a very short and condensed period of time. Nor can Jewish views, lacking as they do any sort of coherent or central animating institutional focus like the church, turn around suddenly.

Add to this fact the reality that the Jewish people have suffered an assault — the genocidal attack of the Nazis — which is simply unprecedented historically and which I think has created a wound that will take a long time to heal. How could it be otherwise? All of us are still coming to terms with the Holocaust. This is a process of progressive understanding that began with John XXIII and was carried forward admirably and extraordinarily by John Paul II. This is a *process*, and I think that we need to keep in mind that total transformation of attitude and view can only be envisaged by utopians.

All that acknowledged, I have to say that the sainting of Pius XII is not entirely helpful coming as it does at a time when we are still in the process of coming to terms with the insufficiencies of Vatican policy during the war. Yes, we may say that it is wrong to criticize Pope Pius XII using twenty-first-century hindsight, that that does not make sense, but on the other hand any objective assessment will have to recognize that there were extraordinary insufficiencies, that there were things *not* done, there were options that were *not* taken, a prophetic voice *not* heard, etc.

So when Jews think about a saint, they conventionally think of someone who has risen above an ordinary level of standing to act in an exemplary way, who has served as an exemplary demonstration of the kind of person who responds in an exceptional way in exceptional circumstances. Pius XII, whatever else one can say of him, does not, in my view as an historian, rise to that level. I should also add that Roosevelt does not rise to that level, nor even Churchill, who had the deepest awareness of all of what was happening to European Jewry, who was the most philo-Semitic of all the world leaders on the stage at the time — even Churchill doesn't make the standard.

As you can see, Jews have a tough time with the contention that Pius XII is a saint, although I hasten to add that this is not my business, so to speak, as I have no locus standing in the debate. Friends owe it to friends to speak honestly. I think that Jews are appreciative of the directions that the church has taken on Jewish issues, but we have some obligation to say to Catholics who are involved in the sainting process that "we don't get it" — it doesn't seem right, it doesn't make sense, and perhaps the better part of wisdom would be to postpone this action for another time, waiting for more information, more knowledge, more background, more documentation, for a deeper understanding on all sides.

Without question, Catholics and Jews are divided on the wisdom of proceeding with the cause of Eugenio Pacelli, but not universally so. There are Jews who are well disposed toward Pius XII, although reluctant to speak on his eligibility for saint-hood — as that is, in Marrus's words, an internal matter — and there are Jews overtly hostile to any move on the church's part to defend the record of Pius during the war years. More signifi-cantly, however, there is a very deep chasm that exists among Catholics themselves over the reputation, legacy, saintliness, and political savvy of Pacelli, with those on one side fiercely defensive of the Pope and those on the other side adamant in their opposition to any and all efforts at rehabilitation. In addi-tion, Catholics have staked out positions that, although explicitly about Pius, the Jews, and the Holocaust, are implicitly about competing views of the papacy and church reform. Far more than was the case with either Padre Pio or Mother Teresa, Roman Catholic opinion — popular, official, and scholarly — is severely discordant on the matter of Pius's cause, not only in terms of timeliness and historical sensitivity, but also in terms of the essential merits of the cause itself and of the theological and ecclesiological fallout guaranteed to follow formal conferral of sainthood.

The case against Pacelli has been advanced by many, but perhaps the two most egregious opponents of the cause are the Roman Catholic John Cornwell and the Jewish Daniel Goldhagen.

Cornwell, brother of espionage and spy novelist John Le Carré, a former student for the priesthood — a Fellow of Jesus College, Cambridge University — journalist, papal-affairs analyst (he wrote the highly successful investigation into the death of Pope John Paul I — *A Thief in the Night* [1989]), and arch-critic of the pontificate of John Paul II (*The Pontiff in Winter: Triumph and Conflict in the Reign of John Paul II* [2004]), Cornwell is no stranger to controversy. But his incendiary study of Pacelli, *Hitler's Pope: The Secret History of Pius XII* (1999), created a firestorm similar to Hochhuth's *The Deputy*, not only in Catholic circles but throughout the world. It injected a new tone into the debate, upped the ante on the issue of Pacelli's eligibility for sainthood, and polarized the positions around the scientific assessment of the Pacelli papacy. The concluding paragraph of Cornwell's jeremiad leaves his readers in no doubt about his view of Pope Pius: "I am convinced that the cumulative verdict of history shows him to be not a saintly exemplar for future generations, but a deeply flawed human being from whom Catholics, and our relations with other religions, can best profit by expressing our sincere regret."[18] Ouch.

Cornwell faults Pacelli for his silence, argues that he was, if not an outright anti-Semite, certainly inclined in that direction; that he allowed his Germanophilia to blind him to the dangers of Nazism; that he placed the preservation of the church's institutions over the lives of non-Catholics; that, as a diplomat, he had been prepared to sacrifice Catholic opposition to Hitler to secure a concordat with the regime; and that he was so blinkered and mystified by his office that he could not see the demands of common humanity in the dark days of universal barbarism. Historians, biographers, and political scientists have seriously disputed many of the main theses of *Hitler's Pope*, queried Cornwell's objectivity and use of sources, and attacked him for playing fast and loose with some of the historical facts in addition to deploring his penchant for inferring where the evidence is insubstantial and for deducing where the data is most suspect. For instance, without categorically rebutting Cornwell's condemnation of Pacelli for failing to speak out on behalf of the Jews, Owen Chadwick, the foremost church historian of the period, notes in his review of *Hitler's Pope* the broader complexities, moral quandaries, and political quagmires that regularly faced lesser prelates:

If a defending attorney were desirable in a historical subject, the main line of the plea would need to be something like this. Take the two contiguous German dioceses of Bishops Galen and Berning. We revere Galen for his courage and have no use for Berning because of his silence. But many more priests in Galen's diocese ended in concentration camps than those from Berning's. The brutes did not take it out on the person of the bishop but knew where it would hurt most. If a higher than Galen behaved like him, how many thousands more would end in concentration camps?[19]

Surely Chadwick's point is to illustrate the dilemma Pacelli faced with disturbing frequency. To choose one course of action over another was not simply a matter of electing the option with the minimal risk. Pacelli had to weigh in the balance a whole array of sometimes-competing priorities that Solomon in all his wisdom could not have solved with alacrity and assuaged conscience. Cornwell's sweeping denunciation of Pacelli predictably spawned a series of tracts, critiques, and reviews that sought to discredit not only Cornwell's scholarship — his lack of professional credentials as an historian, for instance — but also his motivation (entrepreneurial, if not venal) and his very fidelity to his Catholic faith (so outraged was Cornwell by the insinuations and outright assaults on his integrity as a believing Catholic that he wrote his own riposte in the form of an apologia — *Breaking Faith* [2001] — underscoring his spiritual pedigree, rootedness in the Catholic tradition, and abiding piety.)

But no one has more consistently, if not ruthlessly, called into question Cornwell's qualifications and intentions than Pacelli's relator, Peter Gumpel:

I got a phone call from a member of the Vatican's Secretariat of State asking me if I would be willing to receive a certain Mr. Cornwell, who is writing a book on Pope Pius XII. I said yes, of course, but I wanted to know with whom I was dealing, so I rang two university professors in England who are close collaborators and I asked them if they knew anything about Mr. Cornwell. Does he have a degree in history, or theology, or law? What is their respective opinion of him?

In very short time I got an answer to my queries. He does not have the appropriate degrees and, apparently, does not read German — a serious omission, given the subject. But I met with him anyway, provided him with all sorts of literature and testaments of sworn witnesses and I conducted the session courteously and without any malice.

Now, at the time the book was to be published, I was contacted by several editors and asked to write a pre-publication review — positive, obviously, for publicity purposes. I didn't want to write anything until after it was published. And what I discovered shocked me. I found mistake after mistake.

For instance: Cornwell accuses Pius XII of anti-Semitism from the very beginning. When he was a child he went to school where the founder and headmaster was the fiery Giuseppe Marchi, who, according to papal biographer Nazareno Padellaro, was fond of delivering speeches from his high desk, thundering against the "hard-heartedness of the Jews." Perhaps Cornwell fell victim to a bad translation, but if he had gone to the original Italian he would have understood the author's intention and the pedagogue's taste for drama better. As a consequence, he would have interpreted the event the opposite way from which he did.

Let me give you one more example among too many. On the flap of the English edition there is a picture of Pacelli that identifies him at the Presidential Palace in 1939. This could not be. Pacelli became pope on March 2, 1939, and Hitler had subsumed the function of president when he came to power in 1933. The impression is thereby given that Pacelli was paying a visit to Hitler, when in truth the photo was taken of Pacelli, as Dean of the Diplomatic Corps, leaving the Presidential Palace following his attendance at a reception honouring the eightieth birthday of the then president of Germany, Paul von Hindenburg. The year was 1927. The publishers subsequently, although it took a long time, ordered the copies back for the correction to be made.

Gumpel's dismissal of Cornwell's work on the basis of its perceived methodological sloppiness, its historical inaccuracies, its blatant anti-Pacelli bias, and its indifference, in Gumpel's mind, to the very principles of scholarly integrity, resulted in a thirteen-page fax sent to the Vatican's Secretariat of State outlining the most egregious of Cornwell's errors. Clearly, Cornwell had struck a nerve.

And he wasn't the only one to do so.

Daniel Goldhagen's *A Moral Reckoning: The Role of the Catholic Church in the Holocaust and Its Unfulfilled Duty of Repair* (2002) is, in the words of Michael Marrus, "an ambitious work, deeply flawed by the author's selective use of evidence, a sneering disparagement of his opponents and a righteous indignation that blinds him to historical complexity."[20] Simply put, Goldhagen has painted his canvas with broad strokes, insensitive to effective coloration and more inclined to impress with outrage rather than represent the truth with measured objectivity. The subtitle nicely sums up the book. But multi-textured moral arguments elude simple summaries. History demands something more than the enraged sputterings of the polemicist.

In an early piece, "Pope Pius XII, the Catholic Church, and the Holocaust: What would Jesus have done?" a 27,000-word essay that ran in *The New Republic* (January 21, 2002) and served as an adumbration for *Moral Reckoning*, Goldhagen reserves his special bile for the hapless Gumpel, whom he attacks as "an antisemite and an historical falsifier," particularly in terms of his role as Pacelli's relator and keenest public apologist. If anything, Gumpel reciprocates Goldhagen's derision and contempt and proceeds full steam in his determination to bring Pius to the altars.

People have repeatedly published in the United States the assertion that the cause has been abandoned or shelved. This is totally absurd!!! Why do people like *The New York Times* staff publish notices that indicate that the cause of Pius XII has been stopped when it is not true? Are they overly enthusiastic in their desire to see the Holy Father beatified and are coming out with unreliable statements to advance his cause? Or are they coming from a completely different angle fuelling the polemical discussion in order to prevent closure on Pius XII?

Let me be clear. Causes for beatification and canonization are an internal Catholic Church matter. I am aware of the fact that the Pacelli cause may once again heat up the controversy. This is a serious problem. But I for one, and I think at least our Holy Father as well, are not going to stop the process for anything. Our task will be — and we are making progress on this, thanks be to God — to make people understand what the real situation of Pius XII was and to remove as many of the problems as possible that people have regarding him. We will not succeed in every single case, but I can tell you through my numerous contacts that the tide is turning. There are more and more people saying that they have been misled by the media and certain sections of society, and in several countries people are beginning to feel that something shameful has been going on with regard to Pius XII.

Gumpel can be quite specific in identifying "these" people. They include ex-priests like James Carroll, novelist and author of *Constantine's Sword: The Church and the Jews* (2001); ex-seminarians like the biographer, essayist, and classicist Garry Wills, who observed caustically in *Why I Am a Catholic* (2002) that "in terms of basic decency, the average president of the United States has been a better human being than the average pope"; and certain sections of the Jewish community, liberal establishment, and collegium of professional historians.

Gumpel takes special pleasure in noting that Pacelli has prominent defenders among Jewish leaders and scholars, including Rabbi David Dalin and Sir Martin Gilbert. Dalin, author of *The Myth of Hitler's Pope: How Pope Pius XII Rescued Jews from the Nazis* (2005) and a member of the board of directors of the Center for Christian-Jewish Understanding of Sacred Heart University in Connecticut, is persuaded, like many of his Catholic colleagues, that "the 'silence' of the Pope is becoming more and more firmly established as settled opinion in the American media," and that the focus and unanimity of approach of the Catholic Pacelli detractors is not about Pius at all.

For Jewish leaders of a previous generation, the campaign against Pius XII would have been a source of shock. During and after the war, many well-known Jews — Albert Einstein, Golda Meir, Moshe Sharett, Rabbi Isaac Herzog, and innumerable others — publicly expressed their gratitude to Pius. In his 1967 book *Three Popes and the Jews*, the diplomat Pinchas Lapide (who served as Israeli consul in Milan and interviewed Italian Holocaust survivors) declared that Pius XII "was instrumental in saving at least 700,000, but probably as many as 860,000 Jews from certain death at Nazi hands."

This is not to say that Eugenio Pacelli — the powerful churchman who served as nuncio in Bavaria and Germany from 1917 to 1929, then as Vatican Secretary of State from 1930 to 1939 before becoming Pope Pius XII six months before World War II began — was as much a friend to the Jews as John Paul II has been. Nor is it to say that Pius was ultimately successful as a defender of the Jews. Despite his desperate efforts to maintain peace, the war came, and, despite his protests against German atrocities, the slaughter of the Holocaust occurred. Even without benefit of hindsight, a careful study reveals that the Catholic Church missed opportunities to influence events, failed to credit fully the Nazis' intentions, and was infected in some of its members with a casual anti-Semitism that would countenance — and, in a few horrifying instances, affirm — the Nazi ideology.

But to make Pius XII a target of our moral outrage against the Nazis, and to count Catholicism among the institutions delegitimized by the horror of the Holocaust reveals a failure of historical understanding. Almost none of the recent books about Pius XII and the Holocaust is actually about Pius XII and the Holocaust. Their real topic proves to be an intra-Catholic argument about the direction of the Church today, with the Holocaust simply the biggest club available for liberal Catholics to use against traditionalists.[21]

Dalin supports the Novak reading on the Catholic anti-Pacellists and subscribes to the view that "Pius XII felt the tragedy of the Jewish people . . . [and] that Pius XII was, genuinely and profoundly, a Righteous Gentile." In fact, Dalin has lobbied to have Yad Vashem, Israel's Holocaust memorial and museum, formally recognize Pius as one of the "righteous gentiles." Dalin is not the only Jew to think this way. Sir Martin Gilbert, distinguished historian of the Holocaust, official biographer of Winston Churchill, prolific author, and a major authority on the Second World War, revealed a remarkable depth of pro-Pacelli sympathy in an interview published in 2003:

> The Vatican, under Pius XII, had taken a public stand against Nazi atrocities in Poland, very early on. That is something on the public record which cannot be taken away, denied or disparaged. To assert Pius XII was "silent" about Nazi mass murder is a serious error of historical fact.
> But there was always the reality of Nazi reprisals. . . . This was obviously a factor in Pius XII's judgements about how far he can speak out during the War. He did speak out, but acted with caution, understandably so, in light of the reprisals. . . . Whenever someone says, "Why didn't the Pope speak out more?" I say, let us start with his December 1942 message, which spoke out for "the hundreds of thousands of innocent people put to death or doomed to slow extinction, sometimes merely because of their race or descent," a message which, as the Nazis themselves recognized, put the Pope squarely and publicly against the Holocaust . . . all things considered, morally and politically, Pius XII acted appropriately and made the right decision.[22]

This is surely music to the ears of Peter Gumpel. Gilbert's scholarship, international prestige as an historian and biographer of record, as well as his high standing in the Jewish community, combine to make him an ally in Gumpel's advocacy of Pacelli. Gilbert has strenuously avoided the kind of polarizing polemics that only too obviously distinguish the current debate on the holiness or culpability of Pope Pius XII. In fact, like most Jewish scholars and religious leaders, Gilbert holds John Paul II in high esteem, and in his 1997 book *Holocaust Journey: Travelling in Search of the Past*, he recounts the story of Wojtyla's special sensitivity to Judaism. After the war, Wojtyla was approached by a Polish Catholic woman seeking guidance with regard to a Jewish child, Shachne Hiller, whom she had hidden and raised during the Nazi occupation. Shachne's parents perished, and the Polish woman wanted to know if she could have the boy baptized in the church. When Wojtyla inquired what the intentions of the parents were, he was told that they had requested that their son be told of his Jewish origins and "returned to his people." The future pope judged that it would be unfair to proceed with the baptism as long as there was hope that Shachne could be united with his relatives. Which, in fact, happened.

In addition, in his 2003 generous compendium *The Righteous: The Unsung Heroes of the Holocaust*, Gilbert painstakingly profiles the not insignificant, although still woefully sparse, select number of individuals who imperilled their own lives to save Jews. Indeed, some died in the process. Although the examples he draws upon reflect a wide spectrum of backgrounds, ethnicities, political creeds, and motivations, an impressively large number were people of faith, and among this number, many were clergy and nuns. French bishops like Pierre Cardinal Gerlier of Lyons, Jean-Baptiste Maury of Reims, Pierre-Marie Théas of Montauban, Gabriel Piguet of Clermont-Ferrand, and Paul Remond of Nice were especially proactive. As well, the exceptionally brave Benedictine Father Bruno — Henri Reynders — saved hundreds of Jewish children in Belgium, while various high-ranking clerics in Italy, including Elia Cardinal Della Costa of Florence, Pietro Palazzini in Rome, and Rufino Niccaci, the abbot of the Franciscan monastery in Assisi, defied the Nazi authorities and laboured relentlessly to save Jewish lives. Gilbert, not unnaturally, is viewed favourably in Rome.

But other Jewish historians worry over the possible, indeed real, manipulation of Jewish opinion by Vatican authorities keen on marshalling as much support as they can to advance Pacelli's star in the constellation of saints. Marrus is especially concerned that a new politics of division not surface in Catholic-

Jewish relations as a consequence of the deployment of what he sees as a questionable tactic.

I don't think there is an important body of Jewish Pacellists who are speaking from within a particular Jewish vantage point. That is to say, there are views on all sides of this issue, but let me come to the heart of it: there is something about the Catholic polemics on this issue that seeks to identify specific Jewish spokespersons and then say, "Look at so and so, who happens to be Jewish and who is pro–Pius XII." How many times have I heard Golda Meir's cable-gram to the Vatican cited? [It read: "We share in the grief of humanity at the passing away of His Holiness Pope Pius XII. In a generation afflicted by wars and discords, he upheld the highest ideals of peace and compassion. When fearful martyrdom came to our people in the decade of Nazi terror, the voice of the Pope was raised for the victims. The life of our times was enriched by a voice speaking out on the great moral truths above the tumult of daily conflict. We mourn a great servant of peace."]

So, when Pius XII died in 1958 Golda Meir, whom I believe at the time was Israeli foreign minister, said some nice things about the Pope. I doubt that she wrote those words or even reflected deeply upon them — she is hardly an authority one could point to as someone with deep insight into Pius XII — and yet over and over and over again her voice is mentioned. Why?

Because I think there is a hunger to find Jewish voices that can be used to legitimate a particular point of view that says, "Look, the Jews that feel otherwise than Meir, etc., have got it wrong." I don't think, for instance, that the views of Dallin and Gilbert are well grounded historically — certainly Sir Martin's are better grounded — and that their point of view has any special significance in the Jewish world. It is simply a point of view and needs to stand or fall on its own merits.

I recognize that wounded sensibilities may well want to marshal as many voices as possible in order to legitimate the defence of Pius XII as a polemical strategy. But I am calling to attention a particular aspect of that strategy that would isolate those Jewish voices that say otherwise. In other words, Jewish voices are being co-opted as part of an anti-Cornwell attack because they are seen as enjoying extra standing precisely because they are Jewish.

There is also the unpleasant possibility that Jews who are not like Golda Meir or Sir Martin Gilbert or the Chief Rabbi of Italy, who happened to convert to Catholicism — in other words, Jews who have been critical of Pius XII — are being contrasted unfavourably as displaying a certain ingratitude.

I think that we can do without these polemics.

It is not likely that the polemics will cease as the cause for sainthood proceeds. There is simply too much at stake on both sides of this unbridgeable gap to anticipate any kind of rapprochement. Both factions — and they are factions — grab every new bit of information, every helpful disclosure, every unearthed document, discovered letter or memoir, to give it their respective spin. The publication in 2004 of the memoirs of Harold Tittmann, *Inside the Vatican of Pius XII*, is a case in point.

Tittmann was a U.S. career diplomat who was assistant to Myron Taylor, President Franklin Roosevelt's personal representative to the Holy See, and when Italy declared war on the United States in December of 1941 he sought refuge in the Vatican, where he remained until the arrival of Allied troops three years later. Tittmann described Pius XII as "a political pope [and] . . . very possibly, the future will rate him a saint." Gumpel sees great advantage in this assessment and gave interviews to that effect.

Meanwhile, those who would discredit Pius XII look for additional ammunition wherever they can, even if it is only marginally related. Historical data used to discredit Pius IX — incipient anti-Semitism, pretensions to inerrancy, and distrust of non-Catholic states — are deployed against Pacelli by association, as if by sharing the same name and holding a similar conception of their exalted office, they are guilty of the same "misdeeds" and hubris.

Succinctly put: Pius is seen as a failure because, when forced to choose between state and faith, he, in the categorical judgement of Suzanne Brown-Fleming of the Center for Advanced Holocaust Studies at the United States Holocaust Memorial Museum, like "so many members of the Church, chose the former, [which] testifies to the ultimate and wrenching failure — and futility — of the Roman Catholic faith as they understood it."[23] Or: Pius is seen as a noble if tragic figure, fervently denouncing all forms of racism until the end of his life — as was repeatedly illustrated, according to Ronald J. Rychlak, author of *Hitler, the War, and the Pope* (2000) and a professor at the University Mississippi School of Law, in the numerous citations, tributes, and awards that came his way from a variety of sources, including most prominently many U.S. and international Jewish bodies.[24]

In the end, it is, of course, Gumpel's job to investigate, weigh, and argue the cause through its Roman phase, and none can gainsay his passionate commitment to Pacelli. Not infrequently he has been caricatured and pilloried by the media, portrayed as an unregenerated anti-Semite, a pre-conciliar troglodyte, and an historian seriously compromised by his own ideological impulses. In fact, Gumpel is an urbane polyglot — charming, rigorously intelligent and professional, seriously deficient in media savvy, trusting to a fault, and less than impartial. And it is true that he has invested a great deal of personal interest in the cause. He met Pacelli when a child and was impressed by him, suffered the death of many relatives and associates who opposed the Nazis, including his grandfather, was forced to flee Germany, and grew up in a family resolute in its loyalty to the church.

Gumpel's zeal and the support of Pope John Paul II ultimately may not be enough to bring the cause to its desired conclusion. Even if the controversies surrounding Pacelli's "silence" find some kind of resolution, and even if new and unsubstantiated allegations of papal malfeasance arise, there are at least two outstanding reasons for stalling the process. One is the disturbing charge of Pius's involvement in providing assistance to Fascist war criminals seeking escape to South America, and he did this — conspire to smuggle Nazis and their associates via the "ratline" to safety — not because he approved of their behaviour, for he clearly abhorred and condemned it, but because, according to Uki Goni's *The Real Odessa* (2002), he was convinced that they would become archenemies of Communism and therefore of use to the church in its life-and-death struggle with the creed of Lenin and Stalin. Michael Phayer, professor emeritus at the Jesuit Marquette University and author of *The Catholic Church and the Holocaust, 1930–1965* (2000), poses the relevant questions in a stark manner:

If Pius was so saddened about Europe's Jews — as he wrote Berlin Bishop [Konrad von] Preysing in 1944, why did he later help their killers to escape? Why have advocates for Pius's canonization failed to address the ratline issue? Wouldn't it be better for them to admit the facts and then place these failings in the full context of Eugenio Pacelli's life? Perhaps his advocates can make an argument that, because of the Communist threat, the ratline does not disqualify Pius from sainthood. That argument has yet to be made, however.[25]

Phayer's charge of Pius's complicity with the ratline has not gone unchallenged, but his sources and scholarship are solid and the questions he asks have yet to be satisfactorily addressed.

The second outstanding reason for arguing that the process be delayed, if not aborted, can be found in a surprising source and in a surprising publication. Martin Rhonheimer is a priest of the Opus Dei Prelature, an ethics and political philosophy professor at Rome's Opus Dei University of the Holy Cross, and a Swiss Catholic whose family is three-fourths Jewish. In November 2003 he published an article in *First Things* titled "The Holocaust: What Was Not Said," in which he spoke of the sobering fact that, following the November 9–10, 1938, pogrom of the Jews — *Kristallnacht* (The Night of Breaking Glass) — the *only* person to speak out against the infamy was Bernard Lichtenberg, provost of the Berlin Cathedral, who ultimately paid with his life for his witness to the truth. He was canonized by John Paul II (interestingly, Hochhuth includes Lichtenberg in his dedication to *The Deputy*) and is used by Rhonheimer as a reminder of the devastatingly mute response of the church to the unfolding and intensifying persecution of the Jews.

Although Rhonheimer does not pronounce on the Pacelli cause, he does lament the church's timidity on the matter of the Jews, highlights the convergence of both the Vatican and the German episcopate's limited opposition to the persecution of the Jews — at the same time that he notes that they took a more proactive role in protesting the incarceration and deportation of those Jews who had converted to Catholicism — and deplores the fact that the church strove at all costs to avoid confrontation with the state by always seeking some kind of *modus vivendi* that would protect the church's pastoral interests (although never losing sight of the true nature of the negotiating beast).

The church could and did resist Nazi ideology and persecution, argues Rhonheimer, when it came to the faithful, but it failed the Jews abysmally.

> Well-intentioned Catholic apologists continue to produce reports of Church condemnations of Nazism and racism. But these do not really answer the Church's critics. The real problem is not the Church's relationship to National Socialism and racism, but the Church's relationship to the Jews. Here we need what the Church today urges: a "purification of memory and conscience." The Catholic Church's undeniable hostility to National Socialism and racism cannot be used to justify its silence about the persecution of the Jews. It is one thing to explain this silence historically and make it understandable. It is quite another to use such explanations for apologetic purposes.[26]

Rhonheimer would not be unaware of the numerous ironies that beset any discussion of Pacelli, his "silence," and his cause. After all, it was John Paul II, the very pope who inaugurated the new millennium with a liturgy of purification of memory, who was steadfast in his support of Peter Gumpel and the Vatican-inspired efforts to rehabilitate the reputation of Pius XII. He was the Pacelli supporter par excellence, and no advance would be made were it not for his commitment. At the same time, as Rhonheimer well knows, no greater progress was made on Jewish-Catholic relations than during the pontificate of the Polish pope.

Gumpel is proceeding apace, controversy continues unabated, apologists and critics alike refuse to temper their inflammatory rhetoric, moderates feel unheard or sidelined, and in the words of an editorial in the Toronto-based *Catholic Register*, we have all had enough of "intellectual thuggery masquerading as history."

The politics of saint-making calls for a solid dose of pastoral wisdom and a courageous injection of papal diplomacy: shelve the cause for at least a generation. Various factors mitigate against such a development, however. The German Pope Benedict XVI recognizes that his predecessor's commitment to the Pacelli cause jeopardized neither his high standing in the Jewish community nor his commitment to the purification of memory, and that by proceeding with the sainting process he will honour the memory of John Paul II at the same time that he acknowledges the church's need to address its past. Disaffected Catholics who recall, personally or via a mediated nostalgia, the heady days of Catholic triumphalism prior to John XXIII and the Second Vatican Council era are likely to be at least partly mollified by the canonization of a pope who represents the high peak of Catholic self-confidence. It is a propitious time to stem the secular scapegoating of Pius XII as the weak leader during the Second World War and for setting the historical record straight now that *both* his great ideological enemies — Nazism and Communism — have been effectively ground to dust. The Vatican has invested so much energy, time, and personnel in defending its wartime record that to pull back now may be easily construed as either acknowledgement of the weakness of the Pacelli cause or as cowardice in the face of aggressive lobbying tactics.

If Pacelli is one of the church's "monsters of love," recognition of his natural holiness has been sabotaged by the embattled polemics over his "silence." A new purification of memory is needed.

CONCLUSION

PERHAPS ART CRITIC and writer John Bentley Mays said it best in his Civitas Mundi column for *The Catholic Register* when he observed: "I find it reassuring that so many cranky blundering people have become saints. Maybe there's hope for me. After all, sainthood is not about being nice. It's a matter of saying 'yes' to divine love so often you simply forget how to say anything else."[1]

But how do you say yes to divine love? And what are the personal and communal costs of that yes?

In his bestselling work *The Heart of Christianity* (2003), Marcus Borg identifies the Celtic notion of "thin places" as non-specific geographically, as places where our hearts are opened — a sacrament, a channel of grace, indeed saints, "known and unknown, Christian and non-Christian, were (and are) thin places."

But we most directly encounter the saints through that ancient human endeavour: storytelling. In fact, as Kenneth Woodward would have it, storytelling is a form of canonizing:

> . . . those involved in the process by which saints are recognized should appreciate that canonization is a form of story-telling: it locates the life of a saint (itself a form of narrative) within the wider story of God's grace. In this respect, the Catholic imagination still tends to produce impossibly pious biographies of the saints — including, I must say, many of the *positios* produced by the congregation itself. Who can identify with a figure who never committed serious sin, which is the implicattion in nearly all the *positios* I have read?[2]

The squeamishness of dealing with less-than-immaculate dossiers of less-than-immaculate lives underscores the contorted attitude of officialdom when it comes to chronicling the lives of the saints. Take sex, for instance. As soon as it comes into the picture, officials are sent scattering in all directions, rationalizing its presence as if this is the power that can undo everything. Only the most antiseptic, fully laundered, and emasculated (in the gender-free sense of the term) of *positios* ever moves forward. And even the hint of a sexual scandal, an affair, or a less-than-Manichean approach to pleasure can seriously jeopardize the requisite *gravitas* of a case and compromise the possibilities of success.

Peter Gumpel provides a perfect illustration, if unwittingly, of the Vatican's skittishness when it comes to sex: the case of Salvo D'Acquisto.

My Jesuit confrere, Dr. Molinari, along with the chief commander of the *carabinieri* and myself were invited to respond to a television program aired on the state network — RAI — that purported to deal with the life of an heroic member of the *carabinieri* during the German occupation of Italy. A young officer by the name of Salvatore D'Acquisto offered his own life to spare others. Evidently, an attack against the Germans resulted in their determination to exact revenge by executing twenty-two innocent civilians. This prompted D'Acquisto to step forward and accept responsibility (although he knew nothing of the incident) because he thought it best that he be the sacrifice necessary to spare the twenty-two family men. The Germans obliged.

The RAI film demeans D'Acquisto by showing him in bed with a woman. He is represented as a woman chaser, when he was in fact a very pure man who went to Communion daily. The commander, Molinari, and I were outraged and we were part of a two-hour interview to counter the false claims of the film.

Gumpel and the others have every right to be outraged by the misrepresentation of facts, by the sensationalizing of D'Acquisto's love life, and by the egregious introduction of juicy fiction to embellish the story. Nothing to fear, though, as D'Acquisto has passed all the hurdles for beatification. At the same time, Gumpel and his associates may well have missed the real point. D'Acquisto's flesh-and-blood life, sexual struggles and tensions, and spiritual conflicts are the stuff of interest. Their exclusion from the narrative drains the lifeblood out of the *positio*. As writer Ben Okri aphoristically notes in *A Way of Being Free* (1997): "the fact of storytelling hints at a fundamental human unease, hints at human imperfection. Where there is perfection there is no story to tell."

The saints are not perfect. That is the point. And that is why their stories *should* be interesting, were they not so frequently sanitized.

In fact, they can be interesting even when they don't exist. As Eamon Duffy baldly remarks:

A staggering number of the figures who have evoked the most passionate veneration and the most elaborate and popular of cults have in fact been entirely fictitious, or at least no more than a name round which legend congealed. These include some of the most celebrated figures in the calendar, whose images and legends have inspired countless great works of art: Agatha, Barbara, Catherine of Alexandria, Crispin, Christopher, George — the list seems endless.[3]

Those were the old days. Or were they? The canonization in July 2002 of Juan Diego, a Mexican Indian of the sixteenth century on whose cloak was miraculously imprinted an image that became known as Our Lady of Guadalupe, provoked a controversy around the paucity of documentation attesting to his very existence. Historians, ecclesiastics, anthropologists, and theologians all waded in, arguing the comparative merits of moving forward with a case of dubious authenticity. One historian, Fernando Cervantes of Bristol University, argued that since Juan Diego failed to meet the requirements of historicity as laid down by the Congregation of Saints itself, the credibility of the canonization process was called into question. But David Brading, professor of Mexican History at Cambridge University and author of the definitive study *Mexican Phoenix — Our Lady of Guadalupe: Image and Tradition Across Five Centuries* (2001), more sagely concluded that as "Mary is the type of the Church, so Juan Diego is the type, the symbolic, representative figure, of all the Indians whose devotion to Our Lady of Guadalupe brought them into the Mexican Church." In other words, Juan Diego's story — Juan Diego *as* story — is compelling, efficacious, and deeply meaningful.

And we all have our stories of mundane, ordinary holiness that shine incandescently in our own lives. Robert Ellsberg speaks of saintliness as something that can be approximated, touched, and experienced, something nobly mundane rather than "other-worldly":

When I say that I recognize that I am called to be a saint, as we are all called to be saints, it doesn't mean that I am called to be canonized. I doubt very much that is going to happen. I guarantee that it is not going to happen! I don't live and operate in that kind of arena. But it also doesn't mean that I have the ambition to have a church named after me or that anybody at all might recognize my sanctity. It is simply another way of saying that if I call myself a Christian, my vocation is to really live as if that is true in some sense, and that can't be measured by whether I obeyed all the rules, believed all the right things, or went to church every Sunday. If it is real, this Christian life, then it is going to be expressed not through the books I write but in the way I live, the way I express love towards those around me, towards strangers, and even towards my enemies.

Some people are Christian in their behaviour in an heroic fashion, and these are the people who tend to be officially recognized as saints, but that is not the only measure of whether we have achieved our purpose in life or not.

For instance, I came back the other day from the funeral of my son's godmother and one of our closest friends. I can truthfully say that I think that everybody who was at her funeral — there were nine hundred people there — saw her as one of the holiest of persons. Truly a saint. This was never so well expressed as during the last three years when she suffered with a terrible cancer — multiple melanoma — that was diagnosed just after the birth of her second child. She died at the age of forty-five.

Being a martyr means bearing witness to Christ, even to laying down your life. There are few people who are called to be martyrs on some public stage, defending their faith in the face of idolatry or whatever. There are people who bear witness to their faith, to the truth they believe in, by the way they face the difficult challenges of life, by the way they face death.

Right to the end, my friend was a person who made you glad to be in her presence. There was joy in her, and no sense that her suffering, though it was very real, deprived her of access to that truth she lived by.

If her life had been in the recorded annals of the saints, what happened next would have been a certified miracle. After her funeral, we all went back to her brother's house for the reception. It was a beautifully clear day. There were just some wispy clouds in the sky. No rain. We looked up and there was a rainbow literally over the house. It was astonishing. I had never seen that before. I have seen rainbows, of course, after a storm, but I have never seen a rainbow on a nice, clear, sunny day. What did this mean? Her husband, a very pragmatic, mathematically minded Jewish scientist, who was very different from her, who saw things very differently, responded to my observation that the rainbow was just one of the first of many signs. He quipped that "she would have to do a lot better than that to convince me." But in terms of what it means as a miracle, a lot of times it is in the eye of the beholder.

And for Ellsberg the beholder, the rainbow was a sign of the transcendent, his "thin place," his friend, the sacrament. For Jesuit Michael Czerny, saints are icons or windows:

If a person functions as a window that opens out from this flat world of suffering and hopelessness, of materialism, self-indulgence and self-centeredness, if this person, fifty years, five hundred years, or a thousand years ago opened a window for people so that they could and can perceive the other world and at the same time live differently here and now with God and others, then that to me is a valid saint, a valid icon.

An example for me, I think, is St. Aloysius Gonzaga, who until recently was pictured as a nearly unattainable model of purity and religious dedication but who is today the parton saint for those who have AIDS and for those who care for them. St. Aloysius, of course, had never heard of AIDS (he was, after all, a sixteenth-century Jesuit), but he responded with heroic simplicity and generosity to the victims of the plague of his day, and that is what people need to do today for those who have AIDS: respond as he did.

He is a window, for he says to those who have AIDS and their caregivers, "Don't worry if you're discouraged, don't worry if you're suffering, don't worry if you don't have what you need to get better. There's hope and there's life and that's all we really need to know and hear."

We need windows, in the end, not in order to be looking at ourselves and at what our hands have made. No, we need windows, we need icons, we need these saints, because both seeking and finding God is a perilous journey, and you can easily go off the rails. Saints — prophets and martyrs both — help to keep us on the highway to God, I would say. And that's why we need them.

They knew — they know — what "saying yes to divine love" means. The monsters of love teach us how to be fully human.

Epilogue
SAINTHOOD NOW!

SANTO SUBITO! Santo subito! Santo subito! The cry was thunderous, unrelenting, and seemingly spontaneous. The thousands gathered in St. Peter's Square for the funeral Mass of Pope John Paul II on April 8, 2005, left no doubt in the minds of the millions watching the sacred ceremony on television that the late Pontiff was a worthy and popular candidate for sainthood. In fact, if those in the large crowd carrying placards calling for his immediate sainthood and chanting in unison for action to that very same end are illustrative of the widely held view that John Paul II has the stuff for sainthood — and there is strong evidence that this view has wide currency — then it seems a fitting end to a pontificate irreverently dubbed the "sainting machine." After all, John Paul beatified more than 1,300 persons and canonized over 480. There are those who think he should now be added to the list. And among their number is his successor, Benedict XVI.

The new Pontiff waived the five-year waiting period that follows the death of a potential candidate and the opening of the process, as indeed John Paul had in the case of Mother Teresa, and chose to make the announcement himself at a meeting of the Roman clergy in his own church, St. John Lateran, on May 13, 2005. The date is significant because it is the anniversary of the 1981 assassination attempt on the life of John Paul. Wojtyla would have liked that touch. Fond of anniversaries, symbols, providential signs, and supernatural interventions, John Paul's cause may well be fast-tracked — once again, it was the same pontiff who accelerated the process when he saw great value in proceeding with candidates whose sainting could assist greatly with his evangelizing mission. Benedict may have a more qualified fascination with religious epiphenomena, a more skeptical approach to visionaries and stigmatics than his predecessor, but he understands the high importance of sainthood, the labours expended by John Paul II to identify and celebrate the friends of God, and he gives every evidence of responding to the popular request of the masses that John Paul the Polish Pope, John Paul the Great, become St. John Paul II.

On June 28, 2005, Camillo Cardinal Ruini, papal vicar of Rome, formally opened the sainting process in St. John Lateran in the presence of thousands congregated in the church proper and in the palazzo, joined in the service of solemn vespers by John Paul's private secretary, Stanislaw Dziwisz, and the Polish postulator of the Wojtyla cause, Oder Slawomir. Ruini has made no secret of his desire that the pope be beatified quickly, and not a few prelates have even suggested that John Paul should be considered a martyr, given that he shed his blood in St. Peter's Square on May 13, 1981, and continued to offer his blood throughout the rest of his life, "uniting him to Christ and the humanity he redeemed." Given that John Paul broadened the definition of martyr, that he altered the rules so that a miracle is not needed for the beatification and only one is required for the canonization of a martyr, and given the ground-swell of support from so many quarters from both within and outside the Catholic communion for Wojtyla's sainting, the speed with which his cause will be advanced may shatter all records since the first major codification of the rules by Pope Urban VIII in 1642.

As those responsible for preparing the official biography of the Servant of God for the cause undertake their work, they will have much to draw upon. John Paul inspired scores of biographies in numerous languages, ranging in approach from the idolatrous to the hypercritical, from the reverential to the tendentious. In addition, in a manner quite atypical for a supreme pontiff, John Paul published several volumes of autobiography during his lifetime. It was as if he wanted to help guide future scribes in order that they get the record straight.

And what is that record?[1]

The broad outline of Karol Wojtyla's rise from relative obscurity to the pinnacle of ecclesiastical power has been told many times, including in comic-book form. He was born to Wadowice, Poland, in 1920, the second son of Emilia Kacrorowska and Karol Wojtyla, a retired noncommissioned officer. He lost his family very early in life — his mother in 1929, his physician-brother Edward in 1938, and his father in 1941. He lived in a time of unspeakable horrors and of great national turbulence. Poland had emerged from the First World War a fully consti-tuted sovereignty, only to subsequently have its nationhood obliterated by the invading armies of the Third Reich and Soviet empire. Both principalities possessed an abiding hatred for the Poles, who were repeatedly subjected to harsh rule, mass deportations to the camps, arbitrary executions of intellectuals and clergy, and ruthless efforts to implant a "culture of the lie" in the very heart of Polish society and governance.

Like many young Poles, Wojtyla realized that he would have to hold his dreams in check while he survived the tyranny of the moment, so he pursued studies in Polish philology at the school of letters in Krakow's Jagiellonian University until the Nazis closed the university. He picked up work first in a stone quarry and later at the Solvay chemicals factory (he recounts these experiences in some of his verse). He resumed his studies in 1942, this time with the intention of becoming a priest. He did this clandestinely, and after the Warsaw Uprising of 1944 the Prince Cardinal of Krakow, Adam Sapieha, hid his seminarians in the archiepiscopal palace for the duration of the occupation. Wojtyla was ordained in 1946 and immediately sent to Rome to pursue doctoral studies at the Pontifical University of St. Thomas, also known as the Angelicum. He returned to Poland in 1948, and with remarkable speed became head vicar of the

most important parish in Krakow (St. Florian), pursued a
doctorate in philosophy on the eminent German phenomenologist Max Scheler, taught in the faculty of theology in Krakow,
and assumed a professorship of ethics at the Catholic University
in Lublin, where he also founded an institute of moral theology.
And then, barely two weeks before his death on October 9,
1958, Pope Pius XII named him an auxiliary bishop of Krakow
at the age of thirty-eight. At the time, he was the youngest
bishop in the country.

His episcopal career was largely confined to Krakow —
auxiliary bishop, interim administrator, archbishop, and by
1967 cardinal-archbishop — but he was not without influence at
the Second Vatican Council and throughout Communist Europe.
Although not a major player on the universal scene, he sat on
many of the senior bodies at the Vatican, preached the Lenten
retreat at the Holy See at the request of Pope Paul VI, and
began a serious schedule of travelling outside of Poland to
familiarize himself with the Catholic world beyond Europe.
Cardinals of various backgrounds got to know him. And then
the man who made him a cardinal died in 1978.

Paul VI was succeeded by John Paul I (a thirty-three-day
pontificate), and Wojtyla quickly found himself the new pontiff.
A surprise to the world, but not, I wager, to either the electors
or Wojtyla himself. He was installed pope on October 22, 1978.
He would rule the Roman church for twenty-six years.

Such a long and forceful pontificate as the Johan-Pauline is
bound to produce a controversial legacy. On some matters of
doctrine and practice, John Paul II earned global respect and
affection. He championed freedom throughout the world
and confronted those leaders with a taste for the dictatorial in
ways that often indirectly destabilized them. Presidents Marcos
of the Philippines and Duvalier of Haiti rued the day he came to
their shores. The Soviet empire ceased to exist during his
pontificate, and he played a major part in its peaceful disman-

tling. He supported labour rights, advocated on behalf of the rights of indigenous peoples throughout the world, denounced trade sanctions and war (he opposed both Gulf Wars), fostered the dialogue of nations at every level — encouraging peace and harmony among all peoples and creeds — and he struggled nobly and tirelessly up to and including his own very public dying to create a planetary culture of life.

John Paul's openness to new ecumenical initiatives to achieve church unity — his repeated overtures to the Orthodox communities, for instance — disclosed a willingness to find common ground that one did not usually see when it came to internal Roman Catholic matters. He was a firm disciplinarian with little patience for those who departed from the rubrics and canons that define church governance. More important still, in spite of his very public avowal of the rights and liberties of Catholic intellectual life and the demands of rigorous scholarship, he was stern with dissident theologians, not inclined to brook loyal opposition, and balked at any change that threatened to collapse the differences that exist between the clerical state and the lay state. His philosophical anthropology was traditional — man is man and woman is woman — the vocations of the ordained, the consecrated, and the lay are ontologically or essentially discrete and cannot be confused, and his teaching in the areas of sexual morality made no allowance for changing paradigms.

Both a progressive and a restorationist, John Paul was open to new ways of promoting the goals of the church. He celebrated youth when others despaired of them, he saw the media as his ally and not as his intrepid foe, he injected joy and hope into the lives of millions (Catholics and others alike) by affirming their inviolable dignity as human beings, he roused the lukewarm, provoked the cynical, and inspired untold numbers with his courage. In fact, more than any other religious leader in his day, including Billy Graham, he personalized his leadership office, stamped the papacy with his signature, brought Rome to the world, and did it with panache. He was, after all, an actor, a poet, a dramatist, a man who knew his audience. In many ways, he knew them better than they knew him. Because he could be tough, very tough. And he played tough. That's why he survived the Nazis and the Communists and that is why his church has flourished in many parts of the world — and, in many ways, in spite of the divisions he either generated or exacerbated. John Paul was not an irenic figure. He took the world on, with nothing short of a full-frontal strategy. Catholics more than non-Catholics are in sharp disagreement over his legacy, a legacy marked not only by grand and brave gestures and a formidable body of writings, but by a temerity whose granite-like resolve was sometimes shocking. The debates over his universal pastorship, his style of exercising authority, his judgement, and the very direction he took the church will continue for generations because the effects will be felt for generations.

But if there is one ground of consensus, one position around which Catholics of every hue and stripe can coalesce, it is the matter of his personal holiness. That holiness may be daunting, inexplicable, mystical even, and it may puzzle as much as it intimidates, but there is no question as to its authenticity.

But what are the roots of Wojtyla's spirituality? What traditions, devotional practices, modes of prayer, and cultural and historical influences shaped the making of the holy in Karol Wojtyla?

It all began in his native Poland. Polish culture, spirituality, thought, and history made him. He was moulded by the great literary and religious thinkers and artists of Poland, and not just remotely through their writing and art, but sometimes directly, as in the case of Jan Tyranowski, a man Wojtyla considered a mystic and a saint and who introduced him to St. John of the Cross and Carmelite spirituality. But the primary leitmotif that runs through his spirituality is the "Marian thread."

It was during the war, while working in the Solvay plant, that he read the work that he identified as a turning-point: *Treatise on the Most Excellent Devotion to the Most High Virgin* by St. Louis-Marie Grignion de Montfort. The treatise provided him with the intellectual substructure that justified, and made theologically organic, his own personal devotion to the Virgin. Mary was everywhere: his parish church in Wadowice is named the Presentation of the Blessed Virgin Mary; the Marian sanctuary of Kalwaria Zebrzydowska was a favourite haunt during his youth and throughout the early years of his priesthood; he wore the scapular of Our Lady of Mount Carmel from the time he received it at the age of ten at the Carmelite monastery of St. Raphael Kalinowski to the end of his life; and his episcopal motto, *totus tuus* (totally yours), was taken from Montfort himself and defines Mary's total self-oblation. In short, Mary was critical to all that Wojtyla did. He acknowledged her importance in countless ways: his reflections on the Marian aspect of his presbyteral life in *Gift and Mystery: On the Fiftieth Anniversary of My Priestly Ordination*; his encyclical dedicated specifically to Mary, *Redemptoris mater*; his numerous invocations of Mary in his apostolic exhortations, papal locutions, Wednesday-afternoon sermons, and encyclicals of both broad and narrow focus; his public recognition in a talk to the Roman curia that the church, including the Petrine Office that he exercised as pope, took its fundamental form from Mary in her self-surrender to God with her *fiat*; and the special significance that he attached to Marian apparitions, shrines, and titles.

Although there is a theological sophistication to the Pope's Mariological reflections, including some interesting if unconventional exegetical interpretations, the appeal of Marian devotion is at a level of deep personal meaning, indeed mystical. For instance, although Wojtyla professed a strong attachment to such Polish shrines as Czestochowa — home of the Black

Madonna and the last point of resistance to the Swedish invaders of the seventeenth century, thereby underscoring the cultural significance of Marian devotion in his homeland — he had a personal familiarity with, and great attraction to, many of the great (and some more recent) Marian moments in Catholic history: Our Lady of Guadalupe, the patron saint of all the Americas, and a devotion we noted earlier that is associated with St. Juan Diego (of dubious existence) and which actually originated in sixteenth-century Mexico; Our Lady of La Salette, named the Reconciler of Sinners, a nineteenth-century French devotion; Our Lady of Lourdes, also a nineteenth-century French devotion, with the most famous and popular of shrines, which John Paul visited not long before his death; and Our Lady of Fatima, a twentieth-century devotion originating in Portugal, which holds special importance in the life and ministry of John Paul II.

It was on May 13, 1917, that it all began. Three young Portuguese shepherd children — Lucia de Jesus and Francisco and Jacinta Marto — witnessed an apparition of a "Lady brighter than the sun," from whose hands there hung a rosary. The Lady instructed them to pray frequently and invited them to return to the spot of the apparition on several occasions where they could find her. During the last apparition, October 13, 1917, the Lady appeared in the presence of some 70,000 people and informed the children that hereafter she was to be known as Our Lady of the Rosary. In an earlier apparition — July 13 — the Lady had requested that Russia, then in the throes of the Communist Revolution, be consecrated to her Immaculate Heart. This request was subsequently known as the "Secret of Fatima." In time, a commanding shrine would be built on the site of the apparitions. Francisco would die on April 4, 1919, and his sister Jacinta on February 20, 1920, while Lucia would become a Dorothean nun and witness several subsequent apparitions in convents in Pontevedra and Tuy, meet with John Paul personally, and die two months before his death.

The "secret" consists of three parts, two of which were disclosed, and the third of which was rumoured to be known to popes alone. The secret became the subject of great speculation — wild, apocalyptic, millennarian, doomsday — and stories of popes overcome by the power of the message were rampant. On May 13, 2000, the Vatican revealed the third part at a Mass for the beatification of the two Marto children celebrated at the Shrine of Our Lady of Fatima by John Paul himself. Angelo Cardinal Sodano, the Vatican secretary of state, read an address at the Mass that both revealed the content of the third part and provided a context for interpreting its meaning. The text includes a prophetic vision that graphically describes a scene in which "a bishop clothed in white" makes his way with great effort toward a cross. His path is strewn with the corpses of the martyred — bishops, priests, women and men religious, and laypeople as well — and then he too falls on the same cluttered ground, apparently dead, felled by a fusillade of bullets.

On May 13, 1981, John Paul was wounded in St. Peter's Square in an assassination attempt by Turkish terrorist Mehmet Ali Agca. The Pontiff concluded that, as he said in a meditation with the Italian bishops at the Gemelli Polyclinic in 1994, it was "a motherly hand which guided the bullet's path, enabling the dying pope to halt at the threshold of death." In time, the Pope would send this very bullet to be set in the crown of the statue of Our Lady of Fatima in Portugal.

In addition to the special intervention by the Blessed Virgin Mary to spare his life — a conviction he held unwaveringly — the Pope attached special significance to her intercessory role in the collapse of the Soviet empire that commenced in 1989. She was a player on both the private and the international plane.

Wojtyla is not the only modern pope with a private devotion to Mary. Pius XII has been called the Pope of Mary for his 1950 exercise of papal infallibility when he defined as dogma the Assumption of the Blessed Virgin Mary, for consecrating Russia

— and then the whole world — to the Immaculate Heart of the Virgin, for solemnly proclaiming a Marian Year, and for instituting the Feast of the Queenship of Mary, in addition to other things. John XXIII had a strong devotion to Mary, as one can easily see in his popular *Journal of a Soul*, and Paul VI authored the sane, measured, and insightful 1974 apostolic exhortation on Marian devotion, *Marialis cultus*.

But for John Paul II, Mary forms the essential part of his spiritual triptych. The other two parts — his Polish blood and the contemplative tradition of the Carmelites — combine with his love of Mary to find unique expression in his veneration of Maria Faustina Kowalska of the Most Blessed Sacrament. A religious of the Congregation of the Sisters of Our Lady of Mercy, she spent her entire life as a nun — about thirteen years in total — given over to the imitation of Christ through sacrifice, humility, and compassion. On February 22, 1931, she had a vision in her cell of Christ with rays of mercy streaming from his heart. He instructed her to have an image painted to represent this vision, which was to bear the legend "Jesus, I trust in you." Christ also commanded her to write a diary so that others could come to know and trust him — a work that was eventually published as *Divine Mercy in My Soul* — and she continued to have revelations between 1931 and 1938. Christ continually emphasized the unlimited and non-discriminating nature of his mercy, and it was this aspect of Jesus that most appealed to her. She died of tuberculosis on October 5, 1938, a year before the war she is said to have predicted.

Throughout the years of Nazi domination of Poland, her cult spread, and she was, as John Paul II has remarked, "a particular support and an inexhaustible source of hope." Faustina's emphasis on the divine mercy greatly appealed to John Paul, and he made a special visit to the Shrine of Divine Mercy in Lagiewniki in 1997 to pray at her tomb. Located in the Archdiocese of Krakow and adjacent to the Solvay chemical plant, Wojtyla would have known it well. In fact, speaking of the message of the Divine Mercy, the Pope identified it as "a message that has always been near and dear to me . . . and in a sense forms the image of this pontificate." As Archbishop of Krakow he promoted her cause for sainthood, and as pope he canonized her — the first of the new millennium — thereby underlining the significance he consistently attached to the contemplative life, to the self-emptying quality of Mary's total love, and to the unique mosaic that is Polish culture and spirituality. Not insignificantly, John Paul II introduced the causes, beatified, and canonized more Poles than any previous pontiff. Some, like Adam Chmielowski, were nationally recognized figures. Chmielowski was a religious brother, a patriot who lost a leg during the January Uprising of 1864, a painter, mendicant, and radical Christian who walked, as John Paul II notes, "in the footsteps of Saint Francis of Assisi and Saint John of the Cross." He was beatified in Blonia Krakowskie during a papal visit to Poland in 1983, and canonized in Rome six years later. Others who were either raised to the altars or poised for such were more local and personal. They include Wojtyla's schoolmate Jurek Ciesielski, Polish bishops Jozef Bilczewski and Jozef Sebastian Pelczar, pastoral servant of the sick and suffering Hanna Chrzanowska, Communist resister Franciszek Blachnicki, and educator Urszula Ledochowska.

Wojtyla took to heart the words of the priest-founder of the Congregation of St. Michael the Archangel, Blessed Bronislao Bonaventure Markiewicz, that "when a nation lacks saints, darkness invades people's minds and they no longer see the paths to follow." John Paul would see to it that not only Poland, but as many nations as possible, would not lack saints.

Benedict XVI, Joseph Ratzinger, Wojtyla's intellectually formidable prefect of the Congregation for the Doctrine of the Faith and now his successor as pontiff, is a theologian of greater stature than Wojtyla himself, has in many ways a different spirituality than his predecessor, and does not appear to be as interested in adding to the roll call of saints. His pastoral strategies and priorities are different. But both men are profoundly christocentric in their theology, not inclined to compromise the deposit of the faith, engaged in vigorously promoting a philosophical framework at odds with the legacy of the Enlightenment, and utterly persuaded of the burdens and mandate of the Petrine Office. Benedict entertains no doubts over the personal holiness of his former boss, although for a pope to canonize another pope is not a regular ecclesial occurrence. The last canonized pope is Pius X, who ruled from 1903 until 1914 and was canonized by Pius XII in 1954. Before him was Pius V, who ruled from 1566 through 1572 and was added to the list in 1712. Quite a gap.

Although it was Paul VI who introduced the causes of Pius XII and John XXIII in the last year of the Second Vatican Council, it was John Paul II who beatified John and his nineteenth-century predecessor, the long-reigning *bête noire* of all things liberal, Pius IX. Pius XII, as we have seen, is still embroiled in controversy. The cause of the Germanophile pope is now in the hands of a German pope.

Benedict has also revived the practice of reserving beatifications for cardinal-designates, leaving canonizations for himself, an established papal prerogative for a millennium. John Paul II, by contrast, beatified 1,330 Servants of God himself. Another difference.

Still, there is every evidence that Benedict would welcome the opportunity to preside over the canonization of Karol Wojtyla. Time is of the essence. In spite of the popular support and the echoes of *santo subito* reverberating in the ears of the dicasterial cardinals of the Congregation for the Causes of Saints, the process, although abbreviated, is not likely to be overridden, and Benedict was elected in his late seventies. Still, as theologian Joseph A. Komonchak noted earlier, pressure on Pope

Paul VI to canonize John XXIII by acclamation at the end of the Second Vatican Council could suggest that Benedict XVI might well find himself lobbied at an episcopal synod, extraordinary consistory, or World Youth Day to do what has yet to be done in modern times: bypass the procedures and acclaim Karol Wojtyla a saint. After all, sainting, in the end, is a papal prerogative.

Still, it's all a matter of eternity, as I am sure Karol Wojtyla and Saint Pancratius would both agree.

Notes

Introduction

1. Robert Ellsberg, *The Saints' Guide to Happiness* (New York: North Point Press, 2003), p. xiv.
2. Robertson Davies, *Fifth Business* (Toronto: Penguin Books, 1977), p. 164.
3. Bernard Shaw, *Saint Joan* (Toronto: Penguin Plays, 1975), pp. 137–38.
4. *The Tablet* (23 January 1988), pp. 85–86.
5. Michael W. Higgins, "The Jesuit Mystique," episode of *Ideas*, CBC Radio One, originally aired in 1995.
6. Ann-Marie MacDonald, *Credo*, Vision TV, February 3, 2004.
7. Ron Rolheiser, *The Catholic Register*, February 23, 2004.
8. Joanna Manning, "The Communion of Saints," *The Social Edge* [e-zine], November 20, 2002.
9. George Steiner, *Nostalgia for the Absolute* (Toronto: CBC Publications, 1974), pp. 5–6.
10. Richard P. McBrien, *Lives of the Saints: From Mary and St. Francis of Assisi to John XXIII and Mother Teresa* (San Francisco: HarperSanFrancisco, 2001), p. 4.
11. Nicholas Zernov, *Eastern Christendom* (1961), as quoted by Anthony M. Coniaris, *Introducing The Orthodox Church: Its Faith and Life* (Minneapolis: Light and Life Publishing, 1982), p. 102.
12. Peter Henderson, "Nicholas declared martyr and saint," *The New York Times*, August 21, 2000.
13. Donald Smith, "A Sign for Russia," *The Tablet*, 30 September 2000, pp. 1293–94.

14. Kathleen Jones, *The Saints of the Anglican Calendar* (Norwich: Canterbury Press, 2000), p. viii.
15. *Lives of the Saints*, p. 54.
16. Robert Ellsberg, "Joy's silver thread," *The Tablet*, 1 May 2004, pp. 6–7.
17. Robert Coles, Introduction, *A Tremor of Bliss: Contemporary Writers on the Saints*, ed. Paul Elie (New York: Harcourt, Brace & Company, 1994), p. xxv.

Chapter One: The Process and the Controversies

1. Ron Hansen, "What Stories Are and Why We Read Them," *A Stay Against Confusion: Essays on Faith and Fiction* (New York: HarperCollins, 2001), p. 39.
2. "Lumen gentium," *Vatican Council II: The Conciliar and Post-Conciliar Documents*, ed. Austin Flannery, O.P. (Boston: St. Paul Editions, 1988), p. 411.
3. Robert J. Sarno, "Theological Reflections on Canonization," *Canonization: Theology, History, Process*, ed. William H. Woestman, O.M.I. (Ottawa: Saint Paul University, 2002), p. 9.
4. James Fitzpatrick, O.M.I., "Commentary on the Present Legislation and Norms — Glossary of Terms," *Canonization: Theology, History, Process*, p. 140.
5. John F. Coverdale, "The Anticlericalism of the Early Second Republic," *Passionately Loving the World: The Message of Saint Josemaría Escrivá*, eds. Elmar J. Kremer and Teresa A. Tomory (Toronto: Legas, 2004), p. 48.
6. Michael Walsh, *The Secret World of Opus Dei* (London: Grafton Books, 1990), p. 144.
7. Michael W. Higgins and Douglas R. Letson, *Power and Peril: The Catholic Church at the Crossroads* (Toronto: HarperCollins, 2002), p. 380.
8. Annabel Miller, "Opus Dei in England: 1, Saints in the office," *The Tablet*, 10 November 2001, p. 1598.

9. Douglas R. Letson, ed., *Sex and Marriage in the Catholic Tradition: An Historical Overview* (Ottawa: Novalis, 2001), p. 11.

10. Jack Dominian, letter to the editor, *The Tablet*, 3 November 2001, p. 1568.

11. J. L. Granatstein, "Georges Vanier: As governor-general, he spoke for both founding peoples," *Maclean's*, July 1, 1998.

12. Claude Ryan, Foreword, *Only to Serve: Selections from Addresses of Governor-General Georges P. Vanier*, ed. George Cowley and Michel Vanier (Toronto: University of Toronto Press, 1970), p. xi.

13. Kathleen Norris, *The Cloister Walk* (New York: Riverside Books, 1996), p. 234.

14. *The Cloister Walk*, pp. 234–35.

15. Rudolph M.Bell and Cristina Mazzoni, *The Voices of Gemma Galgani: The Life and Afterlife of a Modern Saint* (Chicago: University of Chicago Press, 2003), p. xi.

16. Catherine Sasanov, "Reassembling the Bodily Relics of St. Gemma Galgani," *Commonweal*, June 18, 2004, p. 11.

17. Hilary Mantel, "Sisterhood of Saints," *The Tablet*, 6 March 2004, p. 13.

18. Frances Kennedy, "Gianna's choice," *The Tablet*, 22 May 2004, p. 4.

19. Thomas Rosica, "Saint Gianna Beretta Molla: Mother, Doctor, and Lover of Life," *Legatus*, May 2004, p. 14.

20. As quoted by Frances Kennedy, *The Tablet*, p. 5.

21. Leslie Scrivener, "Modern saint loved fashion, family, fast cars," *Saturday Star*, July 17, 2004, p. A22.

22. Michael Valpy, "Canonization of pediatrician expected to fuel abortion battle," *The Globe and Mail*, May 12, 2004, p. A3.

23. Kathleen Jones, *Women Saints: Lives of Faith and Courage* (Maryknoll: Orbis Books, 1999), p. ix.

24. Paul Mariani, *Thirty Days: On Retreat with the Exercises of St. Ignatius* (New York: Viking Compass, 2002), p. 79.
25. *Friends of God and Prophets*, pp. 242–43.

Chapter Two: The Causes and the Controversies
1. Gerard Noel, "An Emperor heads for sainthood," *The Catholic Herald*, 16 January 2004, p. 6.
2. As reported by Christa Pongratz-Lippitt in "The Church in the World," *The Tablet*, 3 May 2003, p. 28.
3. Geoffrey Gneuhs, "A saint from Brooklyn," *The Tablet*, 23 May 1998, p. 663.
4. Patrick Jordan, "A model disciple," Letters, *The Tablet*, 29 July 2000, p. 1017.
5. Joseph A. Komonchak, "Remembering Good Pope John," *Commonweal*, August 11, 2000, p. 14.
6. Eamon Duffy, "It takes all sorts to make a saint," *The Tablet*, 9 September 2000, p. 1182.
7. Philippe Levillain, general editor, *The Papacy: An Encyclopedia*, Volume 2 (London: Routledge, 2002), p. 855.
8. Donald Nicholl, "Saints for peace," *The Tablet*, 4 January 1992, p. 8.
9. Robert J. Sarno, "Theological Reflections on Canonization," *Canonization*, p. 14.
10. Michael W. Higgins and Douglas R. Letson, as quoted in *The Jesuit Mystique* (Toronto: Macmillan, 1995), p. 126.

Chapter Three: Padre Pio: Saint and Stigmatic
1. John Cornwell, "Why I am still a Catholic: Graham Greene on God, sex and death," *The Tablet*, 23 September 1989, pp. 1086–87.
2. Gennaro Preziuso, *The Life of Padre Pio: Between the Altar and the Confessional*. Trans. and ed. Jordan Aumann, OP (New York: Alba House, 2000), p. 106.
3. Ibid., p. 103.

4. Ibid., p. 107.

5. G. K. Chesterton, *St. Francis of Assisi* (New York: Image Books/Doubleday, 1957), pp. 131–32.

6. Donald Spoto, *Reluctant Saint: The Life of Francis of Assisi* (New York: Viking Compass, 2002), pp. 190–91.

7. "The Word from Rome," *National Catholic Reporter*, December 28, 2001.

8. As found reprinted from *Inside the Vatican* on Catholic Culture web site, http://www.catholicculture.org/index.cfm.

9. As quoted on the American Atheists web site in "Fleeing Sex Scandal Coverage, Pope Canonizes Huckster Friar," posted June 17, 2002, at http://www.atheists.org/flash.line/vat12.htm.

10. As quoted in Douglas Johnson's review of *Padre Pio: The True Story* by C. Bernard Ruffin, *Homiletic & Pastoral Review*, January 1983, p. 76.

11. Rev. Father Jean, OFM.,Cap., *Blessed Padre Pio*, reprinted in *Catholic Family News* and available online from http://olrl.org/lives/padrepio.html.

12. *Padre Pio: In My Own Words* (London: Hodder & Stoughton, 2001), compiled and edited by Anthony F. Chiffolo, p. 110.

Chapter Four: Teresa of Calcutta: God's Pencil

1. Gillian Girodat, "Life in Canada is the dawn of a new era," *The Catholic Register*, December 29, 2002–January 5, 2003, p. 9.

2. Donald Nicholl, "Holiness: A Call to Radical Living," *Grail: An Ecumenical Journal*, Volume 5, Issue 4, 1989, pp. 70–72.

3. Mario Cardinal, *Blessed Mother Teresa of Calcutta: The Making of a Saint* (Ottawa: Novalis/CBC Radio-Canada, 2003), p. 58.

4. *No Greater Love: Mother Teresa* ed. Becky Benenate and Joseph Durepos (Novato, Calif.: New World Library, 2002), p. 194.

5. *Blessed Mother Teresa of Calcutta: The Making of a Saint*, p. 62.

6. Paul Williams, *The Life and Work of Mother Teresa* (Indianapolis: Alpha Books, 2002), p. viii.

7. Christopher Hitchens, *The Missionary Position: Mother Teresa in Theory and Practice* (London: Verso, 1995), p. 98.

8. Christopher Hitchens, "The Devil and Mother Teresa," *Vanity Fair*, October 2001, p. 172.

9. Jim Holt, "The Life of the Saint," *The New Yorker*, August 13, 2001, p. 78.

10. Germaine Greer, "Unmasking the Mother," *Newsweek*, September 22, 1997, p. 33.

11. As quoted in *Blessed Mother Teresa of Calcutta: The Making of a Saint*, p. 97.

12. *The Life and Work of Mother Teresa*, p. 119.

13. John Allemang, "In God's fast lane," *The Globe and Mail*, October 11, 2003, p. F4.

14. "Miracles under the microscope," *The Economist*, April 22, 2000, p. 79.

15. Mary Catherine Hilkert, *Speaking with Authority: Catherine of Siena and the Voices of Women Today* (New York: Paulist Press, 2001), p. 140.

16. Malcolm Muggeridge, *Conversion: A Spiritual Journey* (London: Collins, 1988), p. 138.

Chapter Five: **Pope Pius XII:**
Christ's Embroiled Deputy

1. Shirley Williams, *God and Caesar: Personal Reflections on Politics and Religion* (South Bend, Ind.: University of Notre Dame Press, 2003), pp. 2–3.

2. Justus George Lawler, *Popes and Politics: Reform, Resentment, and the Holocaust* (New York: Continuum, 2002), p. 138.

3. As quoted in Owen Chadwick, *Britain and the Vatican during the Second World War* (Cambridge: Cambridge University Press, 1986), p. 316.

4. José M. Sánchez, *Pius XII and the Holocaust: Understanding the Controversy* (Washington: The Catholic University of American Press, 2002), p. 179.

5. *The Papacy: An Encyclopedia* (London: Routledge, 2002), Philippe Levillain, general editor, p. 1214.

6. David Remnick, "The Spirit Level," *The New Yorker*, November 8, 2004, p. 86.

7. Primo Levi, *The Drowned and the Saved* (New York: Vintage International, 1989), p. 21.

8. Istvan Deak, "Jews and Catholics," *The New York Review of Books*, December 19, 2002, p. 44.

9. Michael R. Marrus, "Men of Their Time and Place," *Commonweal*, May 7, 2004, p. 30.

10. Michael R. Marrus, "The Ambassador and the Pope: Pius XII, Jacques Maritain and the Jews," *Commonweal*, October 22, 2004, p. 18.

11. John Wijngaards, "A saint from Holland," *The Tablet*, 2 November 1985, p. 1152.

12. As quoted in Mary Craig, "Maximilian Kolbe," *CTS Twentieth Century Martyrs: Victims of the Nazis* (London: CTS Publications, 1997), p. 14.

13. As quoted in Michael W. Higgins and Douglas R. Letson, *Power and Peril: The Catholic Church at the Crossroads* (Toronto: HarperCollins, 2002), pp. 61–62.

14. As quoted in Mary Frances Coady, *With Bound Hands — A Jesuit in Nazi Germany: The Life and Selected Prison Letters of Alfred Delp* (Chicago: Loyola University Press, 2003), p. 140.

15. Thomas Merton, Introduction, *The Prison Meditations of Father Alfred Delp* (New York: Herder and Herder, 1963), p. xxiii.

16. For a fuller discussion of Merton and the Eichmann Affair, please see my *Heretic Blood: The Spiritual Geography of Thomas Merton* (Toronto: Stoddart, 1998), pp. 163–67.

17. Rolf Hochhuth, "Should the Theater Portray the Contemporary World?", *Essays on German Theater* (New York: Continuum, 1985) ed. Margaret Herzfeld-Sander, p. 268.

18. John Cornwell, *Hitler's Pope: The Secret History of Pius XII* (New York: Viking, 1999), p. 384.

19. Owen Chadwick, "Was Pius XII 'Hitler's Pope'?" *The Tablet*, 23 September 1999, p. 1285.

20. Michael Marrus, "One-sided assault links Catholic Church to Holocaust," *The Globe and Mail*, November 2, 2002, p. D2.

21. David G. Dalin, "Pope Pius XII and the Jews," *CCJU Perspective*, Fall 2001, p. 22.

22. "The Untold Story: Catholic Rescuers of Jews," an interview with Sir Martin Gilbert conducted by William Doino Jr., *Inside the Vatican*, August 2003, pp. 28–29.

23. Suzanne Brown-Fleming, "The Wartime Role of Pope Pius XII," H-German Internet (German History newsgroup), February 8, 2005.

24. See Ronald J. Rychlak, "Goldhagen vs. Pius XII," *First Things*, June/July 2002.

25. Michael Phayer, "Canonizing Pius XII: Why did the pope help Nazis escape?" *Commonweal*, May 9, 2003, p. 23.

26. Martin Rhonheimer, "The Holocaust: What Was Not Said," *First Things*, November 2003, p. 27.

Conclusion

1. John Bentley Mays, "Saying 'yes' to divine love," *The Catholic Register*, January 12, 2003, p. 13.
2. Kenneth Woodward, "Slow up on saint-making," *The Tablet*, 13 November 1999, p. 1540.
3. Eamon Duffy, *Faith of Our Fathers: Reflections on Catholic Tradition* (New York: Continuum, 2004), p. 40.

Epilogue: **Sainthood Now!**

1. The following material on John Paul II's biography and spirituality is in part a distillation of a more detailed argument that I make in "Peter's Unsteady Barque," *Power and Peril: The Catholic Church at the Crossroads* (Toronto: HarperCollins, 2002).

Interviews

John Allen, author and columnist, Rome, Italy, June 20, 2002

Rudolph Bell, historian, Rutgers University, New Brunswick, New Jersey, September 11, 2003

Mary Frances Coady, author and teacher, CBC, Toronto, Ontario, December 6, 2004

John Corriveau, Capuchin friar, Rome, Italy, June 17, 2002

Michael Czerny, Jesuit scholar and activist, Rome, Italy, June 18, 2002

Istvan Deak, professor emeritus of history, Columbia University, New York, New York, September 12, 2003

Gerardo di Fiumeri, vice-postulator for the Capuchins, Rome, Italy, June 17, 2002

Robert Ellsberg, publisher and author, Maryknoll, New York, September 25, 2004

Peter Gumpel, Jesuit relator, Rome, Italy, October 17, 2003

Ron Hansen, novelist and screenwriter, Santa Clara, California, April 18, 2000

Elizabeth Johnson, sister of the Congregation of St. Joseph and theologian, Fordham University, New York, September 12, 2003

Brian Kolodiejchuk, priest of the Missionaries of Charity and postulator, Rome, Italy, October 16, 2003

Susannah Malarkey, Dominican nun, Santa Sabina Retreat
Center, Dominican University, San Rafael, California,
April 17, 2000

Michael Marrus, historian and Holocaust Studies Chair, CBC,
Toronto, Ontario, December 1, 2003

Robert Mickens, reporter and columnist, Rome, Italy,
June 20, 2002

Paolo Molinari, Jesuit postulator, Rome, Italy, June 19, 2002

Robert Sarno, Vatican official in the Congregation for the
Causes of Saints, Rome, Italy, June 20, 2002

Kathryn Spink, biographer, Rome, Italy, October 18, 2003

Wieslaw Spiewak, postulator for the Congregation of the
Resurrection, Capranica, Italy, June 19, 2002

Florio Tessari, postulator for the Capuchins, Rome, Italy,
June 17, 2002

Lucinda Vardey, author, Rome, Italy, October 17, 2003

Kenneth Woodward, journalist and religion editor emeritus,
Newsweek, New York, New York, November 27, 2001

Sources Cited

Allemang, John. "In God's Fast Lane." *The Globe and Mail*, October 11, 2003.

Allen Jr., John L. "The Word from Rome." *National Catholic Reporter*, December 28, 2001.

American Atheists Inc. "Fleeing Sex Scandal Coverage, Pope Canonizes Huckster Friar." *American Atheists*. Posted June 17, 2002. http://www.atheists.org/flash.line/vat12.htm.

As found reprinted from Inside the Vatican on Catholic Culture website, http://www.catholicculture.org/index.cfm. *Inside the Vatican*. Martin de Porres Lay Dominican Community. Trinity Communications, 2004.

Bell, Rudolph M. and Cristina Mazzoni. *The Voices of Gemma Galgani: The Life and Afterlife of a Modern Saint*. Chicago: University of Chicago Press, 2003.

Benenate, Becky and Joseph Durepos, eds. *No Greater Love: Mother Teresa* ed. Novato, Calif.: New World Library, 2002.

Borg, Marcus J. *The Heart of Christianity*. Toronto: HarperCollins, 2003.

Brading, David. *Mexican Phoenix — Our Lady of Guadalupe: Image and Tradition Across Five Centuries*. Cambridge: Cambridge University Press, 2001.

Brown-Fleming, Suzanne. "The Wartime Role of Pope Pius XII." H-German Internet (German History newsgroup). As provided by Scott Kline, Assistant Professor of Religious Studies, St. Jerome's University.

Butler, Fr. Alban. *Lives of the Saints*. Edited, revised, and supplemented by Herbert Thurston and Donald Attwater, New York, 1956.

Cardinal, Mario. *Blessed Mother Teresa of Calcutta: The Making of a Saint*. Ottawa: Novalis/CBC Radio-Canada, 2003.

Chadwick, Owen. *Britain and the Vatican during the Second World War*. Cambridge: Cambridge University Press, 1986.

———. "Was Pius XII 'Hitler's Pope'?" *The Tablet*, September 23, 1999.

Chesterton, G. K. *St. Francis of Assisi*. New York: Image Books/Doubleday, 1957.

Chiffolo, Anthony F., ed. *Padre Pio: In My Own Words*. London: Hodder & Stoughton, 2001.

Coady, Mary Frances. *With Bound Hands — A Jesuit in Nazi Germany: The Life and Selected Prison Letters of Alfred Delp*. Chicago: Loyola University Press, 2003.

Cohen, Leonard. *Beautiful Losers*. Toronto: McClelland & Stewart, 2003. As quoted by S. T. Georgiou, *The Way of the Dreamcatcher: Spirit Lessons with Robert Lax: Poet, Peacemaker, Sage*. Ottawa: Novalis, 2002, p. 281.

Coles, Robert. Introduction. *A Tremor of Bliss: Contemporary Writers on the Saints*. Edited by Paul Elie. New York: Harcourt, Brace & Company, 1994.

Cornwell, John. "Why I Am Still a Catholic: Graham Greene on God, Sex and Death." *The Tablet*, September 23, 1989.

———. *Hitler's Pope: The Secret History of Pius XII*. New York: Viking, 1999.

Coverdale, John F. "The Anticlericalism of the Early Second Republic." *Passionately Loving the World: The Message of Saint Josemaría Escrivá.* Edited by Elmar J. Kremer and Teresa A. Tomory. Toronto: Legas, 2004.

Craig, Mary. "Maximilian Kolbe." *CTS Twentieth Century Martyrs: Victims of the Nazis.* London: CTS Publications, 1997.

Dalin, David G. "Pope Pius XII and the Jews." *CCJU Perspective,* Fall 2001.

Davies, Robertson. *Fifth Business.* Toronto: Penguin Books, 1977.

Day, Dorothy. *The Long Loneliness.* Toronto: HarperCollins, 1981.

Deak, Istvan. "Jews and Catholics." *The New York Review of Books,* December 19, 2002.

Dominian, Jack. Letter to the editor. *The Tablet,* November 3, 2001.

Duffy, Eamon. "It Takes All Sorts to Make a Saint." *The Tablet,* September 9, 2000.

———. *Faith of Our Fathers: Reflections on Catholic Tradition.* New York: Continuum, 2004.

El Feki, Shereen. "Miracles Under the Microscope." *The Economist,* April 22, 2000.

Ellsberg, Robert. *The Saints' Guide to Happiness.* New York: North Point Press, 2003.

———. "Joy's Silver Thread." *The Tablet,* May 1, 2004.

Fitzpatrick, James, O.M.I. "Commentary on the Present
    Legislation and Norms — Glossary of Terms."
    Canonization: Theology, History, Process. Edited by William
    H. Woestman. Ottawa: Faculty of Canon Law, Saint Paul
    University, 2002.

Gilbert, Sir Martin. "The Untold Story: Catholic Rescuers of
    Jews." Interview conducted by William Doino Jr. *Inside the
    Vatican*, August 2003.

Girodat, Gillian. "Life in Canada Is the Dawn of a New Era."
    The Catholic Register, December 29, 2002–January 5, 2003.

Goddard, Peter. "The Art of Faith." *The Toronto Star*, May 19,
    2002.

Goldhagen, Daniel. "Pope Pius XII, the Catholic Church, and
    the Holocaust: What Would Jesus Have Done?" *The New
    Republic*, January 21, 2002.

Gneuhs, Geoffrey. "A Saint from Brooklyn." *The Tablet*, May
    23, 1998.

Granatstein, J. L. "Georges Vanier: As Governor-General, He
    Spoke for Both Founding Peoples." *Maclean's*, July 1, 1998.

Greer, Germaine. "Unmasking the Mother." *Newsweek*.
    September 22, 1997.

Hansen, Ron. "What Stories Are and Why We Read Them." *A
    Stay Against Confusion: Essays on Faith and Fiction*. New York:
    HarperCollins, 2001.

Henderson, Peter. "Nicholas Declared Martyr and Saint." *The
    New York Times*, August 21, 2000.

Higgins, Michael W. "The Jesuit Mystique," episode of *Ideas*,
    CBC Radio One, originally aired in 1995.

Higgins, Michael W. and Douglas R. Letson. *Power and Peril: The Catholic Church at the Crossroads.* Toronto: HarperCollins, 2002.

Hilkert, Mary Catherine. *Speaking with Authority: Catherine of Siena and the Voices of Women Today.* New York: Paulist Press, 2001.

Hitchens, Christopher. *The Missionary Position: Mother Teresa in Theory and Practice.* London: Verso, 1995.

———. "The Devil and Mother Teresa." *Vanity Fair*, October 2001.

Hochhuth, Rolf. "Should the Theater Portray the Contemporary World?" *Essays on German Theater.* Edited by Margaret Herzfeld-Sander. New York: Continuum, 1985.

Holbock, Ferdinand. *Married Saints and Blesseds Through the Centuries.* Ignatius Press, 2002.

Holt, Jim. "The Life of the Saint." *The New Yorker*, August 13, 2001.

Johnson, Douglas. Review of *Padre Pio: The True Story* by C. Bernard Ruffin. *Homiletic & Pastoral Review*, January 1983.

Johnson, Elizabeth A. *Friends of Gods and Prophets: A Feminist Theological Reading of the Communion of the Saints.* New York: The Continuum Publishing Company, 1999.

Jones, Kathleen. *Women Saints: Lives of Faith and Courage.* Maryknoll: Orbis Books, 1999.

———. *The Saints of the Anglican Calendar.* Norwich: Canterbury Press, 2000.

Jordan, Patrick. "A Model Disciple." Letters, *The Tablet*, July 29, 2000.

Kennedy, Frances. "Gianna's Choice." *The Tablet*, May 22, 2004.

Komonchak, Joseph A. "Remembering Good Pope John." *Commonweal*, August 11, 2000.

Lawler, Justus George. *Popes and Politics: Reform, Resentment, and the Holocaust*. New York: Continuum, 2002.

Letson, Douglas R., ed. *Sex and Marriage in the Catholic Tradition: An Historical Overview*. Ottawa: Novalis, 2001.

Levi, Primo. *The Drowned and the Saved*. New York: Vintage International, 1989.

Levillain, Philippe, ed. *The Papacy: An Encyclopedia*, Vol. 2. London: Routledge, 2002.

Lieven, Anatol. "A Saint of Islam." *The Tablet*, November 24, 1990.

"Lumen gentium." *Vatican Council II: The Conciliar and Post-Conciliar Documents*. Edited by Austin Flannery, O.P. Boston: St. Paul Editions, 1988.

MacDonald, Ann-Marie. *Credo*. Vision TV, February 3, 2004.

Manning, Joanna. "The Communion of Saints." *The Social Edge*, November 20, 2002. http://www.thesocialedge.com/archives/joannamanning/columns-nov2002.htm.

Mantel, Hilary. "Sisterhood of Saints." *The Tablet*, March 6, 2004.

Mariani, Paul. *Thirty Days: On Retreat with the Exercises of St. Ignatius*. New York: Viking Compass, 2002.

Marrus, Michael. "One-Sided Assault Links Catholic Church to Holocaust." *The Globe and Mail*, November 2, 2002.

———. "Men of Their Time and Place." *Commonweal*, May 7, 2004.

———. "The Ambassador and the Pope: Pius XII, Jacques Maritain and the Jews." *Commonweal*, October 22, 2004.

Mays, John Bentley. "Saying 'Yes' to Divine Love." *The Catholic Register*, January 12, 2003.

McBrien, Richard P. *Lives of the Saints: From Mary and St. Francis of Assisi to John XXIII and Mother Teresa*. San Francisco: HarperSanFrancisco, 2001.

Merton, Thomas. Introduction. *The Prison Meditations of Father Alfred Delp*, by Fr. Alfred Delp. New York: Herder and Herder, 1963.

Miller, Annabel. "Opus Dei in England: 1, Saints in the Office." *The Tablet*, November 10, 2001.

Morris, Michael. "Christ's Passion and Gibson's Lynching." *New Oxford Review*, February 2004.

Muggeridge, Malcolm. *Conversion: A Spiritual Journey*. London: Collins, 1988.

Nicholl, Donald. "Holiness: A Call to Radical Living." *Grail: An Ecumenical Journal* 5.4 (1989).

———. "Saints for Peace." *The Tablet*, January 4, 1992.

Noel, Gerard. "An Emperor Heads for Sainthood." *The Catholic Herald*, January 16, 2004.

Norris, Kathleen. *The Cloister Walk*. New York: Riverside Books, 1996.

"Notebook." *The Tablet*, January 23, 1988.

Novak, Michael. "Pius XII as Scapegoat." *First Things*, August/September 2000.

Okri, Ben. *A Way of Being Free*. Toronto: McArthur & Co/ Orion Con Trad, 1997.

Phayer, Michael. "Canonizing Pius XII: Why Did the Pope Help Nazis Escape?" *Commonweal*, May 9, 2003.

Pongratz-Lippitt, Christa. "The Church in the World." *The Tablet*, May 3, 2003.

Pope John Paul II. Preface. *Divinus perfectionis Magister*, 1983.

———. *Veritatis splendor*, 1993.

Preziuso, Gennaro. *The Life of Padre Pio: Between the Altar and the Confessional*. Translated and edited by Jordan Aumann, O.P. New York: Alba House, 2000.

Remnick, David. "The Spirit Level." *The New Yorker*, November 8, 2004.

Rev. Father Jean, O.F.M., Cap. *Blessed Padre Pio*. Reprinted in *Catholic Family News* and available online from http://olrl.org/lives/padrepio.html.

Rhonheimer, Martin. "The Holocaust: What Was Not Said." *First Things*, November 2003.

Rolheiser, Ron. "We've Lost Our Faith's Romantic Ideal." *The Catholic Register*, February 23, 2004.

Rosica, Thomas. "Saint Gianna Beretta Molla: Mother, Doctor, and Lover of Life." *Legatus*, May 2004.

Ryan, Claude. Foreword. *Only to Serve: Selections from Addresses of Governor-General Georges P. Vanier.* Edited by George Cowley and Michel Vanier. Toronto: University of Toronto Press, 1970.

Rychlak, Ronald J. "Goldhagen vs. Pius XII." *First Things,* June/July 2002.

Sánchez, José M. *Pius XII and the Holocaust: Understanding the Controversy.* Washington: The Catholic University of American Press, 2002.

Sarno, Robert J., "Theological Reflections on Canonization." *Canonization: Theology, History, Process.* Edited by William H. Woestman. O.M.I. Ottawa: Saint Paul University, 2002.

Sasanov, Catherine. "Reassembling the Bodily Relics of St. Gemma Galgani." *Commonweal,* June 18, 2004.

Scrivener, Leslie. "Modern Saint Loved Fashion, Family, Fast Cars." *Saturday Star,* July 17, 2004.

Shaw, Bernard. *Saint Joan.* Toronto: Penguin Plays, 1975.

Smith, Donald. "A Sign for Russia." *The Tablet,* September 30, 2000.

Spoto, Donald. *Reluctant Saint: The Life of Francis of Assisi.* New York: Viking Compass, 2002.

Steiner, George. *Nostalgia for the Absolute.* Toronto: CBC Publications, 1974.

Tittmann, Jr., Harold H. *Inside the Vatican of Pius XII.* New York: Doubleday, 2004.

Thurston, Herbert. Introduction. *The Lives of the Saints,* by Fr. Alban Butler. New York: Attwater, 1956.

Valpy, Michael. "Canonization of Pediatrician Expected to Fuel Abortion Battle." *The Globe and Mail*, May 12, 2004.

Walsh, Michael. *The Secret World of Opus Dei*. London: Grafton Books, 1990.

Wijngaards, John. "A Saint from Holland." *The Tablet*, November 2, 1985.

Williams, Paul. *The Life and Work of Mother Teresa*. Indianapolis: Alpha Books, 2002.

Williams, Shirley. *God and Caesar: Personal Reflections on Politics and Religion*. South Bend, Ind.: University of Notre Dame Press, 2003.

Wills, Gary. *Why I Am a Catholic*. Boston: Houghton Mifflin, 2002.

Woodward, Kenneth. *Making Saints: How the Catholic Church Determines Who Becomes a Saint, Who Doesn't, and Why*. New York: Simon and Schuster, 1990.

———. "Slow Up on Saint-Making." *The Tablet*, November 13, 1999.

Zernov, Nicholas. *Eastern Christendom* (1961). As quoted by Anthony M. Coniaris, *Introducing The Orthodox Church: Its Faith and Life*. Minneapolis: Light and Life Publishing, 1982.

Index

Stepinac, Alojzije, 101
stigmata, 115–20
    Francis of Assisi, 118–20, 125,
        129
    Padre Pio, 115–17, 122, 125, 129
    stories of saints, 2, 14, 98, 227, 229

Teresa Benedicta a Cruce, *see* Stein,
    Edith
Teresa of Avila, 116, 195
Teresa of Calcutta, *see* Mother
    Teresa of Calcutta
Tessari, Florio, 126–27
Thérèse of Lisieux, 125–26, 143, 161
Third World countries, 51
Thomas à Becket, 4–6, 11–12
Thurston, Herbert, 98
Tittmann, Harold, 220–21
transverberation preceding stigmata,
    116

Udalricus, 32
unrecognized saints, 75, 230–32
Urban VIII, Pope, 32, 236

Vanier, Georges and Pauline, 59–60
Vardey, Lucinda, 148–50, 158–59,
    167–68
Vatican
    Concordat with Nazi regime, 188,
        189
    popes, *see* individual popes
    vulnerability to Italy, 175
    Veritatis splendor, 36, 98
    vision, 8

Walsh, Michael, 41–42
Watt, Helen, 69
"wildness," 90–91
Williams, Paul, 145, 158
Williams, Shirley, 173–74
Wills, Garry, 215
Wojtyla, Karol, *see* John Paul II,
    Pope
women saints, 60–72, 77, 86–87
    see also married saints; Mother
        Teresa of Calcutta
Woodward, Kenneth, 34, 38–40,
    42–44, 45–46, 53–55, 73, 227